Other Books by the Author

Condo Buying Made Easy

Home Buying Made Easy

Mortgages Made Easy

Mortgage Payment Tables Made Easy

The Complete Canadian Small Business Guide (with Diana Gray)

Home Inc.: The Canadian Home-Based Business Guide (with Diana Gray)

The Canadian Small Business Legal Advisor

Be Your Own Boss (with Norm Friend)

So You Want to Buy a Franchise (with Norm Friend)

The Complete Canadian Franchise Guide (with Norm Friend)

Raising Money (with Brian Nattrass)

The Canadian Snowbird Guide (Everything You Need to Know About Living Part-Time in the USA or Mexico)

The Canadian Guide to Will and Estate Planning (with John Budd)

Risk-Free Retirement (with Dr. Des Dwyer and others)

Start a Successful Consulting Business

Start and Run a Profitable Business Using Your Computer

Marketing Your Product (with Donald Cyr)

Have You Got What It Takes? (The Entrepreneur's Complete Self-Assessment Guide)

Making Money in Real Estate

THE CANADIAN GUIDE TO PROFITABLE INVESTMENT IN RESIDENTIAL PROPERTY

Revised Edition

DOUGLAS GRAY

John Wiley & Sons Canada, Ltd.

National Library of Canada Cataloguing in Publication Data

Gray, Douglas A.
Making money in real estate: the Canadian guide to profitable investment in residential property/Douglas A. Gray. — Revised ed.

Includes index.
ISBN-13 978-0-470-83620-0
ISBN-10 0-470-83620-2

1. Real estate investment. 2. Real estate investment--Canada. I. Title.

HD1382.5.G73 2005   332.63'24   C2005-900322-7

The material in this publication is provided for information purposes only. Laws, regulations, and procedures are constantly changing, and the examples given are intended to be general guidelines only. This book is sold with the understanding that neither the author nor the publisher is engaged in rendering professional advice. It is strongly recommended that legal, accounting, tax, financial, insurance, and other advice or assistance be obtained before acting on any information contained in this book. If such advice or other assistance is required, the personal services of a competent professional should be sought.

Production Credits:

Cover design: Natalia Burobina
Interior text design: Pat Loi
Printer: Friesens

John Wiley & Sons Canada Ltd
6045 Freemont Blvd.
Mississauga, Ontario
L5R 4J3

Printed in Canada

10 9 8 7 6 5 4 3

Contents

Preface

Many people seriously consider investing in real estate, but they hesitate due to concern over their lack of knowledge of investment techniques that will reduce their risk and maximize their return. Other people proceed to invest without caution or any clear plan or objective, and without a clear understanding of the pitfalls, and they end up having problems and losing money. Still others proceed in a prudent and informed fashion, and they create financial wealth and independence, as well as a feeling of personal satisfaction.

This book provides a practical step-by-step format to assist you in attaining your financial and investment objectives through real estate, by giving you a realistic awareness of the market and helping you to apply sound judgment.

It has been 13 years since the first edition of this book was published. This second edition has retained the core content of the original edition, but has been substantially revised and updated.

There are two new chapters. Chapter 8: Understanding the Insurance Aspects covers the key elements of insurance that you need for informed and prudent decision making. Chapter 12: Understanding Financial and Estate Planning discusses matters that are vital to your long-term financial security and your retirement-planning needs. These additions will prove very important to your sense of financial well-being, protection, and peace of mind.

The Internet, search engines, and advances in computer technology and software have radically changed the investment marketplace. Now any real estate investor can obtain instant data on any property at any time, and perform detailed comparative and specific research. This second edition includes key Web sites of interest throughout the various chapters and, where relevant, at the end of many chapters.

New content has been added to existing chapters. For example, in Chapter 2: Types of Residential Real Estate, new sections have been added on commercial and industrial condominiums, and dealing with condominium disputes. In Chapter 4: Selecting Your Advisory Team, the section regarding selection criteria has been expanded, and ways of resolving disputes with different types of advisers has been added. In addition, there are new sections on selecting a financial planner, insurance broker, and building/home inspector.

Chapter 5: Understanding the Financing Aspects has a new section on using a variety of on-line mortgage amortization tables for free. Chapter 6: Understanding the Legal Aspects has a new section on legal cautions and protections to consider when purchasing real estate. This discussion includes how to limit your personal and estate liability exposure, as well as how to avoid the pitfalls of litigation. It also includes how to keep peace in the family when asking for a loan or investment money.

New sections have been added to Chapter 7: Understanding the Tax Aspects. These include a section on investing in U.S. real estate, and how to take money from your investments in a tax-strategic fashion. Chapter 10: Managing Your Property has new sections on avoiding homeowner maintenance problems and how to avoid common fire hazards.

I hope you enjoy this book and find the information helpful and encouraging. Your candid feedback on how this work can better meet your needs is welcomed and will assist in preparing future editions. Please refer to my contact information and Web site at the back of the book under "Further Education and Information."

Good luck and good fortune!

Douglas Gray
Vancouver, B.C.
www.homebuyer.ca
April 2005

Acknowledgements

I am grateful for the kind assistance given me by many parties, including the Canada Mortgage and Housing Corporation, GE Mortgage Insurance Canada, Canadian Real Estate Association, and Royal LePage.

Many thanks to Steve Reed, CA, of Manning Jamison, Chartered Accountants (Vancouver, B.C.), for his review of the chapter on tax. I would also like to thank Ken Chong, of Davidson and Company (Vancouver, B.C.), for all his helpful assistance from time to time on tax implications of various business and investment scenarios.

I am grateful for the high quality of professionalism contributed by Sieg Pedde of Phoenix Accrual Corporation (London, Ontario) in providing chart calculations in the Appendix.

I would like to thank Valerie Ahwee for the superb quality of editing and professionalism that she has demonstrated throughout. Her insights, creative suggestions, and positive attitude made the editorial experience a most pleasurable one.

Last but not least, I would like to express my appreciation to Don Loney of John Wiley & Sons for his patience, encouragement, and insightful suggestions in the development of this new edition. I have had the pleasure of knowing Don for over 14 years, since the first edition of this book was released. I have indeed been fortunate to work with such a consummate professional in the publishing business.

CHAPTER 1

Understanding Real Estate Investment

Many Canadians have become financially secure by investing in real estate. The skills they have employed to safely and prudently invest in real estate can be learned and practised. This book will provide you with that knowledge so that you can make informed decisions about investing in real estate, plan the increase in your net worth, minimize risks, maximize profits, and enjoy the attainment of a personal challenge.

Many Canadian households have a net worth that exceeds $1 million. Most of the people who live in these households, unless they have inherited money or been successful business owners, owe their financial wealth to real estate. In many cases, the wealth has been accumulated simply through owning a principal residence for 25 years or longer and carefully tending to their pension plans. Many of the millionaires—who are 55 to 65 years of age, and have worked at relatively ordinary jobs—live in Toronto, Calgary and Vancouver, where real estate value has increased substantially over the years. They have accumulated their wealth due to inflation in real estate on their tax-free principal residence and the tax-free compounding of their RRSPs.

As you can see, there are distinct advantages to starting your real estate investment by purchasing a principal residence, so that you can get into the market and start benefiting from the growth of tax-free equity. Statistics from the Canadian Real Estate Association show that the average compounded annual increase in real estate value through MLS listings nationally has been 5% a year over the past 25 years, since 1980. Depending on the real estate cycle at any given time, the geographic location and type of property, the percentage annual increase could be substantially higher of course. Residential real estate appreciates more than the annual rate of inflation over time.

This first chapter will help you in understanding the real estate market. Whether you are buying your first home or other residential revenue property, you can't operate in a vacuum in terms of the market. Knowing how the market works will develop your self-confidence, your "street-smarts," and improve your chances of making the right choices.

This chapter covers investing in real estate, understanding the real estate market, establishing your investment strategies, buying with others, and avoiding the pitfalls.

Advantages of Real Estate Investment

Here are the main advantages that make real estate investment, compared to other types of investments, attractive. As mentioned earlier, many are inter-related. There are also some disadvantages, which will be discussed later.

Low Risk Compared to Other Investments

Any investment has a potential risk, and you can indeed lose money in real estate. The reasons why will be covered in this book. Real estate, however, has traditionally been a secure, stable investment compared to other investments, especially if you buy prudently and carry out due diligence. There are various reasons for the relatively low risk, which naturally will vary depending on the geographic area, stability of the market, and other factors. These reasons include increases in population density a scarcity of land for development, interest rate stability and flexible financing terms, the intrinsic need and demand for residential real estate, and consistent history of land value appreciation exceeding inflation. The market is cyclic and, depending on location and other factors, eventually will increase.

Minimal Starting Capital

You can make a real estate purchase with a minimal amount of money, possibly only $5,000 to $10,000, and borrow the rest using the property as a security. For example, you could buy a condominium for $150,000, put 10% down ($15,000), and finance the balance (90%). This is called high-ratio financing, where the ratio between the debt (mortgage of 90%) and equity (your down payment of 10%) is high. You will be required to take out high-ratio mortgage insurance (explained in greater detail in Chapter 5: Understanding the Financing Aspects) through Canada Mortgage and Housing Corporation (CHMC). It is even possible to borrow 100% of the purchase price.

Investment Skills Can Be Learned

Compared to other investments, buying your own home can be a relatively easy process. You don't need a lot of experience. It just takes motivation, drive, and a desire to acquire the knowledge and skills. The fact that you are reading this book clearly shows that you have the necessary attitude. Naturally, if you are buying real estate for investment other than your principal residence, more knowledge and skills must be acquired. The essential knowledge will be covered in this book.

Investors Do Have a Life

Investing in real estate need not take up all of your free time. Once you learn the techniques, you will be more efficient, selective, and confident, which will save you time. You should decide at the outset how much time you are prepared to spend researching the market, and negotiating for, buying, managing, and selling properties. If you find yourself spending more time than you want to or have available on your real estate dreams, you have to analyze the causes and fix them. Various strategies are provided in later chapters.

Using Leverage

The concept of leverage simply means using a small amount of your own money and borrowing the rest—using other people's money (OPM). Many people have become wealthy by applying the OPM principle of leverage. The discussion under "Minimal Starting Capital" provided an example of a highly leveraged investment. Basically the ratio was 9:1; that is, nine times as much money was borrowed as invested. The risk to the lender is low or non-existent, as the property is the security. If the lender has to sell, the net proceeds after the sale should at least cover the amount of the mortgage, especially considering historical appreciation in value.

If the investor leverages up the property too high (that is, has a high-ratio debt of, say, 95%), and the market moves into a declining part of the cycle, then the investor and the lender could be at risk. That is why the higher the amount of the mortgage, the greater the risk for the lender and therefore the higher the interest rate paid by the borrower unless the mortgage is insured. For example, if you are buying a $100,000 property and have three mortgages—the first at $75,000, the second at $10,000, and the third at $5,000—the interest rates could be 5%, 7%, and 10%, respectively. The last mortgage has the highest risk because it is the last to be repaid upon the sale of the property. On the other hand, if you have a first mortgage that represents 90% of the purchase price, and it is insured against default and loss as a high-ratio mortgage, your interest rate could be the basic 5% in the above example. The two companies that insure high-ratio mortgages are CMHC (www.cmhc-schl.gc.ca), and G.E. Mortgage Insurance Canada (www.gemortgage.ca).

Here is another example to show the power of leverage. Let's say you bought a house for $100,000, put down 10% ($10,000), and borrowed 90% ($90,000). The home appreciated by 10% over a year in this scenario. What would be the return on your original investment of $10,000? The answer is 100%. In other words, the increase in the value of your home of $10,000 (10% appreciation of the $100,000 original price) is a 100% return on your down payment investment of $10,000. Conversely, if you put all your own money into the home—that is, $100,000—your return on your original investment, due to appreciation of 10% over the year ($10,000) would be 10%.

A related concept to leverage is pyramiding, in which you would borrow on the increasing equity (due to appreciation) of your existing properties, applying the principal of leverage to buy even more properties over time. This compounding effect of equity buildup through appreciation in a prudently selected real estate portfolio can result in the accruing of considerable wealth.

Appreciation

This term simply means the increase in value of the property over time. It is the growth in value of your original capital investment. As mentioned earlier, the national average has been approximately 5% per year. As a note of caution, it should be stressed that it is an *average*. Certain geographic areas or locations will be less than the average, and some considerably less. Conversely, a well-selected, located, and maintained property in a growing community could be higher than the average. If the real estate cycle is going up in a high-demand area, the appreciation could go up as much as 25% or more in one year. A basic axiom in real estate is that what goes up rapidly and in a sustained fashion tends to come down sometimes rather suddenly. (See the section on real estate cycles, page 9.)

Equity Buildup

When you make payments on your mortgage, you are paying down the principal over time. As you reduce your debt, you build up your equity—that is, the portion of your original house price on which you no longer owe any debt. This is independent of the percentage increase in appreciation or value of the property. In practical usage, most people commonly refer to equity as the amount of clear value in the property that the investor owns, free and clear of any debt. It is the amount of equity that a lender will lend further money on and place a mortgage on as security. In realistic terms, your actual equity is what you would net upon the sale of the property, after all real estate commissions and closing costs are taken into account. Lenders understand this, which is why they generally do not like to base a loan on more than 90% of the equity in order to minimize risk and leave a margin for safety in the event that the loan goes into default and a forced sale is required. Under the federal *Bankruptcy Act*, all first mortgages over 75% of the appraised value or purchased price, whichever is lower, must be insured by high-ratio insurance. However, in certain situations, CMHC will provide purchasers who qualify with insurance on a mortgage up to 100% of the purchase price of a principal residence, with some conditions, of course. If borrowers want more money than what is available under a first mortgage, they would need to obtain additional funds from a lender in the form of second or third mortgages.

Inflation Hedge

You are probably well aware of the concept of inflation. As a review, inflation means the increasing cost of buying a product or service. In other words, it is the decrease in your purchasing power; for example, an item that cost $1 ten years ago now costs $10. People on fixed incomes that are not indexed (increased) for inflation are very aware of the erosion of the purchasing power of the dollar. The inflation rate in Canada varies at different times of the year and in different regions across the country. At one time Canada had double-digit inflation, but currently has a policy of keeping inflation single-digit and as low as possible.

Naturally, the appreciation of property value over time includes an inflation factor. Historically, land appreciation value for residential homes has been approximately 4% to 5% greater than the inflation rate. Another benefit of real estate investing is that you are paying off the mortgage in inflated dollars. That is, you are probably getting more money now in terms of salary increases to pay off lesser-value money when you took out the original mortgage.

Tax Advantages

There are numerous types of tax advantages to investing in real estate, whether you have a principal residence or investment income property. Many of these are covered in Chapter 7: Understanding the Tax Aspects. It would be hard to find another investment that has as many benefits as real estate. For example, all the interest you receive from your bank account, term deposit, or guaranteed investment certificate (GIC) is fully taxable as income. So, if you are obtaining interest of 6% (the nominal rate) on your deposit, and the inflation rate is 4%, the "effective" or "real" rate of return is 2%. If you are paying tax at a 35% rate (2% based on the 6% nominal rate), then effectively you have a zero, or possibly negative, rate of return on your money. In practical terms, taking inflation and taxes into account, you have lost on your investment in bank deposits. Real estate does not have this problem, so wisely investing in real estate—starting with a principal residence—is clearly an attractive form of investment.

Some of the key tax advantages of real estate investment include the following:

- √ tax-free capital gain on your principal residence
- √ ability to write off principal residence suite rental income against your home expenses
- √ ability to write off a portion of a home-based business income against your home expenses (the home-based business could even be to manage your residential investment income)
- √ reduced tax rate of 50% of capital gain from investment in real estate
- √ flow through of losses from negative cash flow against other sources of income
- √ deduction of real estate property investment expenses against income
- √ write-off of depreciation of the building against income

Income Potential

A prudent real estate investment can result in a net positive cash flow income to you every month—that is, after all expenses and debt servicing have been taken into account. Not only can the income provide you with additional money, but the fact that you have a positive cash flow is one factor that automatically increases the value of income-producing real estate, sometimes very substantially. This is discussed in greater detail in Chapter 3: Finding and Evaluating the Right Property.

Attractive Return on Investment

For all the reasons outlined in earlier points, clearly the potential for an attractive return on your investment—before and after tax—is very high in real estate. Keep in mind that it is not what you make before tax, but what you can keep after tax that is the important investment criterion.

Increasing Demand for Land

Due to increasing population and a decreasing supply of land, real estate prices go up. Many communities have slow growth or no-growth policies because they cannot meet rapidly expanding needs for community services. This restricts land availability for new development, causing existing land to go up in value. Real estate is a commodity that the public needs. Other investment commodities are not so reliable because they don't constitute a public need and, therefore, demand. In addition, many people want to have a second home as a retreat, vacation property, or place of retirement. This creates further demand for land.

Disadvantages of Real Estate Investment

To provide some balance, there are some limitations to investing in real estate, but if you are aware of these limitations, you will be able to invest realistically in terms of expectations and planning. Most of the limitations can be dealt with or eliminated satisfactorily. Here is a brief outline:

Subjective Feelings

Some people make decisions based on emotion rather than sound preparation, knowledge, and objective assessment, particularly when buying their first home. After you read this book, that problem should not affect you.

Lack of Liquidity

This means that you can't convert your real estate investments into cash quickly, as far as a sale is concerned, because many factors have to be taken into account. You could have the option of borrowing on your property, though.

Extended Holding Period

Most real estate investments are held for long periods, for example, 5 to 10 years. You will have to wait some time, therefore, to get your return on your investment. However, there are alternative investment options in terms of time. Some of these are discussed in later chapters.

Time Expenditure

The investment could take up a considerable amount of your time, but with advance planning, this should not happen unexpectedly. If it does, you have other options, as explained in Chapter 10: Managing Your Property.

Potential High Risk

The potential for high risk, of course, exists, but with prudent and cautious decision making and following the tips and strategies outlined in this book, the risk should be minimal or non-existent, in practical terms.

Lack of Accurate Comparisons

The very nature of real estate makes comparing two or more properties difficult because each property is unique. On the other hand, there are rules of thumb and other formulas that are effective, especially in combination. These are explained in detail later in this book.

Exposure to Government Control

Governments at all levels have an impact on real estate. There are government laws and regulations covering a wide range of areas, including planning, zoning bylaws, use of property, building codes and licences, rent controls, property transfer taxes, and environmental regulations. In addition, governments can expropriate and require rights of way. All these factors could certainly affect your investment. The best way to eliminate a potential problem is to avoid it to begin with. That is why you have to do your research thoroughly and obtain expert legal advice, especially in the case of income real estate investment.

Understanding the Real Estate Market

In order to have a better appreciation of how the real estate market operates, and how to operate prudently within that market, you need to understand the cycles and factors that influence prices. The market is a fluid, dynamic entity, and no buying or selling decisions should be made without an accurate market assessment.

The Real Estate Cycle

Real estate is a cyclical industry. As in any such industry, the cycle historically creates shortage and excess, which is related to supply and demand in the marketplace. Too much supply creates a reduction in value. Too little supply creates an increase in value. It is essential to know where you are in the cycle relative to the property you are considering to purchase. It is also important to appreciate that different provinces, regions, and communities are in different parts of the economic cycle. Timing in the cycle is important when making buying and selling decisions.

One of the reasons for the cycle is that many developers are entrepreneurial by nature and operate primarily by short-term planning. If financing and credit are available, developers tend to build without regard for the overall supply and demand. If a consequent glut occurs and the demand is not there, prices come down as houses and condominiums go unsold. The phases of the real estate cycle will be discussed later in the chapter.

External Factors that Can Affect the Real Estate Market

General Business Economic Cycles

The economy historically goes through periods of increased economic growth followed by periods of recessions. The economic impact is greater, of course, in certain parts of the country than in others in any given cycle. In a recession, people lose their jobs and have to put their houses on the market. Real estate prices become depressed as potential purchasers decide to wait until the economy is more secure.

It is difficult to know for certain when the economy will turn around, but various indicators should give you some insight. (See the section on obtaining information in Chapter 3: Finding and Evaluating the Right Property.) Later in this chapter other indicators to look for will be discussed. If the economy has been in a recession for a sustained period, there could be opportunities to buy. Once the economy comes out of a recession, prices tend to climb. Conversely, if the economy has been on a buoyant growth trend for an extended period, be very cautious in purchasing because a change in the cycle, and therefore a drop in real estate prices, could be imminent.

Local Business Cycle

Each local economy has its own cycles and factors that affect real estate prices. These factors may not be greatly influenced by the general (provincial or national) business cycles just discussed.

Community Cycle

Certain geographic locations within a community can have their own economic cycles as well as supply and demand, all of which affect real estate prices. In addition, a community has its own life cycle from growth to decline to stagnation to rehabilitation. Look for areas of future growth.

As you can see, being aware of economic, business, and community cycles is critical to prudent decision making. Before buying or selling real estate in a certain area, determine what external factors are prevalent and how they affect the cycle of the real estate market. Different types of real estate—for example, condominiums, new houses, resale houses, and small apartment buildings—can be at different points of a cycle.

There are four distinct segments to a real estate cycle. Each of these segments has certain identifiable characteristics and therefore helpful clues for assessing the state of the real estate cycle. (Refer to Chart 1 in the Appendix.)

Three Types of Real Estate Markets

You undoubtedly are familiar with the common terms used to describe the three types of real estate markets. As a brief review, they are:

Seller's Market

In a seller's market the number of buyers wanting homes, for example, exceeds the supply or number of homes on the market. This type of market is characterized by homes that sell quickly, an increase in prices, a large number of buyers, and a minimal number of available homes. These characteristics have implications for the buyer, who has to make decisions quickly, must pay more, and frequently has his or her conditional offers rejected.

Buyer's Market

In a buyer's market the supply of homes on the market exceeds the demand or number of buyers. Characteristics of this type of market include a longer selling period for homes on the market, fewer buyers compared to the number of available homes, more homes for sale, and a reduction in prices. The implications for buyers in this type of market are more favourable negotiating leverage, more time to search for a home, and better prices.

Balanced Market

In a balanced market, the number of homes on the market is equal to the demand or the number of buyers. The characteristics of this type of market include a reasonable selling period for houses on the market, demand that equals supply, sellers who accept reasonable offers, and stable prices. For the buyer in this type of market, the atmosphere is more relaxed and there are more homes to choose from.

Factors that Affect Real Estate Prices

There are many factors that influence the price of real estate. Whether you are a buyer or seller, you need to understand which factors are affecting the market so you can make the right decisions at the right time and in the right location. Many of these factors are interrelated.

Position in the Real Estate Cycle

As described in the previous section, the position of the particular real estate market in the cycle will have a bearing on prices.

Interest Rates

There is a direct connection between interest rates and prices. The higher the rates, the lower the prices. The lower the rates, the higher the prices. When the rates are low, more people can afford to buy their first home or an investment property. This puts pressure or greater demand on the market.

Taxes

An area of high municipal property taxes can be a disincentive to a purchaser. A rise in taxes could cause real estate prices to drop. Provincial taxes, such as a property purchase tax or speculators' tax, will limit the number of buyers. Federal tax legislation on real estate, such as a downward change in capital gains tax, could have a negative influence on investors. All these factors would affect the overall amount of real estate activity, as well as prices.

Rent Controls

Naturally, provincial rent controls and related restrictions could have a limiting effect on investor real estate activity, thereby resulting in fewer buyers in the market for certain types of homes. Rent controls are set and governed by provincial legislation. Not all provinces have rent control, but any province can introduce them or modify their existing legislation at any time. To find out whether there are caps on rent increases, check out the landlord/tenant legislation in your province. Go to *www.google.ca* and then type in the key words "landlord tenant law" and the name of your province. If your province has rent controls, you will see the criteria for increasing rents, including any special permitted circumstances for additional rent increases.

Economy

Confidence in the economy is important to stimulate homebuyer and investor activity. If the economy is buoyant and the mood is positive, more market activity will occur, generally resulting in an increase in prices. Conversely, if the economy is stagnant, the opposite will occur, resulting in decreased homebuyer and investor activity and lower prices. If real estate purchasers are concerned about the same problem, a predictable loss of confidence occurs in the market.

Population Shifts

A geographic location with attractive business, employment, tourism, and retirement opportunities will attract immigrants from outside the country and emigrants from other provinces. The increased demand will increase property prices. Conversely, if there is net migration out of the area due to closure or potential closure of industry, environmental problems, or other factors, prices will go down.

Vacancy Levels

High vacancy levels could reduce investor confidence due to the potential risk, and real estate sales could go down. On the other hand, low vacancy levels could stimulate investor activity as well as first homebuyers. Renters who can't find a place to rent may borrow from relatives or find other creative ways to enable them to purchase a home.

Location

This is an important factor. Highly desirable locations will generally go up in price more quickly and consistently.

Availability of Land

A natural shortage of land, municipal zoning restrictions, limits on development, or provincial land-use laws that restrict the utilization of existing land for housing purposes will generally increase prices. Again, it relates back to the principle of supply and demand.

Public Image

Public perception of a certain geographic location or type of residential property or builder will affect demand and therefore prices. Some areas or types of properties are "hot" or trendy, and some are not at any given time.

Political Factors

The policy of a provincial or municipal government in terms of supporting real estate development will naturally have a positive or negative effect on supply and demand and therefore prices.

Seasonal Factors

Certain times of year are traditionally slow months for residential real estate sales, so prices decline. The same seasonal factor affects recreational property. There are ideal seasons for purchase and sale.

Establishing Your Investment Strategies

To attain the maximum financial benefit from real estate investment with a minimum of risk, you need to have clearly defined goals and objectives, and a plan for achieving them. There are various steps in the process of determining your plan. Completing a self-assessment is step 1. Determining your current financial need is step 2. Assessing your future personal and financial needs is step 3. And step 4 is planning your investment strategies.

Step 1: Personal Self-Assessment of Skills and Attributes

Your success in real estate investment has a lot to do with the qualities that you bring to the process. It is important to know your strengths and weaknesses so that you can capitalize on your strengths and compensate for your weaknesses. This self-assessment is particularly important if you are considering group investments or owning several properties. Your self-assessment will identify your areas of interest as well as skills, attributes, and talents that are relevant to the business of real estate investing.

Step 2: Determine Your Current Financial Status and Needs

To obtain this review, complete Form 1: Personal Cost of Living Budget (Monthly) and Form 2: Personal Net Worth Statement (see Appendix). Then complete forms 3 and 4, in which you will calculate your gross debt-service ratio and total debt-service ratio, respectively. Forms 3 and 4 will give you some guidelines in terms of mortgage eligibility. Keep in mind that these are only guidelines. There are exceptions, and there are other creative ways of achieving your financial objectives. This is explained in more detail in Chapter 5: Understanding the Financing Aspects.

Step 3: Determine Your Future Personal and Financial Needs

This is an essential step, as it gives you an idea of the degree of risk you are prepared to take. It will also clarify your time commitment, financial involvement, and realistic short-, medium-, and long-term goals and objectives. For example, maybe you want to be financially independent, primarily through real estate investment, in 10 or 15 years.

Step 4: Plan Your Investment Strategies

Take the time to develop your investment program thoroughly. Like any plan, you will need to monitor and possibly modify it regularly due to changing circumstances. The safest way to make money in real estate is through prudent and cautious investment.

Don't look on real estate as a "get-rich-quick" scheme. There are many who have adopted that attitude, to their misfortune. Avoid the prophets of profit—that is, the self-styled gurus and pitchmen touting U.S.-oriented real estate investment programs. In many cases these real estate investment programs are not directly applicable to the Canadian context (due to differences in legal and tax matters). Some programs are barely ethical or unrealistic. Some real estate seminars and books promote the concept of becoming rich through property tax sales, foreclosure sales, quick flips of property, or the selling (assigning) of the agreement of purchase and sale before closing. In most cases in the Canadian context these options are not applicable or applicable only with considerable difficulty, risk, and skill, so considerable caution is advised.

Key Investment Strategies to Consider

Here are some the key real estate investment strategies to consider:

√   Thoroughly research the market before making any decision. Consider at least three potential investment opportunities, if possible.

√   Give yourself a realistic time frame to achieve your investment objectives. For example, normal real estate cycles are 5 to 8 years and in some cases 10 to 12 years.

√   Buy specific types of revenue property that are in demand and are easy to maintain and/or manage; for example, a single-family house (ideally with a basement suite for separate revenue), a condominium, duplex, triplex, or fourplex. Don't buy an apartment building until you have experience as a landlord with several smaller properties, or unless you are going in with experienced investors.

√ Attempt to make a low down payment (for example, 5% to 10%) unless, of course, you can only obtain a maximum of 75% financing. If you can make a purchase with a low down payment, this frees up your available cash for the purchase of additional properties. Offset a low down payment with a vendor-take-back mortgage, high-ratio financing, or a second mortgage.

√ Strive to have a break-even cash flow. In other words, try to avoid debt servicing the property because of a shortfall of rental income over expenses. Make sure you cover all expenses from cash flow such as mortgage payments, taxes, property management, condominium fees, insurance, repairs and maintenance, and allowance for vacancies.

√ Ensure that you have competent property management, whether you do it yourself or hire an expert.

√ Rely on professionals—including a lawyer, accountant, financial planner, building inspector, appraiser, contractor, realtor, property manager—at all times for peace of mind, enhanced revenue potential, reduced risk, and realistic budgetary projections.

√ Never pay more than fair market value unless there are other collateral benefits to you that you have identified. These types of potential benefits are discussed in more detail in Chapter 9: Negotiating Strategies.

√ Use all the tax-planning strategies available to you after receiving expert tax advice. These options are explained in Chapter 7: Understanding the Tax Aspects.

√ Keep rents at market maximums and manage expenses to keep at market minimum.

√ Buy when no one else is buying and sell when everyone else is buying. This is the so-called contrarian view of investment, which is the opposite of conventional wisdom.

√ Always view and inspect property before you buy. Verify all financial information. Obtain your advisers' guidance.

√ Have a minimum three-month contingency reserve fund for unexpected expenses (repairs) or a reduction in cash flow (vacancies).

√   As a general rule of thumb, buy investment properties within four hours' driving distance of where you live, so you can easily monitor your investment. There are exceptions to this general principle, of course.

√   Consider applying the principle of pyramiding—that is, purchasing selected real estate on a systematic basis. For example, you may purchase one or two or more properties a year—when the cycle is in your favour, of course.

For additional guidance, refer to Checklist 6: Real Estate Assessment Checklist, in the Appendix.

Buying with Partners

Investing with others is not for everyone. Most people prefer to invest on their own, if possible. Occasionally, people may choose to buy in a group. On the one hand, some people prefer to start out investing with a group as it may provide mutual support; shared (and therefore reduced) risk; pooled skills and expertise; greater investment opportunities; shared responsibility and time; and collective energy, synergy, and momentum. On the other hand, if you do not select your group investment wisely, it could be a financial and emotional nightmare. The key is to know the benefits and limitations of the various group investment options and the pitfalls to avoid. Never go into a real estate purchase with others without obtaining prior professional advice from your lawyer and accountant. Always make sure that you have a written agreement in advance.

Factors to Consider When Buying Real Estate with Others

It is important to remember that approximately 80% of business partnership don't work out. The statistical odds, therefore, are very high that any real estate group relationship in which you are involved may not survive. By cautiously assessing the individuals who will make up a potential group, you can minimize the risk immensely. Here are some key factors to consider.

Goals and Objectives

Ensure that your goals and objectives are consistent with those of the rest of the group. For example, some members may want a long-term investment (e.g., five years) with positive cash flow from rents; others may want a medium-term investment (e.g., three years) and be prepared to subsidize the negative cash flow in the hope that the property value will appreciate due to rezoning or subdivision potential; still others may want to flip the property within a few months of purchase because of its desirability or a because of a rapid increase in property values in a hot market.

Expertise

You know what skills you can bring to an investment partnership, and if your partners are friends and relatives, you probably have a clear idea as to what skills they bring to the table. But if you are joining an investment group of strangers or people you know only casually, it is important to clarify exactly what, if any, skills they will bring to the group investment. It may not matter, if they are silent investors—that is, if the investors are just putting their money in and are not actively involved. Sometimes these types of investors are also referred to as passive investors.

If they are active investors and it is a small group, you need to determine what skills they will contribute and in what form. If you are buying into an investment group that will be totally managed by one of the group members, make sure you know the person's credentials and track record, and get it in writing. If you are going to rely on the person to protect your investment, it would be prudent for you to be careful and cautious.

Liquidity

Basically, this means how easily and quickly you can get your money out of the investment. Your financial resources and needs will determine your liquidity needs. For example, if you need to get your investment capital back quickly, then you probably won't want a long-term investment. In addition, you should reconsider the investment if you would suffer if your money was tied up or put at risk. *You should not invest money you cannot afford to lose.* You therefore should be cautious about investing retirement money or contingency reserve funds if you need immediate liquidity.

In practical terms, most investments are tied up for the duration of the deal. That relates back to the investment group's goals and objectives. If you are buying shares in a real estate investment on the public stock exchange, you may have liquidity, but not necessarily at an attractive price. Also, consider having a buy-out clause in the investment group agreement. This means the group would buy you out within a fixed period, although normally at a discount price, to discourage investors from leaving the group early.

Liability

This issue is, of course, a critical one to consider. Make sure, if at all possible, that your risk is limited to the amount of your investment. You want to avoid personal liability for any financial problems that occur, either to mortgage companies, other investors, or the investment group as such. For example, if you are investing in a corporation that is holding the property for the group and the corporation has taken out a mortgage with a lender, the lender may require personal guarantees from the shareholders of the corporation. Another example of risk would be a partnership. If you went into a general partnership with two other investors whose actions resulted in financial problems, you would still be liable for the full amount of the debt if the other two couldn't pay.

A third example of risk would be if you signed an investment group agreement and it stated that any shortfall of funds would have to be paid by the investors on a basis proportional to the percentage interest. A last example of risk would be in a limited partnership. If you stopped being an inactive partner and started to actively manage the investment, you could be liable. Also, some limited partners are asked to sign personal guarantees up to a certain limit. Avoid this scenario. You can see why you need a lawyer to look at the agreement and advise you of the implications and ways of limiting or eliminating personal liability risk.

Legal Structure

There are several types of legal structures—a general partnership, limited partnership, corporation, or joint venture agreement. Group investments fall into these categories or variations of them. Some legal structures allow more flexibility than others. The degree of personal liability exposure varies depending on the structure and the group investment agreement. Some of these were discussed in the previous point. Obtain advice from your lawyer. Also, refer to the sections on legal structures in Chapter 6: Understanding the Legal Aspects.

Control Issues

Certain types of investment groups allow for more investor control than others. Control relates to the degree of influence that you have on the management of the investment and related decision making. Obviously smaller groups tend to allow more individual control than others. For example, in some cases, unanimous consent is required for major decisions; in other cases, 75% consent is required; and in still other cases, a simple 51% majority vote of investors is required. In some instances you do not have any vote at all. You put your money in and hope for the best. If you are buying into a limited partnership or other form of investment that is being touted to you, make sure you thoroughly check out the promoter's previous history, experience, and reputation. You can see why management and quality of management are so important.

Tax Considerations

One of the main reasons for investing in real estate would be for the tax benefits in your given situation. Certain types of investments are more attractive than others from a tax perspective. Be very wary of salespeople or financial advisers who attempt to induce you into buying a tax shelter. That area is fraught with pitfalls and risks. You can see why you need objective and impartial advice in advance from your lawyer and professional tax accountant before making your investment decision. The property should be inherently viable from an investment viewpoint first, with tax benefits then taken into account. Refer to Chapter 7: Understanding the Tax Aspects for a more detailed discussion.

Compatibility

Look at the other people in your investment group. Are there similarities in personality, age, financial position, and investment objectives? What do the other group members think about issues such as control, management, and liability? What contributions, if any, are the other people making to the success of the investment? If the people in the group have diversified skills, this could save the group money and make the investment more secure. In general, people you know are safer than people you don't know. Ego, power, greed, arrogance, and unrealistic expectations are common causes of group stress or disintegration. You can't afford the risk, so be selective with your investment partners.

Risk Assessment

As discussed throughout this section, you need to look objectively at the potential risks—the nature of the investment, the potential for profit, the degree of potential personal liability, the type of legal structure, the nature and degree of control, the quality of management, and the compatibility of other investment group members.

Contribution

Find out what contribution is expected of you in terms of money, time, expertise, management, personal guarantee, and contingency backup capital. Do you feel comfortable with others' expectations of you?

Percentage of Investment

Do you feel comfortable with the percentage of investment that you are getting, relative to the contribution you noted in the above point? For example, let's say that there are four people in an investment who incorporate a holding company. One is an active partner and finds and manages the property, and the other three are silent investors. The active partner has 55% of the investment, did not invest any money, and did not sign any personal guarantees. The three silent partners invested all the money equally, signed personal guarantees to the bank for the mortgage, and hold 15% of the investment each. Would you feel comfortable with that investment percentage if you were a silent partner? What if you were the active partner?

Getting Out or Buying Others Out

One of the important things to consider when investing with a group is getting out. What if you want to leave for any number of reasons? Is there a procedure to follow? What penalty do you pay, how is it calculated, and how long will it take to get your money? Conversely, what if you want to buy out the other investors because of a personality conflict or some other reasons? Can you do so? If there is nothing in the agreement outlining how an investor can leave the group before the property is sold, you could have a problem.

Management

How will the group investment be managed? Will it be managed by a professional management company, a resident manager, a group of investors, one of the investors, or the original promoter? How confident do you feel about the issue of management? What are the management fees? Are they reasonable under the circumstances?

Profits and Losses

Determine how these aspects are to be dealt with. For example, what about excess revenue from the income property? Will that be kept in a contingency fund, or will a portion of it be paid to the investors? What about decisions such as selling the shares of a corporation holding the property or the property itself? How will those decisions be made and who will make them? These decisions have tax implications that will affect you. What about losses? Will the shortfall be covered by a bank loan, or by remortgaging the property, or by the group investors? In practical terms, how will that be done?

Now that some of the key factors have been discussed, you can see why you have to be careful and selective before going into a group investment.

Types of Group Investments

There are many options available in terms of group investing. The most common options are co-tenancy, general partnership, limited partnership, joint venture, syndication, and equity sharing. (See also Chapter 6: Understanding the Legal Aspects and Chapter 7: Understanding the Tax Aspects.) The following discussion will explain how these types of group investments operate.

Co-tenancy

Each co-tenant has a proportional interest reflected in the title to the property filed in the land title office. For example, if three people decide to invest together on an equal basis, the title to the property would show that each party has "an undivided one-third interest each, tenants in common," or other such variation. In law, co-tenants or tenants in common can generally deal with the property without the consent of the other co-tenant(s). In addition, if a co-tenant dies, his or her interest in the title to the property goes to the estate; it does not go to the surviving co-tenants, as it does in a joint tenancy type of legal ownership.

When people buy for investment purposes or buy a property together to live in, but are not living together in a common-law or legal marriage, tenancy in common is often the way they hold the property.

The ownership of the land through tenancy in common reflects percentage ownership on title; it does not involve partnership-type obligations to third parties. To make sure that there will be no misunderstanding on the issue of partnership in case of a co-tenant dispute or creditor problems, a co-tenancy agreement should be prepared and signed. Again, make sure you have your lawyer prepare it or review it carefully if another lawyer prepares it.

Co-tenancy Cautions

In addition to the types of issues discussed in a group investment agreement, which is explained later in this chapter, you would also want to consider including the following points in an agreement:

√   That the co-tenants are not partners of each other, as set out in the provincial partnership act.

√   That the co-tenants do not have the power to act for each other, except as outlined in the co-tenant agreement.

√   That the co-tenants are not agents of each other.

√   That the co-tenants can compete with each other in other real estate investments.

√   That each co-tenant is responsible for any tax or other financial liability relating to his or her percentage interest in the property.

√   That there are no fiduciary duties; in other words, a co-tenant can make money from the co-tenancy without it being considered a conflict of interest.

In addition, the co-tenant agreement should set out the living accommodation rights, duties, and responsibilities if the parties are living in the same dwelling. A sketch map showing the living area should be attached.

It is common for friends or relatives to invest in real estate through a co-tenant arrangement. It is also common for people who cannot afford to buy a principal residence with their own income or down payment to buy with someone else, either a parent, relative, or friend.

One of the key advantages of a co-tenancy is that it is a reasonably simple structure and relatively easy to get out of.

General Partnership

You should be very cautious about going into a general partnership. There are many potential liability risks involved, as well as investment limitations. Never go into one without competent legal and tax advice. A general partnership is governed by the partnership act of each province. The disadvantages of this type of relationship are covered in Chapter 6: Understanding the Legal Aspects. In brief, the risks involve individual liability for all the debts or liability of the partnership, regardless of how many other partners there are. For example, if the partnership owes $50,000 and the other two investors do not have any money or assets and you do, creditors will go after you for the full amount.

Many people don't realize that, and assume that if there are three partners, the liability will be split three ways.

In addition, there are other aspects governed by the provincial partnership act. There are automatic rights that each partner has in law, tax, control, and ownership implications; non-competitive provisions; fiduciary duties (explained in an earlier point); dissolution rights; automatic breakup of the partnership on death of a partner; and inability to pledge the partnership interest as security to a lender. Lack of control and limited management and investor options make the general partnership option an inflexible one, and the implications can be onerous for most investors. Although a partnership agreement can mitigate some of the limitations of a general partnership, it does not eliminate them. General partnerships normally only involve a few people.

Limited Partnership

This is a variation of a general partnership and a corporation. It has fewer of the legal disadvantages of a general partnership, but maintains the tax advantages. For example, the rights and liabilities of the partners are set out in the limited partnership agreement. The liability of each partner is limited to the amount of his or her investment, which is why the partner is referred to as a limited partner. The limited partner is an inactive partner, and has no control over management of the limited partnership, other than voting on the issue of who should be the manager. The general partner is normally a corporation and is responsible for the active management of the limited partnership investment. The general partner can be sued, but usually is operated by a corporation without assets.

It is important that a limited partner not be involved in any fashion with the management and decision making of the limited partnership. To do so could expose the limited partner to unlimited liability as a general partner.

The operation of a limited partnership is governed by various regulations, including a limited partnership agreement, the provincial limited partnership legislation, and possibly the provincial securities legislation. Limited partners hold their interest in the partnership in the form of "units" issued by the limited partnership. These units are similar to shares in a corporation and represent the proportionate share in the limited partnership held by the investor. Units can be sold to other group investors or outsiders, subject to the policies and restrictions set out in the limited partnership document. Many limited partnerships have a large number of investors, as the financial cost of the project can be considerable.

There can be many risks to limited partnerships. Keep in mind that the promoter is out to make a personal profit. This may or may not be consistent with making money for you from the investment. There can be many representations by the promoter (general partner) and agents of the promoter. Minimize the risk by requesting cash flow guarantees from the promoter, secured against assets of the promoter.

Attempt to get a written commitment from the promoter to purchase your unit, if you so wish, after a period of time. Make sure that long-term financing is in place, so that you don't have to come up with more money in a short time. Finally, make sure that your lawyer and tax accountant review the project and documentation, and advise you in advance as to the legitimate tax benefits, degree of risk, and reliability of the financial and operating projections.

Corporation

You may wish to hold real estate by owning shares with others in a corporation. A corporation is usually governed by the provincial company legislation for most real estate investments, rather than a federally incorporated company. A corporation is a separate legal entity and can sue and be sued, but its liability is limited to the assets of the corporation. Individual shareholders are not personally liable for corporate liability, unless personal guarantees of the corporation were signed by the shareholders. Refer to Chapter 6: Understanding the Legal Aspects for a more detailed description of corporations.

It is important to make sure that you sign a shareholders' agreement with the other investors. This agreement contains various provisions, as discussed later.

A corporation can be a convenient vehicle for real estate group investments. It is structured in such a way as to make it easy to sell or transfer shares, subject to the articles of incorporation and shareholders' agreement. If a shareholder dies, the corporation and its investment continues. The shares would go to the estate of the deceased or be purchased by the corporation, depending on the terms of the shareholders' agreement. Generally speaking, there is a limit on the number of shareholders in a corporation, beyond which the corporation could be governed by provincial securities legislation. This would involve stringent public reporting requirements and accountability, as well as limitations in the management of the corporation. For this reason, you have to be cautious and obtain legal advice to ensure that you are not covered by securities legislation. Many holding corporation investments are comprised of a small number of people, generally not more than ten.

Corporations are a popular means of holding revenue property such as apartment buildings. Income from the corporation is tabulated and taxed in the corporation. Investors pay taxes on income only if they receive money by means of dividends or salaries from the corporation. Otherwise, investors have to wait until the property is sold. If the shares of the company are sold to a new owner, the investor could therefore have a taxable gain on those shares. Refer to Chapter 7: Understanding the Tax Aspects for a further discussion.

Joint Venture

A joint venture may involve individuals or corporations who want to pool money, resources, skills, expertise, land, or other assets to make a profit by means of development or investment. Generally it is one specific project. Joint ventures can be formed in different ways, such as a co-tenancy, general partnership, limited partnership, or holding corporation, in which the shareholders are the joint venturers. It is also possible for a corporation to be formed to hold the property in trust for the joint venturers.

The nature and form of joint venture structure depends on various considerations, such as legal, tax, and financial issues, as well as the purpose of the joint venture. Most joint venture groups are small. It is essential to have a joint venture agreement drawn up and signed. Make sure that the agreement makes it clear that the relationship is not one of a general partnership, due to the tax and legal implications. Get advice from your lawyer and tax accountant before committing yourself.

Syndication

This is usually in the form of a limited partnership and is designed to provide silent investors with limited liability, capital appreciation, and tax deferral. The promoter of the syndicate or the company contracted by the syndicate undertakes management of the project. The syndicate makes money from the investors as well as from the investment itself. Generally, the cost to the investor is directly related to the degree of risk and the degree of financial and performance guarantees by the syndicate promoter. As with any investment, there is risk. Have your lawyer and tax accountant give you their unbiased professional opinions before signing any documentation or paying any money. Many syndicates have a large number of investors and are therefore governed by provincial security legislation.

Equity Sharing

There are many variations to this method of investment. In a way, it is a combination of a partnership and co-tenancy. For example, one approach is for an investor to look for a tenant who wants to buy a house but doesn't have the down payment. The investor buys the house and the tenant moves in and pays slightly more than fair market rent. The rent is sufficient to cover all mortgage debt-servicing costs, property taxes, utilities, insurance, and maintenance. Therefore, there is no negative cash flow. The tenants have a place to live and a house to maintain with pride.

The above parties sign an agreement setting out the arrangement. Generally speaking, the investor has title to the property with a stipulation that if the tenant remains for, say three years, the tenant has the option of purchasing the house for the appraised value minus the normal real estate commission that would otherwise be paid, minus an agreed-upon percentage for the equity increase over the three-year period (e.g., 10% to 25%). This could bring the house price down sufficiently that the tenant would be able to get financing and buy it. If the tenant can't or doesn't want to purchase at the end of the term, the tenant loses the option and all equity sharing and purchase rights.

The secret of a successful equity-sharing plan is the selection of the right property at the right price and terms, the right match of investor/tenant, and a well-written agreement that is fair to both parties. The agreement should be drawn up by your lawyer and cover important potential problems such as the following: the tenant stops paying, breaches other terms of the agreement, or dies; the investor declares personal bankruptcy; a disagreement occurs over the appraised value of the property; or the investor does not want to sell after three years because the market is depressed.

Equity sharing can also mean including the tenant on the title for an agreed percentage interest at the outset. This approach is not recommended as it would be difficult for the investor to get the full title back without paying considerable legal fees if a falling-out occurs with the tenant.

From an investor's viewpoint, the equity-sharing concept has some advantages as well as disadvantages. The advantages include the benefits of ideally assured positive cash flow, a committed tenant, and no management problems. From the tenant's viewpoint, the arrangement allows the tenant to choose a house of his or her own and provides a financial backer to get into the market, as well as a share of the equity buildup with an option to buy at a discounted price (net after real estate commission savings are deducted). One of the main disadvantages to an investor, though, is sharing the equity buildup. This has to be weighed against the advantages. You can do equity-sharing arrangements yourself, or invest in companies that offer the service. The problem is that you lose control in these companies, as groups of eight to ten investors are put together. In addition, you will have to pay the equity-sharing management company an administrative fee.

You now have a better idea of real estate group investment options. The smaller the group, the more control and involvement; the larger the group, the less control or no control, and lack of individual identity or involvement with the investment. In some large groups, investors are detached from any involvement or input. Consult your legal and tax advisers before venturing into these waters.

Putting the Arrangement in Writing

After you have considered all the factors outlined above and decided which type of group investment you prefer, the next step is to set out a written agreement. As mentioned earlier, make sure that your lawyer prepares the agreement or reviews an agreement prepared by someone else. Each type of group investment group necessitates a different form of agreement. The agreement you sign should be customized for the specific type of investment in which you're involved, and it should take into account the factors discussed earlier.

The main points and procedures that are common to, although not necessarily all included in, group investment agreements, consist of the following:

√ type of legal structure

√ name and location of investment group

√ goals and objectives of group

√ duration of agreement

√ names and categories of investors (e.g., general, limited, active, silent)

√ financial contribution by investors

√ procedure for obtaining additional capital

√ role of individual investors in the investment management

√ authority of any investor in the conduct of the investment group

√ nature and degree of each investor's contribution to the investment group

√ how operating expenses will be handled

√ how operating income will be handled

√ debts of investment group separate from individual investor

√ separate bank account

√ signing of cheques

√ division of profits and losses

√ books, records, and method of accounting

√ draws or salaries

√ absence and disability of investor

√ death of an investor

√ bringing in other investors

√ rights of the investors

√ withdrawal of an investor

√ buying out other investors

√ management of employees

√ sale of investor interest

√ restrictions on the transfer, assignment, or pledging of the investor's interest

√ release of debts

√ settlement of investor disputes and arbitration procedures.

√ additions, alterations, or modifications to investment group agreement

√ non-competition with the investment group in the event of an investor's departure.

Pitfalls to Avoid

It is probably timely, at this early point in the book, to outline some of the classic pitfalls to avoid in buying real estate. In most cases, investors who have problems have succumbed to a combination of the following traps. Being aware of these problems at the outset will help you place the discussion and cautions in the rest of the book in context. All these issues are dealt with throughout the book.

√ not having an understanding of how the real estate market works

√ not having a clear understanding of personal and financial needs

√ not having a clear focus or a realistic real estate investment plan, with strategies and priorities

√ not doing thorough market research and comparison shopping before making the purchase

√ not selecting the right property, considering the potential risks, money involved, and specific personal needs

√ not verifying representations or assumptions beforehand

√ not doing financial calculations beforehand

√ not buying at a fair market price

√ not buying real estate at the right time in the market

√ not buying within financial debt-servicing capacity, comfort zone, and skills

√ not understanding the financing game thoroughly, and therefore not comparison shopping and not getting the best rates, terms, and right type of mortgage

√ not making a decision based on an objective assessment but on an emotional one

√ not determining the real reason why the vendor is selling.

√ not having the property inspected by a building inspector before deciding to purchase

√ not selecting an experienced real estate lawyer and obtaining advice beforehand

√ not selecting an experienced professional tax accountant when selecting real estate property, and obtaining advice beforehand.

√ not selecting an experienced realtor with expertise in the type of real estate and geographic location you are considering

√ not negotiating effectively

√ not putting the appropriate conditions or "subject clauses" in the offer

√ not buying for the right reasons—in other words, buying for tax shelter reasons rather than for the inherent value, potential, and viability of the investment property

√ not independently verifying financial information beforehand

√ not obtaining and reviewing all the necessary documentation appropriate for a given property before making a final decision to buy

√ not selecting real estate investment partners carefully

√ not having a written agreement with real estate investment partners prepared by a lawyer

√ not detailing exactly what chattels are included in the purchase price

√ not seeing the property before buying it, but relying on pictures and/or the representations of others

√ not managing the property well, or not selecting the right property management company

√ not selling the property at the right time in the market or for the right reasons.

Summary

This chapter has provided a general introduction to the benefits of real estate investment, how the real estate market works, determining your investment strategies, buying with others, and avoiding the classic pitfalls. Now it's time to look at specific types of residential real estate.

CHAPTER 2

Types of Residential Real Estate

There are many types of residential real estate. Deciding which type to buy depends on many factors, such as your budget; how much risk you are willing to take; the amount and speed of return desired; the amount of involvement in managing the investment; whether you are buying property as a principal residence; your past experience (if any) in real estate investment; whether you are buying property with others; and your personal needs and investment goals.

Many people already own a principal residence, such as a house or condominium, and may wish to rent out a suite in order to have the experience of being a landlord before investing in real estate. Some people may not have a principal residence and want to purchase one as an investment for the financial, tax, and other benefits. Others may want to invest jointly with several friends or relatives to buy houses or an apartment building.

This chapter will discuss the seven main types of options when buying real estate used for residential and, in some cases, commercial purposes. The options include condominiums, single-family houses (including resale houses, new houses, or buying a lot and building a house), property for renovation, recreational property, multi-unit buildings, apartment buildings, and raw land. Within many of these main categories, there are several options.

Condominium

What Is a Condominium?

Many people purchase condominiums to live in or as an investment. The concept of condominium will not suit everyone, though, as it involves not only individual ownership in the unit and shared ownership in other property, but also adherence to rules and regulations, and shared management. On the other hand, many people prefer condominium living to the alternatives.

The word "condominium" does not imply a specific structural but a legal form. Condominiums (called co-proprietorships in Quebec) may be detached, semi-detached, row houses, stack townhouses, duplexes, or apartments. They can even be building lots, subdivisions, or mobile home parks. Whatever the style, a residential unit is specified and owned by an individual in a freehold or leasehold format. Freehold means that you own the title to the property outright. Leasehold means that you don't have any ownership rights to the land, only the leasing rights. (These formats are described in more detail in Chapter 6: Understanding the Legal Aspects.) The rest of the property, including land, which is called the common elements in most provinces, is owned in common with the other owners. For example, an owner would own a fractional share of the common elements in the development. If there were 50 condominium owners, then each owner would own one-fiftieth as a tenant of the common elements. The legislation of each province can vary, but it is always designed to provide the legal and structural framework for the efficient management and administration of each condominium project. Once the condominium project documents are registered, the project is brought into legal being.

The part of the condominium that you will own outright is referred to as the unit in most provinces. You will have full and clear title to this unit when you purchase it (assuming you are buying a freehold, not a leasehold, property), which will be legally registered in your name in the land registry office in your province. The precise description of the common elements, and exactly what you own as part of your unit, may differ from development to development, but in any event it will be provided for in the documents prepared and registered for each condominium.

Common elements generally include walkways, driveways, lawns and gardens, lobbies, elevators, parking areas, recreational facilities, storage areas, laundry rooms, stairways, plumbing, electrical systems and portions of walls, ceilings, and floors, and other items. Part of the common elements may be designated for the exclusive use of one or more of the individual unit owners, in which case these are called limited common elements. In other words, they are limited for the use of only specific owners. Examples would include parking spaces, storage lockers, roof gardens, balconies, patios, and front and back yards.

Condominiums can be built on freehold or leasehold properties. A condominium can also be in a stratified format, where a legal description for the unit is allocated in a vertical dimension. In other words, if you live in a condominium apartment on the thirtieth floor, there is a precise legal description in the land titles office for that specific unit in the complex. Another format is a bare-land condominium. In this example, it would be similar to a building lot subdivision with individual units owned by the unit holders, although the units would appear as detached homes. The rest of the land would be considered common elements.

A condominium development is administered by various legal structures set out in provincial legislation.

Types of Condominiums

There are numerous types of condominium formats. These include residential, recreational or resort, or commercial or industrial. Here is an overview of the most common options.

Residential Condominiums

Residential condominiums are found in metropolitan and suburban settings. In a metropolitan setting the most common formats are as follows:

- √ a high-rise apartment building
- √ a three- to five-storey new mid-rise building
- √ a converted older building that formerly consisted of rental apartments
- √ a building where the street-level floor is owned jointly by the condominium corporation members (the unit owners) and rented out to retailers to help offset the common maintenance fees of the residential condominiums in the rest of the building
- √ same format as the previous one, except that the retail space is sold as condominiums.

Suburban condominiums tend to be different and are most often found in the following formats:

- √ cluster housing consisting of multi-unit structures of two or four units apiece, each with its own private entranceway
- √ townhouse-type single-family homes distributed in rows
- √ garden apartments consisting of a group of apartment buildings surrounding a common green, frequently with each of the floors held by separate condominium owners
- √ a series of detached single-family homes in a subdivision format, all utilizing the same land and parking areas
- √ duplexes, triplexes, or fourplexes.

The suburban condominium format tends to make maximum use of the land while creating attractive views, private driveways, and common recreational facilities, such as swimming pools, tennis courts, saunas, and playgrounds.

Many residential condominium developments, offering conveniences and amenities, have created a complete lifestyle experience. The purpose of these separate developments—restaurants, shopping centres, recreational and entertainment facilities, and care facilities for seniors—is to make the condominium community a very distinct and self-contained environment for many people.

Recreational/Resort Condominiums

Recreational condominiums can take various formats, including mobile home parks where the "pad" with utility hookups is owned in fee simple—that is, freehold or the right to the property—with a share in the common property of the rest of the park. Alternatively, it could be in a leasehold format. Another option is a bare-land condominium in rural, wilderness, or waterfront areas. In these examples an owner could build a cabin with fee simple ownership to the land underneath and own a partial interest in the common elements, which could include a marina, beach, farm, or forest. Common recreational facilities could include a playground or community centre, and assets could include boats or farm animals.

The development of condominiums in resort areas is extensive, and condominiums are frequently built on lakeshores, seacoasts or island resorts, or in ski country. There are two main types of resort condominiums: those developed for warmer climates and those developed for winter climates.

The warmer-climate type is generally built around a common recreational facility that can be enjoyed throughout the year by the owners, one that includes such facilities as a seashore, lake, marina, or golf course. The buildings tend to range from high-rise apartments to cluster housing.

Winter resort areas are often built near popular ski resort developments. Many provide recreational facilities for the summer season as well, such as golf courses, tennis courts, and swimming pools, so that it is a year-round resort. The buildings tend to be cluster housing, modular housing, or attached townhouses.

People who purchase a recreational or resort condominium tend to:

√ own it outright and use it throughout the year

√ own it outright and rent it out when not it is in use by using the condominium corporation or management company as an agent, using a real estate agent, or renting it independently

√ own a portion of the condominium as a time-share and use it for one week or more a year; normally each one-week block purchased is equivalent to approximately one-fiftieth ownership in the condominium.

Commercial or Industrial Condominiums

Ownership of a commercial or an industrial condominium is similar in concept to the ownership of a residential one. There are various reasons why condominiums for commercial purposes are an attractive alternative to renting space, buying land with a building on it, or buying land and building on it. Some of the benefits include:

√ tax advantages for an owner-occupier of his own business premises, including depreciation, and expense deductions for mortgage interest

√ a limit on monthly costs by carefully regulating costs through the condominium corporation policies

√ no rent increases

√ shared contribution of costs for features such as maintenance, security, common facilities, and advertising

√ appreciation in value of the condominium over time

√ right to participate in the decision making relating to the condominium development

√ assurance of a unique, commercially attractive location

√ removal of the financial risk of owning in a unique, commercially attractive location

√ provision of an alternative if there is a lack of financial capability or desire to own the whole building.

The three main types of commercial-use condominiums are office buildings, professional buildings, and industrial parks.

Office Buildings

The concept of condominium office buildings is not new. For example, Brazil was the first Western country to pass condominium ownership legislation in 1928, and most office buildings in that country are now owned in that manner. In Canada, it is a popular concept in many major cities, and involves a cross-section of retail and service businesses operating through the condominium structure.

Professional Buildings

A familiar form of office use is the dental or medical condominium, where each dentist or doctor owns a suite. The nature of a dental or medical office is often such that it does not expand in size as other businesses do. Another advantage for the professional is the possibility of sharing reception areas, a central telephone-answering service, accounting services, and expensive equipment. It is fairly common in this type of building to sell or lease the street-level condominiums to retail outlets such as pharmacies, laboratory or X-ray services, magazine stands, and restaurants. Lawyers also own offices in condominium buildings and take the same approach as dentists and doctors in terms of sharing office space, boardroom, reception areas, library areas, and so on.

Industrial Parks

Industrial parks established on a bare-land condominium format are a popular development. They can be advantageous because a business can have an individual unit for its industrial or manufacturing needs, but can share in the common elements such as docks, loading areas, rail sidings and so on.

Additional Expenses Relating to Condominium Ownership

Once you have completed the purchase transaction and are now an owner of a condominium unit, you have to plan for ongoing monthly or annual expenses and other potential expenses. People often don't realize the extra expenses involved in owning a condominium, which is very different from a owning a single-family home. The most common additional expenses, other than mortgage payments, are as follows.

Property Taxes

The municipality assesses each individual condominium unit and the owner has to make an annual payment to cover property taxes. If you have a mortgage, the lender may or may not have required you to include monthly property-tax payments in your mortgage payment. These payments are held in a property tax account so that the lender can pay your municipal property taxes. If you do not have a mortgage, you will have to pay property taxes separately. The common elements are assessed property tax as well, but that tax is covered in your monthly maintenance payments.

Maintenance Payments

Maintenance payments or "assessments for common expenses" cover all the operating costs of the common elements and are adjusted for any increase or decrease in expenses. You are responsible for a portion of the development's total operating costs. The formula for calculating your portion follows below.

Unit entitlement is the basis on which the owner's contribution to the common expenses or maintenance fees of the condominium corporation is calculated. Various formulas are used for the calculation. In some developments the percentage calculated for the unit's share is determined by the original purchase price of each unit in relation to the value of the total property. Another method is to apportion costs on the basis of the number of units in equal proportion, regardless of unit size. But the most common formula is to calculate the unit entitlement by dividing the number of square feet in all the units by the number of square feet in an owner's unit. For example, let's say a condominium development contains 15 condominium units, the total square footage of all units is 15,680, your individual unit is 784 square feet, and the annual cost to maintain the common elements and other related expenses is $40,000. To calculate your monthly financial commitment, you would go through the following steps:

√ Calculate the unit entitlement (15,680 ÷ 784)= 1/20 share in the common property).

√ Calculate the annual share of maintenance costs (1/20 × $40,000 = $2,000 per year).

√ Calculate the monthly share of maintenance costs (1/12 × $2,000 = $166.66 per month).

The payments for common expenses are made directly to the condominium corporation and generally cover the following items:

√ *Maintenance and Repair of Common Property*

This includes costs for maintenance, landscaping, building repairs, recreational facilities, equipment, and other expenses.

√ *Operating and Service Costs*

This includes expenses relating to garbage removal, heat, hydro, and electricity.

√ *Contingency Reserve Fund*

This is a fund for unforeseen problems and expenses (e.g., replacing the roof or repairing the swimming pool or heating system). This fund is for expenses that have not been included in the annual budgeted expense calculations for the common property and other assets of the condominium corporation. Owners contribute monthly to this fund on the basis of a portion of the monthly maintenance fee. The condominium legislation in most provinces requires owners to contribute a minimum amount to the contingency reserve fund (e.g., 10% of annual budget). If you are buying an older condominium, you should check to see what percentage of the monthly payments is being allocated toward this fund, as there is a higher risk of needing to use the fund in older buildings than in newer developments. In older buildings, the fund will possibly be 25% or more, depending on the circumstances. In most cases you are not entitled to a refund of your contribution to the reserve fund when you sell your unit.

√ *Management Costs*

These are the costs associated with hiring private individuals or professional management firms to administer all or part of the daily functions of the condominium development.

√ *Insurance*

Condominium legislation requires the development to carry sufficient fire and related insurance to replace the common property in the event of fire or other damage. Condominium corporations generally obtain additional insurance to cover other payables and liabilities. Note: This insurance does not covers damages to the interior of an individual unit.

Special Assessment

There could be situations in which 75% or more of the condominium members want to raise funds for special purposes. These funds would not come from the contingency reserve fund or from the regular monthly assessments. For example, there could be an interest in building a swimming pool or tennis courts, or it may be necessary to cover the cost of repairs that will exceed the money available in the contingency reserve fund. Once the decision is made to assess members, you cannot refuse to pay the special assessment if it has been approved according to condominium by-laws, even though you might not agree with its purpose.

Condominium Owner Insurance

As mentioned earlier, the insurance on the areas of the building that are covered by the condominium development does not include the interior of your unit. Therefore, you will need to obtain your own insurance to cover the contents as well as damage to the inside of your unit, including walls, windows, and doors. There are several types of insurance, including replacement cost, all-risk comprehensive, and personal liability. It is also common to get insurance to cover deficiencies in the condominium corporation's insurance coverage in the event of fire so that any damage to your unit could be repaired in full; otherwise, the unit owners would have to pay on a proportional basis any deficiency by means of a special assessment. Many insurance companies have developed a specialized program referred to as condominium homeowner's package insurance. Check the Yellow Pages under "Insurance Brokers" and compare coverage and costs. You can also review the Web site for the Insurance Brokers Association of Canada (www.ibac.ca) to obtain a list of local members.

Lease Payments

If you have a leasehold condominium, you will be required to make monthly lease payments in addition to many of the other costs outlined in this section.

Utilities

You are responsible for the utilities you use in your unit, including hydro, water, and heat. In apartment condominiums, these expenses are usually included in the maintenance fee, whereas townhouse condominiums tend to have individual meters. You would be billed directly and individually by the utility companies.

Unit Repair and Maintenance Costs

You will have to allocate a certain amount of your financial budget for repair and maintenance needs relating to the inside of your unit. Your monthly assessment fee would cover common elements outside your unit only.

Advantages and Disadvantages of Condominium Ownership

In any situation of shared ownership and community living, there are advantages and disadvantages. If you are only renting out the condominium, some of the following points may not be as important to you as if you were living in it. An overview of these follows.

Advantages

- √ ready availability of financing as a single-family home
- √ range of prices, locations, types of structures, sizes, and architectural features available
- √ availability of amenities such as swimming pools, tennis courts, health clubs, community centres, saunas, hot tubs, exercise rooms, and sun decks

√ benefits of home ownership in terms of participation in the real estate market and potential growth in equity

√ individual ownership of living units

√ pride of home ownership

√ enables people of moderate and middle income to own their own homes

√ freedom to decorate the interior of the unit to suit personal tastes

√ enhancement of security by permanence of neighbours and, in many cases, controlled entrances

√ elimination of many of the problems of upkeep and maintenance often associated with home ownership, since maintenance is usually the responsibility of a professional management company or manager

√ often considerably less expensive than buying a single-family home because of more efficient use of land and economy of scale

√ investment opportunity for profit if selected carefully

√ good transitional type of home between rental apartments and single-family houses for growing families or singles or couples; conversely, good transition for "empty nesters" who wish to give up their larger family house

√ lower costs due to responsibilities for repair and maintenance being shared

√ enhancement of social activities and sense of neighbourhood community because of residents' relative permanence

√ elected council is responsible for making many business and management decisions

√ owners participate in the operation of the development, such as budget setting and approval; decision-making; determination of rules, regulations, and bylaws; and other matters affecting the democratic operation of the condominium community.

Disadvantages

√ Real estate appreciation is generally not as high as for a single-family house, due to the total ownership of land when owning a house; it is the land that goes up in value.

√ It may be difficult to accurately assess the quality of construction of the project.

√ There may be unacceptable loss of freedom because of restrictions in the rules and bylaws (restriction on the right to rent, restriction on pets, etc.).

√ People live in closer proximity, thereby potentially creating problems from time to time; common problems include pets, parking, parties, people, and personalities.

√ Flexibility may be affected if circumstances require that the condominium be sold in a limited time, as condominiums generally sell more slowly than single-family houses. This is not always the case, of course. It depends on variables. In many instances, condominiums sell faster than single-family houses.

√ One could be paying for maintenance and operation of amenities that one has no desire or intention to use.

√ Management of the condominium council is by volunteers, who may or may not have the appropriate abilities and skills.

√ Owners might be apathetic, so that the same people continually serve on council.

√ Some elected councils behave in an autocratic fashion.

Investing in a Condominium

The first-time real estate investor could find buying a condominium unit as a rental property an attractive option for several reasons. If you are considering investing in a condominium, it is important to consider the advantages and disadvantages of the different types of condominiums—for example, an apartment, townhouse, or hybrid mix, or a conversion of a former rental apartment building to a condominium. Check on whether rental units are permitted in the development before finalizing any offer, and get it confirmed in writing in advance. (This is particularly important, and is covered in Chapter 6: Understanding the Legal Aspects.) You don't want to buy a condo only to find out that the bylaws permit rentals, but the quota has been reached. Check on the current mix of tenants and owner-occupiers.

Here are some of the benefits you may wish to consider:

√ Condominiums generally appreciate in value at a rate that is higher than the inflation rate.

√ Finding an occupant for a condominium apartment is relatively easy in many major Canadian cities because of low vacancy rates.

√ There is an increasing demand for the condominium lifestyle and the convenience that it provides.

√ Because a minimal amount of upkeep is involved, the economic benefits are more attractive for the first-time investor.

√ There is the convenience of having many of the management and maintenance problems taken care of by the condominium corporation and the professional management company, if any.

√ Facilities such as tennis courts and swimming pools are maintained by the condominium corporation, thereby freeing the new investor from the responsibilities of upkeep.

√ The owner is protected by the bylaws and the rules and regulations set by provincial condominium legislation, by the original project documents, or by the condominium council. For example, many condominiums do not allow pets in the building because of the potential wear and tear on the apartment. This type of rule protects and benefits the investor.

If you are looking for higher appreciation (resale value), compare the purchase of the least expensive unit in a luxury condominium townhouse complex versus the largest unit in a modestly priced development, assuming the purchase price is the same. Your research will provide you with the necessary background statistics in your market interest area to determine which of the above options might provide the most attractive return.

Additional tips to look for when selecting a condominium are covered in Chapter 3: Finding and Evaluating the Right Property.

Dealing with Condominium Disputes

In the condominium community there is always the possibility that a problem or dispute may not be resolved quickly and easily. It is important to know your rights and options in that event. This section will cover the most common types of disputes and the means of resolving them.

Nature of Common Disputes

Problems tend to fall into the following general categories:

The Five P's: Pets, Parking, Parties, People, Personalities

The five P's tend to be the most common problems. Some pets can be noisy, roam the property, scare children, or foul the common property. Members or guests can be selfish and irresponsible in using parking spaces. People and parties are too loud for too long at too-late hours. Personalities may become a problem because of people living in close proximity; some owners get annoyed when people use or abuse the common elements, and some people can irritate others with their attitude, arrogance, indifference, or lack of courtesy.

Decisions of the Condominium Corporation or Council

Disputes with the condominium corporation or council can occur, for example, if you believe that the conduct of the corporation or council is oppressive and unfairly prejudicial toward your rights; if you believe that a decision relating to a special assessment was unnecessary and irresponsible; if you were fined for allegedly breaching the bylaws or rules and regulations and you believe the fine was unfair and unwarranted.

Resolution of Disputes

The means for resolving disputes, in ascending order of complexity, are negotiation, mediation, arbitration, and litigation.

Negotiation

It is always best to try to resolve the dispute by discussing the matter directly with the person concerned. That may be all that is necessary, so it is worthwhile to make the attempt.

Mediation

If the first step is not successful, you may wish to contact the condominium council and make a complaint to them by outlining your dispute. If another owner's conduct has contravened the bylaws or rules and regulations, it would be helpful to draw those points to the attention of the council, which has the authority in most cases to deal with infringements of the bylaws or rules and regulations.

Arbitration

If your attempts to have a dispute resolved through using the condominium council have not been successful, you may wish to consider arbitration. Condominium legislation of most provinces sets out the procedures for arbitration. Normally the process is not available if litigation has commenced. Matters that may require arbitration include disputes about contributions to common expenses; fines for breach of bylaws or rules and regulations; damage to common elements, common facilities, and other assets of the condominium corporation; and decisions of the council or the corporation.

The parties should agree on a single arbitrator, but if that is not possible, each party selects its own arbitrator and the two arbitrators select a third who acts as a chairperson. Unless the parties agree other wise, each arbitrator must have been an owner and occupier of a condominium unit in another development for at least one year, but may not be a member of the condominium corporation affected by the arbitration. The arbitrators may accept evidence under oath and may make whatever decision they consider just and equitable. The arbitrators' decision is entered into court as if it were an order of the court. This is a common procedure set out in most provincial condominium legislation, although the procedures may vary in individual provinces.

A list of arbitrators is available upon request from most professional condominium-management companies or provincial condominium owners association, if one exists in your province.

Litigation

If all else fails, you have rights in common law, as well as under most provincial condominium legislation, to commence an action in court. You can proceed against a condominium corporation or council to rectify what you believe is a failure to meet their obligations under the condominium legislation or bylaws, or because you feel that their actions toward you have been oppressive. The court can make any order it considers appropriate, depending on the circumstances.

The difficulty in the litigation process, of course, is that it can be very expensive, stressful, uncertain, and lengthy. If you have a problem and are wondering whether you should choose arbitration or litigation, you should seek a legal opinion from a lawyer who specializes in condominium law. Ideally it would be helpful to obtain a second opinion from another lawyer who specializes in condominium law in order to confirm that the legal advice is consistent.

How to select a lawyer is covered in Chapter 4: Selecting Your Advisory Team. Also, refer to Chapter 6: Understanding the Legal Aspects.

Single-Family House

A single-family house is one of the most attractive investments a beginning investor can make because investors are generally more familiar with a house as often they already live in one or have lived in one. Finding tenants is usually not a problem. In fact, if you have a self-contained suite in the basement, you could rent it out to one or two tenants.

There is generally a wide selection of single-family houses to select from. Land value goes up over time. The price is lower than it is for other types of residential real estate (e.g., duplexes or apartments). Also, financing is easier to obtain, and management effort and time are minimal. You can see why a single-family house is attractive as a principal residence.

However, there are some disadvantages to investing in a single-family house compared to other investments. If a tenant vacancy occurs, you will have to cover the expenses yourself. The small yield in terms of cash flow is lower. You would therefore be relying primarily on resale of the property to make a profit. The opportunity of making a large profit is less than with a multi-unit building. These are general observations, and there are many exceptions.

There are various single-family house choices available: you could buy a resale house, a new house, a lot and build a house yourself or with a builder, or you can assemble a prefabricated house. There are advantages and disadvantages to each option. Note: the terms "builder" and "contractor" are essentially interchangeable. If you are buying a newly built home, the term "builder" is frequently used. When contracting for someone to build you a house on a lot you bought, the term "contractor" is common.

Buying a Resale House

Many people prefer to buy a resale house when purchasing for personal use or as an investment. Here are some of the advantages and disadvantages of buying a resale house rather than a new house. These are general guidelines and do not necessarily apply in every case.

Advantages

√ A resale house is generally less expensive than a new house.

√ A resale house has character or a lived-in feeling.

√ An older home utilizes architectural styles that are unique and generally no longer in common use.

√ A competent professional building inspector can discern any problems in house design or construction (e.g., settling, cracks in the walls).

√ Landscaping is mature.

√ Neighbourhood is established and has developed its own character.

√ Community services are established.

√ Properties are available in and proximate to the centre of the city.

√ A resale house may include extras not normally included in a new home purchase, such as customized features that previous owners have built or installed.

√ You do not pay GST on the purchase. In some provinces, this is a combined federal/provincial tax, referred to a HST or harmonized sales tax, which includes the GST and provincial sales tax (refer to Chapter 7: Understanding the Tax Aspects).

Disadvantages

√ Such a house may not have been built according to current building standards, so it might not meet electrical or insulation codes (e.g., it might have aluminum rather than copper wiring, lead rather than copper pipes, inefficient insulation or UFFI [urea formaldehyde foam insulation]).

√ Defects in the house construction may not be visible or identified unless a thorough inspection is done by a professional building inspector. Buyers of new homes may be protected by a New Home Warranty Program, but buyers of used homes have no warranties.

√ If a resale house is in a metropolitan area, the property could be more expensive because of the higher value of land, whereas a new house in a suburban area could be less expensive due to the lower cost of land.

√ An older home may have been renovated by the owner or a handyman who may have done the work without obtaining a building permit and inspection, so the safety or functional aspects of the house could be deficient.

√ Some older homes do not have an attractive or functional design (e.g., rooms may be too small or the layout is poor); low basement, ceilings can make that area less functional for comfortable use or as a rental suite; the building might have a poor location on the property (e.g., set back too close or too far from front of property line); the bathrooms and kitchens might be too small or outdated. Costs to substantially renovate an older house can be expensive and time-consuming.

√ The equipment (e.g., heating system) and appliances may be outdated and need repair.

Buying a New House

You may wish to purchase a new house for your principal residence or investment needs. Here are some of the advantages and disadvantages of buying a new house over an older resale house.

Advantages

√ New houses tend to be better designed in terms of room layout (e.g., larger kitchen, bathrooms, en suites), functional purpose (e.g., higher ceilings in basement, patios, family room), and brighter atmosphere (e.g., skylights).

√ A builder often offers several house models. You can generally select certain features to customize your needs—such as carpet colour and fabric, kitchen appliance colours, kitchen and bathroom floor coverings, paint colours—if you contract the builder and build from plans or before the house is fully completed.

√ New houses are constructed in compliance with current building code standards (plumbing, electrical, heating, insulation, etc.).

√ It looks clean, modern, fresh, and smells new.

√ You are the first occupant in the house, which is an advantage because you can personalize the house to meet your own or your family's needs rather than remodelling.

√ Market evaluation of the house is easier because of similar comparable houses built in the same area.

√ The price of the house could be lower or the house could be larger (compared to a similar resale house) if a new house is built in a suburb with lower land costs.

√ Many new homes are built by builders who are registered with the New Home Warranty Program in their respective province, so if problems occur after the sale is completed, the builder or the New Home Warranty Program will correct them if the specific problems are covered by the program. Check with your provincial New Home Warranty Program and read the fine print of the coverage, which can vary from province to province.

Disadvantages

√ The builder may not be registered with the New Home Warranty Program, thereby creating a potentially high risk for the purchaser if problems occur.

√ Due to land availability and cost savings, many builders construct new houses a considerable distance from the city core, which means an increase in commuting time and fewer services than are available in more built-up metropolitan areas.

√ It is not uncommon to have construction delays (e.g., in paving driveways, landscaping, finishing touches) and defects, both of which cause
frustration and possible extra expense.

√ Many new houses are purchased pior to construction and are selected
based on an artist's sketch or various model plans. Frequently a model
home is not constructed at this stage. Conceptualizing how the final
house will feel compared to the reality is sometimes not consistent.

√ Purchase documents prepared by the builder tend to be more complex
and detailed than resale house contracts. This is discussed later.

√ You might lose the deposit funds you pay to the company if the builder
ceases to operate. In some provinces there is consumer protection legislation that protects these funds. Unless you put the funds in a lawyer's
or realtor's trust account, though, you could lose your deposit. It is
particularly important that you check the builder's reputation through
the following:

  • If the builder is registered with the New Home Warranty Program,
    in some provinces the deposit funds are protected up to a maximum
    amount. If the builder is not registered with a NHWP, be very cautious
    and don't pay any money or sign a builder's contract without your
    lawyer's advice. The NHWP of each province is similar, but there are
    some differences. The builder adds the fee for NHWP coverage onto
    the house price or builds it into the price. NHWP coverage generally
    includes buyer protection for the deposit, incomplete work allowance,
    warranty protection up to a year, basement protection for two years,
    and major structural defect protection for five years. Although the
    NHWP was designed to protect purchasers of newly constructed
    houses (condominiums can also be covered) against defects in
    construction, there are limitations in coverage. These limitations
    and exclusions could cost you a lot of money. That is why you need to
    check out the NHWP and builder thoroughly.

  • The local or provincial Home Builders' Association will be able to
    confirm whether a contractor is a member or not.

  • The local Better Business Bureau will have a record of any complaints
    against the contractor.

  • Purchasers of houses from other developments the contractor has
    built are good sources of information. Also ask the contractor for
    names and locations of previous development projects. You can
    then knock on doors and ask the owners if they would give you their
    candid opinion as to the quality of the house and responsiveness of

the builder in correcting any problems. Ask if they got what they bargained for. A key question to ask is: "Would you buy from the same builder again, and why?"

- The local (municipal) business licensing office can verify if the contractor is licensed.

If the contractor has no previous history in the industry, be very cautious. The contractor could have been operating under a previous company name but went under, and is now operating under a different company name. Alternatively, the contractor could be a first-timer and be learning at your expense. Take the time to check out the contractor's background and reputation. It will save you time, frustration, and money later on.

Make sure that you take the contract supplied by the house builder to your lawyer before you sign it. Builder's contracts tend to be customized and are designed primarily for the benefit of the builder. Sometimes you can negotiate changes to the contract, but at other times you cannot. It depends on the builder, the changes, and the market. A builder must occasionally be flexible in terms of the contract, especially if an experienced lawyer who is acting on behalf of the purchaser finds them to be unfair. The builder would not insist on retaining these clauses if it would stop the deal from proceeding.

You should have your lawyer advise you in general about the contract, as well as specifically on issues such as the following:

Special Contract Cautions

Deposit

Will the deposit be held in trust and, if so, where? Will interest be paid on the deposit to the credit of the purchaser? There is a risk if the money is going directly to the builder and not being held in trust by a lawyer or real estate company.

Financing

Will the builder arrange financing at a fixed rate through a lender or carry the financing himself? Make sure the payment terms are clearly spelled out. Make sure the rates and terms are competitive and that the financing package is attractive. For example, the builder could provide or arrange for a discounted interest rate for a year. The rate could be artificially low, rather than a prevailing market rate, to attract buyers who might not otherwise be interested or qualify for financing. What if interest rates go up at the end of the year when you have to refinance? Can you handle the increased monthly payments?

Assigning or Selling

Does the builder's contract have a restriction to prevent you from assigning your interest in the contract to someone else before the closing date, or selling your property to someone else after closing, within a certain period of time? Some builders don't want you to assign before closing so that you make potential profit in an increasing market. Other builders don't want you to resell your property after closing and before they have sold out the rest of the project, because they could lose a potential sale, or you could offer your house for sale at a lower price, thereby affecting their pricing structure.

Closing Date

What if the builder does not close on the agreed date? Consider adding clauses to the effect that the house price will be reduced by an agreed sum for a late closing, giving the purchaser the option to back out of the contract and get the deposit money back, plus accrued interest, if the purchaser so wishes (you might not want to exercise this option with a fixed sale price in an escalating market), or adding your own penalty clause that the builder has to pay you a penalty if the building is not completed on time. All these options are negotiable depending on the nature of the circumstances. There is no set formula. An example of a penalty could be a reduction of the purchase price, such as 1%, for every week of delay.

Depending on your needs and objectives, you should ask your lawyer to advise you. Attempt to negotiate a better deal yourself or through your lawyer. If you are not satisfied with the outcome, consider buying from a different builder.

Buying a Lot and Building a House

Some people prefer this arrangement and want to hire a contractor to build the house, build it themselves, or buy a prepackaged type of house (e.g., log cabin, ski chalet) and have it constructed.

If you are building your own house, make sure that you know what you are doing, otherwise it could be very time consuming, frustrating, and expensive. An alternative is to take a school board or college course on building your own house, and then hire a trustworthy contractor on an hourly basis to advise you. Check with your municipal planning department on the steps, building codes, permits, and inspections required. There are many regulations involved. Read how-to books on building your own house. You could save money and obtain personal satisfaction by doing it yourself, but don't overestimate your abilities or the amount of time you have available. Do-it-yourself construction almost always turns out to be more complicated and time consuming than initially expected.

Many of the problems that owners have in their dealings with contractors are due to misunderstanding of the rights, responsibilities, and functions of the various people who are involved in the work.

Homeowner's Responsibilities

Homeowner's responsibilities generally include the following:

- √ Decide what is to be done. Write a description of the work to be done, providing as much detail as possible.
- √ Obtain blueprints from an architect or a "stock" blueprint plan.
- √ Decide on all the features of the house in detail.
- √ Make arrangements with a lender for construction financing.
- √ Select a contractor.
- √ Make sure the written contract describes the job completely, thoroughly, and correctly.
- √ Obtain zoning approval and building permits, if required.
- √ Provide the space and freedom that the workers need to do their work.
- √ Inform the contractor about deficiencies or mistakes as quickly as possible, preferably in writing, so there is no misunderstanding and you will have a dated record.
- √ Pay for the work as required by the contract, holding back a portion to comply with provincial builder's lien legislation (normally 10%).
- √ Make the final decision as to whether or not the job has been done satisfactorily.
- √ Release the builder's lien holdback.

Contractor's Responsibilities

Contractor's responsibilities generally include the following:

- √ Carry out the work described in the contract.
- √ Follow the details in the blueprint (architect or "stock" plan prints).
- √ Decline to do any work that is not covered in the contract without written authorization from the owner for the changes.

√ Maintain public liability and property damage insurance, and workers' compensation coverage for workers. Ensure that the subcontractors carry the same for their workers.

√ Obtain any permits, licences, and certificates required by the municipality, unless there is a written agreement that the homeowner is responsible for them.

√ Adhere to all building codes (federal, provincial, and municipal) and other government construction regulations.

√ Supervise the quality of all work carried out by the contractor, including work done by subcontractors.

√ Pay all workers, suppliers, and contractors.

√ Remove construction debris upon completion of the job.

√ Provide warranties on all work and materials (in addition to manufacturer's warranties) for a period of at least one year if possible.

Finding the Right Contractor

It is important to clearly define your needs before you commit yourself. You should have at least three competitive bids (written fixed-price quotes) from contractors before selecting the one you want. There are various ways of finding names of contractors:

√ check with friends or neighbours for recommendations

√ check with local building material suppliers or hardware stores

√ check with local or provincial Home Builders' Associations

√ check with provincial New Home Warranty Program offices for names of contractors registered with them

√ check in the Yellow Pages of your telephone directory under "Contractors, Building."

Before finalizing your decision, check on the reputation and past performance of the contractor, using the cautions listed in the previous section on "Buying a New House." This is very important. Also, consider the advantages of hiring a contractor who is registered with the New Home Warranty Program. You will pay an extra amount for this coverage protection, but the benefits are obvious. Refer to the discussion of the NHWP in the previous section on "Buying a New House." Ask the contractor for the name of his insurance company, and ask for written verification that he has adequate public liability and property damage insurance. Ask the insurance company for confirmation if you have any doubts or concerns. If the contractor is doing a remodelling job rather than the whole house, ask for the following:

√ plans and/or sketches of the work to be done

√ samples and literature showing different products that could be used

√ photographs of previous work completed.

As mentioned earlier, it is essential that you have a written contract with the contractor. Many Home Builders' Associations have sample contracts available that you can use, so check with them. Have your lawyer look at the contract, and involve him or her in the release of any progress draws— payment to the contractor of an agreed portion of the total contract price—as the work progresses. Depending on the nature of the house construction, there could be from three to five different payments at various stages of construction or it could be every week. At each stage, confirm that the work is complete, and that the subcontractors, suppliers, etc., have been paid, and that there is noth- ing outstanding from the previous draw. It is not uncommon for contractors to use progress draws to pay for subcontractors' services or for supplies. Often lawyers will do lien searches to make sure that no liens have been filed against the contractor before the payment is made.

Your lender will normally require you to make progress draws. If you pay a lot of money to the builder and the work has not been performed or if the contractor goes out of business, you could lose the money you advanced.

Key Contents of a Construction Contract

A construction contract usually includes the following:

√ date of agreement

√ correct and complete address of the property where the work will be done

√ your name and address

√ contractor's name, address, telephone number, cell number, fax number, e-mail address; if a company name is used, the name of the company's official on-site representative should be indicated

√ detailed description of the work, sketches, and list of materials to be used

√ the type of work that will be subcontracted

√ the right to retain a builder's lien holdback as specified under provincial law

√ a clause stating that work will conform to the requirements of all applicable federal, provincial, or municipal building codes

√ start and completion dates

√ the contracted price and payment schedule (remember the lien holdback, which is normally 10%)

√ an agreement on who is responsible for obtaining all necessary permits, licences, and certificates

√ a clause setting out the procedures for confirming in writing any "extras" to the contract requested by the owner

√ signatures of the parties to the contract.

Property for Renovation

There are many types of residential properties that would be profitable after they are renovated. Generally, single-family houses, multi-unit dwellings, and apartment buildings are the most common choices.

When considering a property for investment, the main strategic plan is to locate the right property, improve the property, raise rents to increase the value, and sell at the right time for maximum profit.

Key Factors When Looking for a Property to Renovate

The factors to look for in selecting a real estate investment property are covered later in this chapter. When selecting a property for renovation, though, there are some additional factors to consider.

√ Look for a neighbourhood where people are renovating older houses. This will create a positive image that rejuvenation is taking place.

√ The property should be readily accessible via various forms of transportation and not be isolated.

√ It should be an attractive, high- or middle-income neighbourhood, and the crime rate should be low.

√ The neighbourhood should have more owner-occupiers than tenants and absentee landlords.

√ The property to be renovated should be in a neighbourhood that is not yet in high demand.

√ New residential construction implies that others consider this a growing neighbourhood.

√ New construction of commercial areas (e.g., shopping centre) or other nearby existing commercial areas is a positive sign.

√ The property should have some character and quality construction and craftsmanship.

√ The property should be close to other attractive amenities, such as rapid transit, a college or university, park, downtown area, proximity to lake or ocean view.

√ The property should have potential for renovation without problems from City Hall, e.g., a "non-conforming use" problem. That is, the property conformed to the original zoning or building bylaws, but does not currently conform because of municipal changes to the bylaws. If you decide to renovate, you could be obliged to upgrade many features of the house to conform to the current municipal requirements, which could be quite expensive or financially or structurally unattractive to you from an investment perspective.

√ If the neighbourhood has a community organization to improve the quality of the neighbourhood, that is a positive sign in terms of pride and initiative.

Other factors to consider when finding and selecting a property are covered in the next chapter. Before you buy a property for renovation, review the following.

Steps to Follow before You Buy a Property to Renovate

√ Make sure that you are familiar with the renovation process. If you are not experienced, consider taking courses, reading books and magazines, and getting expert advice.

√ Be realistic and focused on the types of renovations and types of renovation properties you are considering. Certain types of renovations get a better return on your investment in terms of price and general saleability. The highest return generally comes from renovating the kitchen and bathrooms.

√ Make sure that your personal goals and investment goals are clear; e.g., do you intend to purchase a property for a principal residence and then renovate it throughout the year and sell it? If so, you would normally be exempt from paying any capital gains tax on the sale because it would be deemed your principal residence. Or, is it your objective to rent out the property after the renovation?

√ Compare various properties and shortlist them to two or three that have good potential profit return. That way you can negotiate with more leverage because you are considering more than one property.

√ Consider having an architect view the property and give you ideas on how it can be improved. Look in the Yellow Pages under "Architects," or check out the Web site of the Architectural Institute of Canada (www.raic.org). The Web site has sections on how to choose an architect and other helpful information, as well as a directory of architects.

√ Have a professional appraiser give you an idea of the property's current market value. Look in the Yellow Pages under "Appraisers," or visit the Web site of the Appraisal Institute of Canada (www.aicanada.ca). The Web site has a directory of appraisers in your area, as well as consumer information.

√ Have a professional building inspector give you a report on the physical aspects, internal and external, of the building, including what changes would be possible. (Refer to Chapter 4: Selecting Your Advisory Team for tips on how to select a building or a building inspector.) Check out the Web site of the Canadian Association of Building and Property Inspectors (www.cahpi.ca), which has a list of members in your area.

√ Have at least three contractors give you written quotes on the cost of the renovations. Refer to the previous sections on "Buying a New House" and "Buying a Lot and Building a House" for tips on selecting a contractor. Check out the Web site of the Canadian Home Builders' Association (www.chba.ca). You will be able to locate provincial Home-builders' Associations and a list of members in your area. It also has excellent information and tips.

√ Check out the Web site of the Canada Mortgage and Housing Corporation (www.cmhc-schl.gc.ca). They have excellent information on home renovations.

√ Do a feasibility study to determine if the whole exercise makes financial sense. If the property is already a revenue property, analyze the previous expense history and do projections of future expenses. Prepare an income and expense statement and a cash flow projection of income to be derived from increased rents over time. Do a projected budget. You can find sample forms for these types of projections in the Appendix under Forms 5, 6, and 7.

√ Apply the capitalization of net income formula after the projected renovation to determine what the property value would be compared to the present market value, plus the cost of renovations. Will you make money? This formula will be covered in Chapter 3: Finding and Evaluating the Right Property.

√ Finally, if the property still looks attractive after you have followed the previous steps, then have your potential investment objectively reviewed by your accountant and lawyer before you make your final decision.

Recreational Property

For many reasons, the demand for recreational property has increased. You may wish to consider buying recreational property for personal use or investment purposes. Depending on your choices, the purchase could result in an attractive financial return and personal enjoyment over time. The term "recreational property" refers to a range of options, including an existing home (chalet, cabin, cottage, etc.), a condominium, a townhouse, a building lot, or a hobby farm, with recreational amenities nearby, such as fields, mountains, rivers, lakes, the ocean, a ski hill, golf courses, campsites, and recreational vehicle parks. Activities could include snowmobiling, hunting, hiking, climbing, boating, canoeing, sailing, fishing, downhill or cross-country skiing, or other recreational pursuits.

Trends Generating Interest in Recreational Property

Various trends and other motivating factors are generating an interest in rural and recreational property. These are:

√ availability of more leisure time

√ preference for an enhanced quality of life to provide balance for a hectic urban career, or the expense and time involved in commuting

√ desire to combine the best aspects of country and city life

√ desire for a simpler existence

√ desire to be close to recreational interests

√ desire to operate a business out of the home and commute to the city only as required; this could also include telecommuting, e.g., being an employee but working primarily from home and using telecommunications (computer, modem, fax, etc.) to interact with the employer

√ desire for a family retreat, which could be passed on to succeeding generations

√ desire for a future retirement home

√ intention to buy a lot in the desired area, and build when savings are sufficient; in the meantime, the land could be used with a mobile home or recreational vehicle

√ attraction to recreational properties because they are less expensive than urban properties

√ increase in demand for (and therefore value of) recreational or rural property that is proximate (within four-hour driving distance) to a metropolitan area

√ the vendor might be more likely to carry the financing, e.g., provide a vendor-take-back mortgage to the purchaser

√ possibility that the vendor would consider giving an option to purchase the property for a period of time, e.g., one to two years, at an agreed price. The option fee itself is normally nominal.

Potential Downsides of Purchasing Recreational Property

There are some potential downsides to purchasing recreational property. These are general comments, however, and there are many exceptions.

√ lenders are sometimes reluctant to lend money or approve a mortgage for recreational property, especially raw land

√ there may be some restrictions on land use (which will be discussed shortly)

√ if you have a seasonal property and intend to rent it out, you could have a negative cash flow (shortage in revenue to offset expenses) that you would have to subsidize

√ maintenance of the property could be frustrating if you are far from home

√ vandalism is more likely if the property is in a remote location or is used only seasonally

√ if the economy is in a recession, the value of the property can diminish considerably (along with demand) if you need to sell, a recreational property is generally considered a luxury and not a necessity.

Special Considerations When Selecting Recreational or Rural Property

There are special cautions when assessing recreational property for purchase. Chapter 3: Finding and Evaluating the Right Property, which includes a section on "Factors to Consider When Selecting a Property," deals with general factors, although primarily in an urban or metropolitan setting. It is important, though, to read that section thoroughly. Here are some issues that are specific to recreational or rural property.

Location

This is one of the most important aspects. You want to consider proximity to an urban area, what unique features are present (such as tourist attractions or natural beauty of area), desirability of location relative to other areas, and whether the area has seasonal or year-round usage. If you are buying property in a subdivision, try to be among the first to buy, so you can get the best location.

Accessibility to Neighbourhood

The area should be easily and quickly accessible by ferry, boat, plane, or car.

Restrictions on Use

There are various forms of legal restrictions that could affect your land and use of that land. Your lawyer can search the title of the property in the land titles office to see what encumbrances are on title as a condition of any offer you make.

Right of Way

This generally means a statutory (legal) right for certain companies, Crown corporations, or government departments to use or have access to part of your property for hydro, telephone, sewer, drainage, dike, or public access purposes.

Easement

An easement is similar to a right of way, but is the term used when one neighbour gives another neighbour the right to use or have access to a piece of land, e.g., permission to reach a waterfront by crossing a neighbour's land. This agreement is put into writing and filed in the local land titles office.

Restrictive Covenant

In this situation, a developer in a subdivision could make any purchase subject to an ongoing restriction in certain areas, e.g., requiring that all roofs be covered by shakes rather than shingles. The purpose would be for aesthetic uniformity. A document setting out the restrictions would be filed in the land titles office.

Zoning

There could be restrictions on how your property could be used, e.g., only for seasonal use, no mobile homes on the property, no other buildings to be constructed, and so on.

Water Availability

Check on this critical issue. Do you have well water? Is it safe to drink? Is it sufficient for your needs? Do you have a water system, either private or local, available to you? If you don't have a well, what would it cost to drill one?

Waste Disposal

What type of system is required or available? Is it a septic tank or other type of system? Is the soil suitable for a septic field? What about other types of waste disposal, such as garbage?

Crime

Check with the local police division to determine the levels of theft, arson, and vandalism in the area.

Land Boundary

Make sure that the boundaries of your property have been clearly marked and pegged by a qualified surveyor. This is especially important with acreage or waterfront property. You don't want to have disputes with your neighbours.

Amenities

What type of public or private recreational facilities are near the area you are considering? If the developer is establishing facilities, check out the developer's other projects to determine quality and residents' satisfaction.

Local Government

Find out the local government's attitude toward seasonal residents. It might assess higher taxes on seasonal residents to keep the tax base of year-round residents lower.

Existing Building

If you are buying a property with an existing building on it (a home, chalet, or cottage), have the building's structural condition inspected. Rural or recreational properties are particularly susceptible to the elements—wind, sun, ice, rain, and snow—depending on the location. If the building is not regularly or properly maintained, it can deteriorate rapidly. Also check for infestation, wood rot, and other damage.

Time-share Properties

You may also want to consider purchasing a recreational condominium or time-share property. If you are interested in such a property, refer to the earlier section in this chapter on condominiums. If you are interested in time-share properties, there are two main categories—fee simple ownership and "right to use."

Fee Simple Ownership

In this situation you would own a portion of the condominium or cabin, e.g., one-fiftieth of the property. Each portion would entitle you to one week's use of the premises. Other people would also invest in the property. Often you would be allocated a fixed week every year. In other instances, it could be a flexible arrangement, with the exact dates to be agreed upon, depending on availability. If the whole property is sold, you would receive your proportional share of any increase in net after-sale proceeds. You would also be able to usually rent, sell, or give your ownership portion to anyone you wished.

Right to Use

This concept is much like having a long-term lease, but with use for just one-week intervals a year. It is similar to prepaying for a hotel room for a fixed period every year for 20 years in advance. In other words, you don't have any portion of ownership in the property; you only have a right to use it for a fixed or floating time period every year. The "right to use" concept involves condominiums, cabins, chalets, recreational vehicle parks, and other types of properties.

From a real estate investment viewpoint, the opportunity for return on your money is limited or non-existent, especially in the latter case ("right to use"). In practical terms, it is primarily a lifestyle choice. Here are some of the disadvantages and cautions to be aware of.

Disadvantages of Time-share Properties

√ You may tire of going to the same location every year, as your needs may change over time.

√ The time-share programs that include an exchange option (e.g., switching a week in a different location) are not always as anticipated in terms of availability, flexibility, and convenience, or there may be upgrade fee.

√ Make sure you know what you are getting. Some people who purchase the "right to use" type think they are buying a fee simple ownership portion.

√ Be wary of hard-sell marketing techniques. Many time-share promotions, especially the "right to use" type, use aggressive and unethical strategies to get you to sign up. In most instances, the dream fantasy is heavily reinforced and there are "free" inducements (buffet, cruise, etc.) to entice you to hear a sales pitch.

√ High-pressure sales pitches, with teams of salespeople, can go on for hours. They can be very persuasive, if not aggressive, and often use very manipulative techniques to get you to sign a credit-card slip as a deposit. The "freebies" are generally worth from $5 to $10. It is an illusion to think you will get something for nothing. At best, you will only be subjected to an intense one-on-one sales approach. At worst, you will be out a $5,000 to $10,000 deposit charged to your credit card, plus monthly payments over time. Trying to get your money back afterwards, if you suffer from "buyer's remorse," is extremely difficult, if not impossible.

√ Time-share sales in Canada are sometimes covered by provincial consumer protection, in terms of your right to get your money back by "rescinding" (cancelling) the contract within a certain time period. If you are buying in certain U.S. states, in Mexico, or in other destination resort areas, you could have no rights at all if you later have "buyer's remorse." The hard-sell promoters will generally require you to bring your spouse and show your credit card before agreeing to let you into the sales pitch room to be "eligible" for the "freebie." This is a danger sign warning you to stay away. Remember—act in haste, repent at leisure.

√ The legal aspects are generally more complex and expensive when dealing with time-shares outside Canada.

√ There is usually an ongoing management fee for maintaining the premises.

√ Speak to at least three other time-share owners in the project you are considering to get their candid opinions before you decide to buy. Never give out your credit card for any reason as a deposit, or sign any documents requested of you, without first speaking with a local real estate lawyer. Don't let yourself be pressured. Check with the local Better Business Bureau.

Multi-unit Dwelling

These types of dwellings can range from a duplex (two-family house, either side by side or one above the other) to an eight-unit building. Generally, each housing unit is separate, each with exterior access, i.e., you don't need to go through a central lobby to reach each unit. Normally each unit would be self-contained, e.g., have its own bathroom and kitchen. If they were shared, the building would be more like a boarding house.

The multi-unit investment can be ideal for investors who intend to live in one of the units and perform much of the maintenance and repair themselves. This, of course, can also result in tenants bothering you if maintenance problems arise. Multi-unit dwellings are also ideal for splitting into smaller units and renting to singles to maximize the overall income. The return on investment (ROI) in a multi-unit dwelling can be quite attractive as financing is frequently easier to obtain and cash outlays are low or non-existent, compared to larger buildings. Conversely, if a single vacancy occurs, and there is a maximum of eight tenants, for example, the proportional impact on the total rent income will be greater than it would be for a larger building.

Apartment Building

This is not typically the type of purchase for a first-time investor. The usual pattern is to start with a single-family house or condominium, duplex, or triplex, or multi-unit dwelling before considering an apartment building. You want to start your learning experience as an investor and landlord slowly and cautiously before taking on more challenging investments. You may decide to restrict your investments to single-family homes, for example, for many logical reasons. Frequently an investor in an apartment building joins an investment group to share the risk, experience, management, responsibility, financing, and profit. (Refer to the section "Buying with Partners" in Chapter 1: Understanding Real Estate Investment.)

For the purpose of this discussion, an apartment building is defined as a building with eight or more housing units having interior access, i.e., one enters the building first before entering any individual apartment unit. The previous point covered multi-unit buildings up to eight unit. In practical language, though, any building with between six and twenty units is referred to as a small apartment building.

Here are some of the advantages and disadvantages, in general terms, of apartment buildings as an investment.

Advantages

√ Cash flows from medium-size or larger apartments are relatively stable and not as sensitive to tenant vacancies as small buildings such as duplexes and fourplexes.

√ There is usually a good resale market, depending, of course, on location, vacancy rates, cash flow, expenses, economy, etc.

√ Opportunity for profit is generally good, depending on the variables noted above.

√ Financial leverage in terms of borrowing on equity and cash flow is generally good.

√ Rents and therefore profits are often responsive to upgrades and renovations (e.g., buy an apartment building at a price based on its expected return, then upgrade the building, increase the rents, improve the management operation, reduce expenses, and then sell the property to another investor). The new sale price would reflect the more attractive net revenue figure, thereby justifying an attractive profit on sale.

√ A well-located and well-maintained apartment building generally appreciates in value at least with the inflation rate. However, the potential for appreciation is related to an anticipated cash flow increase in the future (no rent control) or land value increase due to an attractive location.

Disadvantages

√ Rents may be subject to provincial rent control legislation, thereby limiting increases in cash flow. This has a more significant impact in a larger apartment building than a single-family home or small multi-unit dwelling.

√ Apartment buildings require more extensive management than other types of properties. Inferior management can quickly lead to increased turnover and rising vacancies.

√ Maintenance costs (e.g., elevators, swimming pools, heating system) can be expensive.

√ If construction quality is poor, the apartment can deteriorate rapidly, thereby increasing operating expenses. If rent control exists, revenue may not be increased sufficiently to offset increased expenses. A related factor is the risk of considerable depreciation of the building, which reduces the refinancing and sale potential.

√ If local market changes occur (e.g., significant unemployment), this can result in a large increase in vacancy rates. This risk is particularly great in a single-industry community.

√ If interest rates drop, many renters will opt to become first-time home-buyers due to the increased amount of mortgage funds available and attractive rates. This would especially be so in a buyer's market. The practical effect is that there could be a sharp drop in apartment occupancy rates, resulting in negative cash flow.

√ New construction of apartment buildings can create competition for tenants due to an oversupply of units on the market.

√ Increased property tax assessments on apartment buildings as a result of a change in municipal tax base policy or new zoning regulations can result in increased expenses and decreased operating profit.

Factors to Consider When Selecting an Apartment Building

There are many factors to consider when selecting an apartment building, most of which will be covered in the next chapter. Other factors include the following:

√ monthly net income (after expenses)

√ quality of construction and condition of the building (affects operating expenses); a detailed property inspection report is a must

√ quality of existing management

√ potential for increase in revenue and reduction in expenses

√ physical attractiveness of property (affects rent levels and demand)

√ nature of amenities

√ mix of apartment units (e.g., studio, one bedroom, two bedrooms); affects nature of demand and type of tenants (e.g., single person, family with children)

√ rent control or the prospect of rent control

√ overall real estate investment climate

√ degree and type of competition

√ history of vacancy/occupancy rates among apartments in general in the community and the specific apartment building in particular

√ thorough research on the population demographics and trends in the community, and clear basis for determining and projecting where tenants will come from

√ federal and provincial tax incentives or tax policies favourable to apartment investment, not only in terms of annual net profit but capital gains on resale

√ availability and attractiveness of financing terms and rates, including the possibility of vendor-take-back mortgage.

Make sure that you get competent professional legal and tax advice before signing any agreement of purchase and sale. Buying an apartment building is a complex business and real estate investment decision, and the potential pitfalls are many. (Refer to Chapter 7: Understanding the Tax Aspects and the section on tax tips when purchasing a revenue property.)

Raw Land

Possibly you are buying raw land so you can build a year-round house or a vacation cottage. If so, you have to take into account many factors, including the cost of servicing the land in order to prepare it for construction, assuming the land is not already in a subdivision. (See also the sections in this chapter on "Single-Family House" and "Recreational Property.")

If you are buying raw land with no building on it, however, for the purpose of holding it as an investment for the future, you should be aware that it is one of the most speculative and risky types of real estate investment. On the other hand, if you are purchasing the land at a reasonable price and you can afford (preferably with cash or a large down payment) to reduce any monthly debt servicing, or if the land is attractive to you and is purchased as a long-term investment without any expectation of profit in the near future, then a raw-land purchase might be an appropriate option to consider. In addition, if the land is a large enough and has good soil, you may be able to generate some revenue by leasing it out to a farmer.

Those who buy raw land and profit from it tend to be sophisticated investors who tie up the property with an option-to-purchase agreement (with a nominal amount paid for the option), spread the risks by going into the purchase with a group of other investors, do their research beforehand, know that the property will increase in value due to rezoning or subdivision potential, or plan to hold it for future development or sale. In other words, you need to be clear and objective about your goals and the degree of risk you are willing to take.

There are inherent problems, though, if you are intending to buy raw land for investment purposes. Due to the risks involved, you should expect a higher rate of return on your investment. Here are some of the advantages and disadvantages.

Advantages

√ Raw land is available at a relatively low cost.

√ There is high potential gain if the land is rezoned, subdivided, developed, or if it increases in value for other reasons such as the building of a road, highway, rapid transit, or if sewers are installed proximate to the property.

√ Diversification of real estate investments—that is, by investing in different types of real estate, you are spreading your risk and therefore minimizing your overall financial and investment risk.

Disadvantages

√ No income will be generated, so there will be a negative cash flow. You have to subsidize the debt servicing of expenses such as a mortgage, interest, and property taxes yourself, unless you paid the entire cost in cash.

√ If the land cannot be converted to a better use or prospects, such as the expansion of the community, do not materialize, the investment could lose money through debt-servicing costs, real estate sales commission fee, reduction in value to other prospective purchasers, or lack of interest by other investors.

√ The municipality may place zoning or environmental restrictions on the use of land, e.g., agricultural use only.

√ The municipality might expropriate the land to expand a highway, designate the land as green space, or request a right of way over part of the land.

√ Financing from banks and other lending institutions to purchase the land is more difficult to obtain because of the speculative nature of raw land and the lack of income to service the debt.

√ Using raw land as security or collateral for raising money for other investment purposes is difficult for the same reasons as noted earlier, so using leverage (borrowing on equity of property) on raw land is reduced.

√ Revenue Canada (CRA) generally considers the profit obtained from the sale of raw land as income from speculation, not a capital gain from an investment. The result is that you will pay more tax. If it were considered a capital gain, you would be taxed on 50% of the gain, e.g., net profit. (Refer to Chapter 7: Understanding the Tax Aspects.)

Web Sites of Interest

Here are some Web sites to assist you in your information and contacts research.

Most of the professional associations provide names of accredited members in your geographic area.

Appraisal Institute of Canada:	www.aicanada.ca
Canadian Association of Home and Property Inspectors:	www.cahpi.ca
Canadian Home Builders' Association:	www.chbi.ca
Canadian Mortgage and Housing Corporation:	www.cmhc-schl.gc.ca
The Royal Architectural Institute of Canada:	www.raic.org

Summary

This chapter discussed the main categories of property available when deciding to invest in real estate: condominiums, houses, property for renovation, recreational property, multi-unit buildings, apartment buildings, and raw land. The various options available within many of these main categories were also explained. The next chapter deals with how to find and evaluate a property.

CHAPTER 3

Finding and Evaluating the Right Property

Whether you are buying a principal residence or investment property, you want to make money on resale and avoid problems and expenses during the interim. Ideally, you want to buy low and sell high. You also want to minimize stress and inconvenience, and maximize tax-free or after-tax profit. There is a good prospect of doing so if you follow the guidelines outlined in this chapter and the rest of the book.

This chapter will explain the main factors to consider when selecting a property, where to find a property for sale, and how to determine its value. Helpful Web sites will also be included.

Factors to Consider When Selecting a Property

There are many factors to consider when selecting real estate for use as a principal residence or for investment purposes. In general, a combination of factors will determine your decision to buy in a particular area. It is important to make a final assessment based on an objective review of the realistic investment potential, taking into account the various factors. This section discusses where to get general and specific real estate information, and the types of issues to consider. Refer to Checklist 1 in the Appendix for an outline of many of the factors you should consider and compare in properties that interest you.

Where to Get General Information

Part of your research to enhance the quality of your decision making is to have a general overview of trends and economic factors that might affect your choice and/or location of investment. There are many sources of information, depending on your available time, personal priorities, and the amount of effort you are willing to expend. The saying that "knowledge is power" is an accurate one. The more general and specific information you have, the better the chance you will have of making the right decision and being aware of opportunities. Here are some sources of general economic and real estate information you may wish to consider. Remember, as discussed in Chapter 1, each market is unique, so general trends may or may not have a direct bearing, but they will give indications. Other factors in your specific geographic area will influence demand and prices.

National Newspapers

There are two main publications—*The Globe and Mail* and *The National Post*—that deal with financial and economic issues and trends, as well as regular features and reports on real estate. Consider subscribing to them. Remember, the subscription fee is a 100% tax-deductible expense against any income from your business or investment.

Regional and Local Business or Real Estate Newspapers

Check with your local newsstand or public library to find out which publications are relevant to your needs. Some publications are free.

Courses and Seminars

These provide another way to increase your awareness and enhance your decision making. There are real estate as well as general business management courses offered from time to time by the school board and college adult-education programs. Also, practical courses for the general public are offered on home buying, home building and renovating, by homebuilder industry associations and the Canadian Mortgage and Housing Corporation. Check out the CMHC site at www.cmhc-schl.gc.ca. Check out the Web site for the Canadian Homebuilders' Association at www.chba.ca to find out contact information for provincial or local homebuilder association seminars or courses.

Books

Check out your local library and bookstore for books on real estate investing, responsibilities of a landlord, and related topics. Also check the Web sites of Chapters/Indigo at www.chapters.ca, and Amazon Books at www.amazon.ca.

Trade Shows

Local home shows or renovation shows, where you can pick up ideas and contacts and attend seminars, are excellent sources of information.

Where to Get Specific Information

The following sources of information will provide helpful assistance or more specific research steps. (Refer to Chapter 1: Understanding Real Estate Investment for further information.)

Internet

The Internet is a valuable research tool. You can find out almost anything you want to know about real estate by using effective search techniques. Google is one of the best search engines currently available (www.google.cw). Other relevant Web sites of interest are mentioned throughout this chapter.

Statistics Canada

This federal government department can provide you with invaluable information relating to population movements, general trends, census data, socio-economic profiles, and other demographic data. Contact your local library for Statistics Canada research data and analysis, or contact Statistics Canada directly. Look in the Blue Pages of your telephone directory under "Government of Canada," or reach them through their Web site at www.statcan.ca.

Canada Mortgage and Housing Corporation (CMHC)

This federal Crown corporation compiles invaluable historical data, analysis of information, and housing trends and projections, among other things. It has superb sources of information, and can provide personalized research consulting services for a fee if you want to know specialized information about a specific area. Many of the publications are free and available upon request or found on their Web site. Other publications are available at market cost. You may want to contact CMHC and ask them to put you on their mailing or e-mail list. To contact the CMHC branch office nearest you, look in the Blue Pages of your phone book, or check out their Web site at www.cmhc-schl.gc.ca. Some of the many CMHC publications available include the following analyses and reports. Obtain a current list of publications:

√ *The Housing Market Outlook* (semi-annual) covers projections of market activity in communities with a population of 100,000 or more

√ *Rental Market Reports* (annual) for all areas with a population of 100,000 or more. Also stats available for communities of 10,000 or more

√ *Local Housing Now* (monthly) covers new and resale home stats for the same type of community populations as noted above

√ *National Housing Observer* (annual) for new and re-sale homes.

Real Estate Survey of House Prices

Royal LePage publishes a quarterly *Survey of Canadian House Prices*. It is free of charge and can be picked up at a local Royal LePage office, or is available through their Web site at www.royallepage.ca. This survey is invaluable and provides information on current (as of survey) estimated "fair market value" house prices, prices three months earlier and one year earlier, and percent change year-over-year. Estimated average taxes and average monthly rentals are also indicated. Four different categories of single-family housing are surveyed, together with a standard and luxury condominium high-rise apartment. Each housing type and its amenities are specifically described, permitting comparisons of value across the country. This includes many regional construction variances for which adjustments have been applied. Naturally, the quality of location has a major influence on real estate values. The properties surveyed are deemed to be within average commuting distance to the city centre and are typical of other housing in the neighbourhood. The survey will also give you an idea of price and rental trends in a particular location.

National Real Estate Firms

All of the major national real estate firms have Web sites with valuable research information available on properties. Check in the Yellow Pages of your phone book for real estate company names and Web sites, or check on the Internet for the Web site address by doing a www.google.ca search.

Real Estate Boards

Most boards keep statistics on historical prices in their geographic area. A real estate agent can provide you with helpful data. If the real estate board operates on a Multiple Listing Service (MLS), there will be even more data available through a member realtor or on the MLS Web site (www.mls.ca).

Real Estate Agents

Agents are a vital source of information about housing in the geographic area of interest that you are considering. (How to select and effectively use an agent is covered in Chapter 4: Selecting Your Advisory Team.) A real estate agent can locate a great deal of information for you through the MLS system, such as price comparisons, historical data and trends, listing profile of property, and more. You can also do your research on the www. mls.ca site.

Municipal Planning Department

This department should be able to advise you if there is a development planned in the community of interest to you. This could include apartment buildings, condominium complexes, shopping centres, or highway expansions, for example. You could also enquire if there is any potential rezoning that might affect the property you are considering. Check to see if there have been any natural disasters such as flooding or mudslides that could affect your property. Also, find out how many building permits have been issued. Which areas have the greatest new construction and renovation activities? If you are interested in applying for rezoning, building a new house, or renovating an old house, ask for the following material as your circumstances dictate: zoning maps, zoning regulations, building codes, building permit application forms and instructions, municipal codes, and regional master plans.

Economic Development Department

This department is normally associated with the municipality or regional district. Its function is to stimulate economic activity and employment in the area. The department should have information about long-term growth plans that will have a positive economic impact on the community. This would include the locations of the growth. Purchasing a residential property near a future growth area could enhance your financial return, e.g., near locations of rapid transport, subways, major shopping mall or office development.

Municipal Tax Department

Find out the basis on which property taxes are calculated. Your municipality might have a high commercial tax base, which effectively subsidizes the residential tax base, thereby keeping residential taxes down. Maybe your municipality is growing rapidly and is becoming, in effect, a bedroom community with lots of families. If the supply of schools and teachers in the municipality is low and the demand is increasing, property taxes could go up to finance the construction of schools and the hiring of teachers.

If you are buying for retirement purposes, you may not want to pay property taxes for services you will not use immediately. Check to see if there are any major property tax increases planned in general and why, and specifically for the property you are considering. In the latter case, a new drainage system or lane paving could be passed on directly to the property owners affected.

Municipal Police Department

Check with the local police department for statistics related to crime in the neighbourhood you are considering. Compare the crime rate with other communities. Determine if it is increasing or decreasing.

Municipal Fire Department

Ask the fire department about the frequency of fires in the neighbourhood you are considering, relative to other areas in the general community. If there are a high number of fires, the neighbourhood could be a risk area, especially if arson is suspected. Also ask about the incidence of false alarms in the neighbourhood you are considering. This also gives an indication of potential problems.

Local Newspapers

These can be an excellent source of information on issues affecting the community in general or a specific location in particular. You can pick up back issues over the past few months from the newspaper office or check with the local library.

Local Homebuilders' Association

The community you are considering may have a Homebuilders' Association. Look in the Yellow Pages or check out the Web site for the Canadian Homebuilders' Association at www.chba.ca. You can obtain contact information about provincial or local Homebuilders' Associations through the site. The association members could tell you which areas of the community have high growth and the trends that indicate future high growth.

Remodelling Contractors

Look in the phone book for contractors who specialize in remodelling. Contact at least three contractors and ask which areas of the community appear to have a high percentage of remodelled homes, which can add value to the property you purchase because they improve the overall attractiveness of the neighbourhood.

Building or Home Inspector

Check with local private building or home inspectors. You can find them in the Yellow Pages or contact the Canadian Association of Home and Property Inspectors through their Web site www.cahpi.ca. Ask them which areas of the community are expanding; which areas have had a lot of remodelling done; which areas have problems such as drainage, insects, etc.; and which areas have resale homes in excellent condition.

Neighbours

Don't forget to ask the people in the area you are considering how they enjoy the neighbourhood. Would they buy there again? Which specific features about the neighbourhood do they like or dislike? What is the ratio of owners vs. renters? Ask for feedback that gives you some feeling for the quality and stability of the community. Whether you are thinking of buying a principal residence or an investment property, these issues are important for peace of mind as well as resale potential.

Important Factors to Consider

Some of the general features and factors are discussed below. Certain factors might be more important if you are buying for personal use (principal residence) rather than as a revenue real estate investment. Remember to refer to Checklist 1 in the Appendix when you are making your selection.

Location

One of the prime considerations is the location. How close is the property to schools, cultural attractions, shopping centres, recreational facilities, work, and transportation? How attractive is the present and future development of the area surrounding the property? You could invest in a property and six months later a high-rise complex could be built across from you, blocking your view and therefore decreasing the resale value of your property. The location should have ample access to parking and other attractive features. Check on the amount of traffic on the streets in your area. Heavy traffic can be a noise nuisance as well as a hazard for young children.

Noise

Thoroughly assess the level of noise. Consider such factors as the location of highways, driveways, parking lots, playgrounds, and businesses relative to the property you are considering. If you are buying a condominium, also consider the location of the garage doors, elevators, garbage chutes, and the heating and air conditioning plant or equipment.

Privacy

Privacy is an important consideration and has to be thoroughly assessed. For example, ensure that the sound insulation between the walls, floors, and ceilings of your property is sufficient to enable you to live comfortably without annoying your neighbours or having your neighbours annoy you. If you have a condominium or townhouse unit, such factors as the distance between your unit and other common areas, including walkways, roads, and fences, are important.

Price

The price of the property you are considering should be competitive with that of other, similar offerings. On the other hand, if you are purchasing a condominium unit, it is sometimes difficult to compare prices accurately without taking into account the different amenities—such as tennis courts, swimming pool, recreation centre, etc.—that may be available in one condominium but not available in another. You may decide that you do not want these extra facilities in view of your lifestyle needs, in which case paying an extra price for the unit because of these features would not be attractive. On the other hand, you have to look at the resale potential, so check with your realtor. He or she can obtain accurate information on comparative pricing and cost per square foot for similar properties.

Common Elements and Facilities

If you are buying a condominium unit, review all the common elements that make up the condominium development. Are they relevant to your needs? What are the maintenance or operating costs that might be required to service these features?

Parking Facilities

Is the parking outdoors or underground? Is there sufficient lighting for security protection? Is it a long distance from the parking spot to your home? Is there parking space available for a boat, trailer, or second car, and is there ample visitor parking?

Storage Facilities

Check out the type of storage space available, including its location and size. Is there sufficient storage space for your needs, or will you have to rent a mini-locker to store excess items?

Quality of Construction Materials

Look thoroughly at your building and the surrounding development to assess the overall quality of the development. If you are buying a condominium, keep in mind that you are responsible for paying a portion of the maintenance costs for the common elements. You may wish to hire a contractor or building inspector whom you trust to give you an opinion on the quality and condition of the construction before committing yourself. An older building will obviously cost money to repair, possibly a considerable amount of money and in a short time.

Design and Layout

When looking at a building, consider your present and future needs. For example, if you are buying a condominium, although you are entitled to use the interior of your unit as you wish, there are restrictions relating to the exterior of your unit or any structural changes that you may make to the unit. If you intend to add a separate room for an expanded family, in-laws, or an office, if that is possible, you should consider the implications beforehand.

For example, you may find that the balcony is very windy and you would like to build a solarium to enclose the balcony for that reason. There is a very good chance that you would not be able to do so without the consent of the condominium council because it would affect the exterior appearance of the development.

Neighbours

Look at the surrounding neighbourhood and determine whether the value of the residences in the neighbourhood will affect the value of your property. For example, are the homes in the area well maintained? Are there children in the same age group as your own children? What sort of people live in the neighbourhood? Are they single adults, young couples (with or without children), or older retired people?

Owner-Occupiers vs. Tenants

If you are buying a condominium, ask how many tenants as opposed to owners there are or will be in the condominium complex, and the maximum number of tenants allowed. The higher the percentage of owner-occupiers, the better the chance that there will be more pride of ownership and therefore more responsible treatment of common elements and amenities. If you are purchasing a house, the same principle applies. Generally you should be concerned if the tenant percentage in the condominium complex or residential area is 25% or more and is increasing.

Management

If you are buying a condominium unit or apartment building, find out whether the building is being operated by a professional management company, a resident manager, or if it is self-managed. (This is discussed in more detail in Chapter 10: Managing Your Property.) Ideally, you should check out the condominium unit or property that you are interested in at three different times before you decide to purchase: during the day, in the evening, and on the weekend. That should give you a better idea of noise level, children, or parties, and the effectiveness of the management control.

Property Taxes

Compare the costs of taxes in the area that you are considering with those of other areas equally attractive to you. Different municipalities have different tax rates and there could be a considerable cost saving or expense. Also, find out if there is any anticipated tax increase and why.

Rental Situation in the Area

If you are thinking of purchasing a revenue property, look for an area that enjoys a high rental demand. You want to minimize the risk of having a vacancy. Check Royal LePage's *Survey of Canadian House Prices*, referred to earlier, to obtain average house rentals in the area. Their site is www.royallepage.ca. On the other hand, you don't want too many rental houses, as that will increase competition and possibly reduce the overall desirability of the neighbourhood. Also, check the CMHC rental stats in the area that interests you. Their Web site is www.cmhc-schl.gc.ca.

Local Restrictions and Opportunities

Check if there are restrictions on use and other matters. For example, is there a community plan? What type of bylaw zoning is there, and is it changing? Is there a rezoning potential for higher or different use? Is there a land-use contract? What about non-conforming use of older or revenue buildings?

Perception of the Area

What perception does the media or the public in general have about a certain area? Is it positive or negative, and why? People's perception of the area may influence rental or purchase decisions.

Stage of Development

A geographic area will typically go through a series of stages, phases, and plateaus over time. For example, the normal stages are development (growth), stabilization (maturing, plateauing), conversions (from apartments to condos), improvements of existing properties, decline of improvements (deterioration), and redevelopment (tearing down of older buildings and new construction, with more efficient use of space).

Economic Climate

This is a major factor to consider. What is stimulating the economy, not only in terms of renters but actual homebuyers? Is there new development such as shopping centres, house and condo construction, office buildings, franchise outlets, and other commercial activity? Will the provincial or federal government construct or move offices to the community? Is a major single-industry employer the main source of economic activity in the area? In the latter case, you can appreciate the risk involved if the industry or main employer has financial problems or decides to close down or move away.

Conversely, in many major cities of Canada, the commercial rent in downtown areas is high and the commuting time and/or downtown residential rents or house prices inhibit employee retention. For this reason, many companies are moving their operations to the suburbs, where commuting, rent, and land costs are cheaper, and employee retention is higher.

Employment

This factor is, of course, related to the economic climate. The closer the tenants live to their workplace, the lower the turnover will be. The closer the workplace to the employee, the higher the demand will be if you sell your property.

Population Trends

Look for the trends in the community you are considering. Are people moving in or out, and why? What is the average age? Type of employment? Income level? Family size? Ethnic origins? Marital status? Many of these demographic statistics can be obtained from Statistics Canada or from your provincial or municipal government. If the population is increasing, it will generally create more demand for rental and resale housing. Conversely, if it is decreasing, the opposite will occur. If the population is older, people may prefer downsizing to condominiums rather than buying smaller houses. There are many variables to consider.

Size and Shape of Lot

This factor has to do with subdivision or rezoning potential, resale marketability, and general enjoyment.

Transportation

A prospective tenant or homebuyer will want to have convenient transportation routes. Whether it's a bus, subway, rapid transit, freeway, ferry, or other mode of transportation, the quality of transportation will have a bearing on your rental or resale price.

Topography

The layout of the land is an important consideration. If the property is low-lying (i.e., adjacent to a rise or hill), water drainage problems could result. Water could collect under the foundation of the house, thereby causing settling, assuming there is only soil under the foundation. Maintaining the property in terms of cutting the grass could be more difficult if the ground is uneven rather than level. These are just some of the issues to consider.

Appearance

Look at the appearance of the property you are interested in. Would it be attractive to someone else if it is resold? Is it well maintained, or does it need repair? What do the other buildings in the neighbourhood look like? Are they new, renovated, or attractive? Or are they poorly maintained with peeling paint, uncut grass, broken windows, and trash lying about?

Crime Rate

Naturally, this is an important issue for purchase or sale. How to obtain this information was covered in an earlier part of this chapter.

Services in the Community

Different services available in the community—for example, shopping, churches, community and recreational facilities, playgrounds or parks, and schools—will attract different types of tenants or purchasers, depending on their needs.

Climate

If you are buying for personal use and eventual resale or buying as an investment, climate is an important consideration. Certain areas of the city or community may have more rain, snow, and wind than others, depending on historical climate patterns.

Unattractive Features

Look for factors that will have a negative influence on a prospective tenant or purchaser: unpleasant odours from an industrial plant, a lack of natural light for the home because of overgrown trees, lack of street lighting that impairs safety, inadequate municipal services such as septic tanks rather than sewer facilities, unrepaired roads, or open drainage ditches. Awareness of these negative factors will also assist you in your decision making and negotiating approach. (This is covered in more detail in Chapter 9: Negotiating Strategies.)

Convenient Proximity

If you are buying real estate as an investment, it is prudent to purchase within a four-hour drive of your principal residence so you can conveniently monitor and/or maintain your property. This is just a general guideline, of course.

Reasons for Sale

One of the important factors to determine is why the property is for sale. Maybe the vendor knows something you don't, which will have a bearing on your further interest. On the other hand, maybe the vendor wants to move to a larger home or downsize to a smaller home or condo, plans to separate or divorce and move out, has lost employment, needs to relocate for a job, or is seriously ill or incapacitated. (A more detailed discussion of a vendor's motives is covered in Chapter 9: Negotiating Strategies.)

Where to Find a Property for Sale

There are some preliminary considerations you need to work through before starting your search. First of all, have a strategic plan:

√ Be clear about what type of real estate you want and which area you are interested in; this will save time and stress. (Chapter 1 dealt with determining your real estate strategies.)

√ Target specific geographic area or areas. This makes your selection process much simpler and gives you an opportunity to get to know specific areas thoroughly. Obtain street maps of the area as well as a zoning map from City Hall.

√ Know the price range that you want to buy in, based on your available financing and real estate needs.

√ Determine the type of ideal purchase package that you want (e.g., price and terms) as well as your bottom-line fallback position. What is the maximum you are willing to pay and the most restrictive terms that you can live with? Make sure that you don't compromise your own position.

√ Do comparisons and shortlist choices. That way you can ensure you get the best deal, in comparative terms.

√ Be realistic in terms of your purchase conditions in accord with the current market situation. Many people fantasize about buying investment real estate for 20% or more below the fair market value and keep searching for this elusive purchase. The reality is, such a purchase could be very difficult to find.

√ Don't wait for mortgage rates to go down before looking. Higher mortgage rates generally mean less demand in the market and therefore lower prices and more negotiating leverage for the purchaser. Conversely, lower mortgage rates generally mean more demand in the market and therefore higher prices and less negotiating leverage for the purchaser. These are guidelines only. The key factor is to buy at the right price, taking all the factors outlined in this book into consideration. If mortgage rates come down, you can renegotiate a lower mortgage rate with or without a penalty, depending on the mortgage you originally negotiated.

√ Remember, the location of a property is very important, especially for a principal residence. Location is, of course, also important for investment property, but it has to be balanced against overall investment goals such as tax benefits, appreciation, resale potential, and net revenue.

√ Consider the issue of distance between your prospective investment property and where you reside. It really depends on several factors, such as type of investment, size of investment, and amount of management required. If it is a smaller investment, you may want to be close to the property so that you can visit it, manage it, attend to any problems, and show vacant suites. If it is a larger investment, you may consider hiring a resident manager or professional management company. In this latter situation, you could live a considerable distance away, even in a different province.

There are various methods of finding out about real estate for sale. Here are some of the most common approaches.

Real Estate Agent

An experienced real estate agent is an invaluable asset. A realtor can save you time, expense, and frustration, and provide advice and expertise. Remember that the vendor pays the real estate commission whether the agent is a listing or selling broker. (Refer to Chapter 6: Understanding the Legal Aspects for a discussion of real estate listing agreements. Refer to Chapter 4: Selecting Your Advisory Team for a discussion on selecting realtors.)

There are many advantages to using realtors. You can use their services to source properties listed on multiple or exclusive listings, or for property being "sold by owner." You can also use them to contact owners of property who wish to sell a property, but who haven't listed it yet. The advantage of using realtors to source unlisted properties is that they might be able to negotiate a better deal for you than you could get yourself.

There are strategic benefits to having an agent present the offer and negotiate on your behalf. Frequently, the owner will agree to pay a commission to the realtor if you buy, although the commission in an un-listed sale would generally be less. This is because the realtor has not had the expense of time or advertising in actively promoting the listing. Alternatively, you could arrange to pay the realtor a negotiated fee if he or she arranges a sale at a price attractive to you.

If you use a realtor to assist your search, be loyal to him or her if you purchase the property. On the other hand, if the realtor is disinterested, then find another. Give your agent a list of your requirements so the agent can refine the search for you. For example, if you want to buy a house, give the agent information such as:

√   price
√   location
√   style of house
√   age of house
√   number of bedrooms
√   square footage
√   basement/non-basement
√   self-contained suite/no self-contained suite
√   lot size
√   exposure of lot
√   fireplace
√   en suite
√   zoning.

Multiple Listing Service

The Multiple Listing Service (MLS) is an excellent source of information. You can research most of the information on the MLS Web site at www.mls.ca. However, a realtor would be able to assist you in your historical or comparative research by accessing the MLS database, which is not accessible to the general public. If you are looking at an MLS book or Web site, look for specific factors that will give you clues as to vendor motivation or the appropriateness of the property. This could assist you in negotiating a lower price. For example, look for the exact area, when the property was listed (how long ago), if it has been relisted, whether the property is vacant, if any price reductions have occurred (for how much and when), and whether there has been a previous collapsed sale. Also look in the remarks/comments section in the MLS listing book. For example, it could say why the property is for sale, such as foreclosure action, order for sale, relocation, the vendor bought another house, etc. All this information is important.

Newspaper Ads

Look in the classified section of your daily or community newspaper under "Houses for Sale," "Homes for Sale," "Condominiums for Sale," "Revenue Property for Sale," or "Apartments for Sale." The weekend section tends to have the most listings. The Monday classified section has the least number of listings. Because fewer people read the Monday section, that could mean more opportunity for you. Ignore the harmless sales puffery. Many ads are designed to entice you with the impression the owner is anxious and therefore imply that you may be able to get a better price. This may or may not be the case. Watch for ads that may imply that the owner has a time pressure, such as "estate sale," "owner transferred," or "foreclosure sale." Also, look in the special real estate newspapers that are available free and come out weekly in many major Canadian cities.

Develop an organized system when reviewing ads. For example, you could circle with a coloured pen those ads that interest you, clip them out, and staple them to an $8^1/_2$"× 11" sheet of paper, and store them in a binder. Date the ads and write the information in summary form when you speak with the owner. Your checklist of questions will keep you on track so that you have information for comparative purposes. Keep the ads for interesting properties for six months (if you are still looking), so that you can track the property to see if it has gone down in price (if it is still on the market). The types of ads described could be listed by a realtor or "for sale by owner." Clearly, the suggestions relate more to a "for sale by owner" research approach. If it is listed, you will go through a realtor.

Putting Ads in Newspapers

You may wish to locate property owners who have not yet put up their property for sale, or who are selling it themselves. One way is to insert an ad in the "Real Estate Wanted" or "Property Wanted" section of the daily or community newspaper in the area that you are considering. Be precise about your needs in the ad, or many people may waste your time phoning you for clarification. Develop a standard checklist of questions you will ask the callers. That will save you time and frustration. Get right to the point to obtain the information you need.

Drive through the Neighbourhood

As mentioned earlier, it is important to become familiar with the area you are interested in. Drive through the area regularly and look for "For Sale" signs, both properties listed with a realtor and "For Sale by Owner." Note addresses, names, and telephone numbers, and other contact information.

Direct Offer to Owner

In the process of becoming familiar with a particular neighbourhood, you might see a property that is not currently for sale but whose owner might be interested in selling. Look for clues that the property is vacant—uncut lawns, peeling paint, broken windows or fence, etc. Also look for signs that say "For Rent," because that owner might be interested in selling.

Once you have determined which properties might seriously interest you, you can find out who the owner is by doing a search in the local land titles office. The documents are on public record. You could do the search yourself or through a lawyer or realtor. You would also be able to discover other information in your search, such as when the existing owner bought it and for how much, the nature and amount of mortgage financing, and if there are any legal problems relating to the property such as liens, judgements, foreclosures, or power of sale. If you want to pursue it further, you could contact the owner yourself, or preferably have your lawyer or realtor contact the owner.

Word of Mouth

Tell your friends, neighbours, relatives, or business associates that you want to buy property, the type of property you are looking for, and the area you are interested in. They might hear of someone who is thinking of selling or see a property for sale in their neighbourhood that might interest you.

Determining the Value of the Property

One of the most important steps is determining the value of the property you are considering. In other words, how much should you pay for it? In theory, a property is worth whatever a buyer is prepared to pay for it. There are various appraisal techniques that you can use, and that are used by professionally qualified appraisers. In addition, there are rules of thumb that real estate investors often use with revenue property. These rules of thumb are guidelines only. There are limitations to some of them, in terms of their accuracy or acceptance.

Appraising a property value is more an art than a science. Two pieces of property are seldom identical. When a professional appraiser writes a report, the estimate of value is given as an opinion, not a scientific fact. This is helpful to you as a basis for negotiation with the owner. Anyone can have an opinion as to value. The appraisal, though, is only as reliable as the competence, integrity, experience, and objectivity of the appraiser and the accuracy of information obtained. Real estate appraisal is only as reliable as the assumptions that are made. There are distinct benefits to having a professional appraisal. The main reasons for an appraisal would be to determine the following:

√ a reasonable offering price for purchase purposes

√ allocation of the purchase price to the land and building (revenue property)

√ the value of a property for financing purposes (your lender will require this)

√ the value of a property at death for estate purposes

√ the value of a property when converting the use from principal residence to investment (rental) use, or vice versa, which would be for Revenue Canada (CRA) capital gains determination purposes, unless you are exempt from this provision (more detail is covered in Chapter 7: Understanding the Tax Aspects)

√ a reasonable asking price for sale purposes

√ the amount of insurance to carry

√ undertaking a feasibility study of a purchase

√ preparation for a property assessment appeal

√ preparation for litigation

√ preparation for expropriation negotiations

√ preparation for taxation records or appeal.

There are several professional designations for property appraisers in Canada. They subscribe to uniform academic, professional, and ethical standards, and are regulated by their professional associations. The most common national designations are Accredited Appraiser Canadian Institute (AACI) and Canadian Residential Appraiser (CRA). There are other national and provincial appraisal designations as well as specialty appraisal areas, e.g., industrial and commercial. Check out the Web site for the Appraisal Institute of Canada at www.aicanada.ca.

Here are some of the basic methods or rules of thumb that professional appraisers, real estate investment lenders, or homebuyers use. Even if you just use the market-comparison approach initially, you should be familiar with the other methods and their limitations, especially if you intend to invest in revenue real estate.

Market-Comparison Approach

This approach is probably the most easily understood concept for a first-time homebuyer or investor. It is also the most common approach that real estate agents use for single-family dwellings. In effect, it is comparison shopping—comparing properties that are similar to the one you are considering.

Because no two properties are exactly the same due to age, location, layout, size, features, and quality differences, you need close comparables to work with. Compare properties whose sale dates are as current as possible so that they reflect the same market conditions. To make more realistic comparisons when you determine prices of comparable properties, you may have to take into consideration such matters as the circumstances of the sale (e.g., forced sale due to financial problems, order for sale, foreclosure, etc.), special features of the property (e.g., flower garden, shrubs, arboretum, etc.), and location of property (view, privacy, etc.).

The market-comparison approach lends itself to situations where the properties are more numerous; there are more frequent sales, so they are easier to compare. Condominiums, single-family houses, and raw land are the most common types of properties for which to use the market-comparison method. At least it gives you a general sense of the appropriate value.

Refer to Checklist 1 and Form 9 in the Appendix as guides for comparing properties. Generally, when an appraiser is doing a market comparison, he or she compares recent sales of similar properties, similar properties currently listed for sale on the market, and properties that did not sell (listings expired). The limitation of the market-comparison approach is that similar properties may not be available for comparison in a particular situation. Also, it is difficult to know the motivations of the vendors of the comparable properties, so in some cases the sale price might not reflect the fair market price.

For example, if you are comparing a condominium for sale against two other identical condos in the same complex that have sold very recently, the data will give you a fairly close comparison. You could calculate the cost per square foot of the two recent condo sales and compare these costs against the cost per square foot of the one you are considering.

If that latter price is higher, you need to know why. Perhaps it has a better view, is on a higher floor, or maybe the previous owner made many interior decorating changes to improve the condo. The point is that the market-comparison approach does have its limitations and provides general guidelines only.

If you are buying an apartment revenue property, some appraisers use various market-comparison approaches to determine value.

√ One approach is to calculate the average price per unit for comparison. For example, if the "average" price of comparables were $50,000 per apartment and the property you were considering had 10 apartments, the purchase price in theory would be $500,000. The problem with this price-per-unit rule of thumb is that it is probably the least reliable in determining the value of a revenue property. When the appraiser researches the area and prepares a list of comparable revenue properties, the following types of factors are, ideally, similar amenities, appearance, size, location, rent structure, condition, and dates of sale. The problem is that it is difficult to find similar comparables in apartment buildings that are reliable. There can be so many variables. The result in terms of estimated market value can therefore be artificial and unreliable. There are more reliable methods for estimating value that will be discussed later.

√ Another approach to determining the value of an income property involves calculating the income per square foot of the building, and comparing this figure with comparable properties. To do this, you calculate the amount of income-generating square footage in the building (excluding square footage of common areas, hallways, and lobbies). Once you have this figure, you can divide it by the gross revenue from rents to end up with the income per square foot. This approach also has some of the limitations mentioned in the point above.

Cost Approach

This approach involves calculating the cost to buy the land and construct an equivalent type of building on the property you are considering with appropriate adjustments, and then comparing the end prices. If you calculate that the replacement cost is below market value, you might want to seriously consider the benefits of buying a lot and building on it, in terms of cost savings. This approach comes, of course, with its own advantages and disadvantages. There are various steps involved in arriving at a figure using the cost approach.

Step 1

Estimate the land value, using the market-comparison approach discussed earlier. The sale price of similar vacant residential lots in the area should be determined, with adjustments made for such factors as use (zoning), size, location, and features (e.g., view).

Step 2

Estimate the cost to construct a new building that is comparable in square footage, features, and quality to the one you are considering. For example, a modest-quality construction could be $100 per square foot to replace, whereas a luxury-quality construction could be $200 per square foot to replace.

Step 3

If the house you are considering is not new, you will have to calculate a depreciation factor, e.g., reduced value of the building, because it is wearing out over time. Calculating the depreciation adjustment factor depends on the building's condition, age, and estimated useful life. Estimated useful life means the point beyond which the building is not economical to repair or maintain. In effect, it would have no market value. If that is the case, you might be buying primarily for lot value and intend to tear down the building or substantially renovate it.

A professional appraiser is usually required to calculate this depreciation factor.

Step 4

To determine estimated property value, add the depreciated cost of the building (Steps 2 and 3) to the cost of the land (Step 1).

For single-family houses and condominiums, the appraiser normally arrives at an estimate of value as of a certain date by adding the market and cost approach values, and dividing by two. An example of this will be shown below.

Example of Estimate of Market Value

This estimate uses market and cost approaches, which is the usual formula for evaluating properties such as houses and condominiums. If you were buying a revenue property (e.g., apartments), you would normally add on the income approach and then take an average of all three approaches.

1. Market-Comparison Approach

Comparison of four similar properties whose prices were $150,000, $155,000, $160,000 and $157,500. Average price is therefore $155,625.

Market Approach Estimate: $155,625

2. Cost Approach Land

30-foot × 150-foot lot =	
4,500 square feet @ $10 per square foot	$ 45,000.00
Value of improvements on land, such as shrubs, trees, fence, garden, tool shed	$ 7,500.00

Construction of building is 1,000 square feet at $100 per square foot construction cost (new) was $100,000

Less 5% depreciation per year because building being purchased is two years old:

$100,000 – 5% = $ 95,000 (Year 1), and

$ 95,000 – 5% = $90,250 (Year 2)

Therefore, depreciated value of building	$ 90,250.00
Cost Approach Estimate:	$ 142,750.00
FINAL ESTIMATE OF MARKET VALUE:	$ 149,187.50

(MARKET VALUE IS DETERMINED BY THE FOLLOWING FORMULA: Market approach estimate of $155,625 plus cost estimate of $142,750 divided by two equals $149,187.50.)

The limitation of the cost approach is that depreciation might be difficult to correctly estimate. In addition, construction costs vary, depending on location, supply and demand, and inflation. Again, the cost approach value is only an estimate.

Income Approach

This approach is the most common one used when estimating the value of income property. In practical terms, though, you will probably use a combination of all three approaches to determine the value of a revenue property. In addition, there are other rules of thumb for revenue investment property that will be discussed later.

Basically, the income approach assumes that the value of the property is the present worth of the future cash flow that the property is expected to generate. For example, the property is worth X times its annual net operating income.

As mentioned, the income approach cannot be viewed in isolation. It is important to use it in conjunction with the previous two approaches so you can consider factors affecting the overall investment climate, such as interest rates, taxes (municipal, provincial, and federal), rent controls, inflation, cost of land, cost of construction and materials, comparative property prices, and supply and demand (of tenants and competitive rental buildings). When you calculate the value of income property for your own investment purposes, be on the conservative and cautious side and use the lowest evaluation. Depending on the nature of the property, however, your investment goals, and the objective of the appraisal, one approach may be better than another.

The most common income approach used by lenders and appraisers to determine a fair market value is the capitalization method. The purpose is to project the value of a property based on the amount, certainty, and length of time of future flow of income (income stream), and then placing a dollar value on that future income stream by applying a capitalization rate. The capitalization (or CAP rate, as it is commonly known) is a rate of return used to derive the capital value (total value) of an income stream.

For example, the net operating income (also referred to as NOI), which is the amount remaining after all expenses of the property have been met but before taxes, is "capitalized" at a certain percentage (say, 10%) to determine a value of a property. If a building is producing an NOI of $30,000 and that is capitalized at 10% (or sometimes referred to as "CAP rate of 10"), then the fair market value would be $300,000. In other words, to achieve a CAP rate of 10%, you would have to attain an NOI of $30,000 in order to justify paying $300,000 for the income property.

The formula just used is a common one and every investor should understand it. It is commonly known as the IRV formula, where the letters represent the following:

I = Income or, more specifically, net operating income (NOI)

R = Rate or, more specifically, capitalization (or CAP) rate

V = Value or, more specifically, fair market value (FMV)

The basic formula is as follows: I ÷ R × V

As long as you know at least two of the three items in the formula, you can determine the third item by removing it from the formula and calculating out the remaining item; in other words, rearranging the components of the formula. For example, the values of I, R, and V can be obtained as follows:

Net operating income (I) = CAP rate × market value, or I = R × V

Example: If you are prepared to pay $245,000 for an income property and you want a 9.5% return on your investment, what net operating income would be required?

Answer: Separate out the unknown factor and fill in the other two letters (factors) with the known information:

$I = R \times V = .095\ (9.5\%) \times \$245,000 = \$23,275$

Therefore, you would need a net operating income of $23,275.

Capitalization rate (R) =Net operating income divided by market value, or R = I ÷ V

Example: A property generating a net operating revenue of $25,000 a year is priced at $220,000. What is the CAP rate on the investment?

Answer: Separate out the unknown factor as you have done previously.

$R = I \div V = \$25,000 \div \$220,000 = 11.3\%$

Therefore, the CAP rate is 11.3%. In other words, as an investor, you will earn 11.3% return on your $220,000 investment (ROI).

Market value (V) = Net operating income divided by CAP rate, or V = I ÷ R

Example: A property is to be capitalized at 11.5%. It has a net operating income of $16,000. How much can you justify paying for it if you want to obtain an 11.5% return on your investment (ROI)?

Answer: Separate out the unknown factor, as you have done previously.

$V = I \div R = \$16,000 \div .115\ (11.5\%) = \$139,130.43$

The most you could justify paying will therefore be $139,130.43.

You can see the benefit of the IRV formula in terms of a quick analysis of the key factors. It is important to remember that the formula does not take financing or mortgages into account. All the results obtained are based on the assumption that the property is clear of all financing.

The IRV formula is also helpful when comparing similar properties. When deciding what CAP rate to use for your investment purposes, remember your investment objectives and the degree of risk you are prepared to take. Ideally you will want at least a CAP rate of 10% (higher than that is better) in terms of your return on your investment. Different investors have different CAP rate criteria.

The types of factors taken into account include the type of property (e.g., small or large apartment building); age (e.g., the older the building, the less future income can be derived from it in its present state); location (e.g., the closer the building to the tenant base, the better); and quality of tenancies (e.g., leases are preferable to month-to-month). As a rough rule of thumb, a low-risk investment or area (or anticipated low inflation in the area) should have a minimum 8% CAP rate, a medium-risk investment or area (or anticipated medium inflation in the area) should have a minimum 10% CAP rate, and a high-risk investment or area (or anticipated high inflation in the area) should have a minimum 12% CAP rate. The greater the risk, the greater the premium you will want in terms of a higher CAP rate.

Another method of estimating the approximate CAP rate value for a building you are interested in is taking the average of the CAP rates of comparable properties in the same geographic area. You can also contact a professional appraiser familiar with the area and type of income property, and request approximate CAP rates.

Remember, if you can get a totally risk-free investment return from Canada Savings Bonds, Treasury bills, or term deposits of 6% (or whatever the prevailing rate would be at any given time), for example, you will want to buffer your risk by ensuring the overall income property package is attractive. (Refer to Form 8, which is an income approach worksheet, as well as Form 9 in the Appendix, which is an investment property analysis worksheet.)

Percentage of Operating Expenses

Once you start comparing various revenue properties in your area, you will see an average overall pattern in terms of the proportion of the various operating expenses relative to the gross income. In Canada, apartment-building expenses tend to be between 35% and 45% of the gross income. That can vary, of course, depending on the circumstances. If you see that the percentage reflected by the vendor's information supplied to you is less than 35% or more than 45%, for example, you should thoroughly verify the data independently.

You should also confirm the accuracy of the information. Some vendors can be less than forthright, in order to make the investment picture appear more attractive. If you rely solely on the vendor's information and it turns out you were misled because it was inaccurate or incomplete, you could lose a lot of money.

Look for individual expense variances from the norm. For example, if the insurance cost is 2% when the norm should be 5%, then the building might be underinsured, and you will have to pay more in insurance premiums to protect your investment. If the property management fee percentage is lower than normal, the management company may not be providing adequate management, or is new and inexperienced and gave a low quote to get the contract.

If the resident manager's costs are too low compared to the normal percentage, possibly the reason is that the costs are artificial. The real costs to hire someone if you buy the building could cost more because the owner's family is performing all the on-site management and not taking a fair market payment for the services provided.

Again, refer to Form 8, which is an income approach worksheet showing the various categories of expenses, and Form 9, which is an investment property analysis worksheet. Before you make any final decision to purchase a particular revenue property, do a projected cash flow statement (Form 5 in Appendix), a projected income and expense statement (Form 6), and a projected balance sheet (Form 7). In other words, you need an accurate idea of what you can make from the property based on realistic projections. The initial analysis you did of the property just dealt with the current situation. Realistic projections will tell you if the current financial analysis will improve or worsen over time. Of course, your professional accountant should thoroughly review all the financial statements of the revenue property for inaccuracies, inconsistencies, shortcomings, and false or unrealistic assumptions.

Gross Income Multiplier

You may hear of real estate investors who use the gross income multiplier (GIM) formula. You should understand how it works. It is an inaccurate method of determining a property value, not only in absolute terms, but in relative terms to other properties. You may wish to use it, but only in combination with the other more realistic rules of thumb described.

Investors use different GIM multipliers, depending on their investment objectives and other factors. For example, if an investor uses a GIM of 6, that would mean that the annual gross income (say $40,000) would be multiplied by 6 to determine the maximum value of the property. In this example, it would be $240,000. The problem is that the GIM method does not take into account such critical factors as mortgage payments or operating expenses, so the formula is rather artificial. Say the average range of operating expenses for the type of income property in the geographic area you are considering is 35% to 45%, as discussed in the previous section. The GIM formula does not take into account that the property you are looking at could have costly operating expenses, at 70% for example. Therefore, the GIM of 6 would arrive at a greater value than the property is really worth. Also, you could be locked into a long-term, high-interest closed mortgage with a six-month interest penalty or cancellation. Current mortgage rates could be 4% lower, for example. The GIM does not reflect these factors. On the other hand, the property could be very efficiently operated and have operating expenses of 30% and a long-term low-interest mortgage. The property could therefore be worth more than six times the gross income. Remember, from an income property purchase viewpoint, the lower the GIM, the better.

The GIM basic formula is:

Gross income multiplier = Market value ÷ Effective gross income

or GIM = MV ÷ EGI

or MV = GIM × EGI

or EGI = GIM × MV

Effective gross income means the actual current income, not a projected or potential income.

Another application of the GIM usage is to determine the amount of time it would take to pay back the investment. The GIM calculated tells the investor how many years it would take to recover the total investment costs (purchase price) if all the gross income were allocated to pay off the purchase price. Again, this formula has limitations, of course, because it is rather artificial in that you would, in reality, be paying operating costs from the gross income. It is just another yardstick to use. For example, if an investor is considering an investment with an asking price of $700,000, and the effective gross income in the first year is $100,000, the GIM would be 7:

GIM = $700,000 ÷ $100,000 = 7

Therefore, in theory, if all the gross income were used to pay for the original total property cost, it would take seven years to recover the total cost of the investment.

Net Income Multiplier

The net income multiplier (NIM) is a more reliable way to determine the number of years it will take to recover the initial investment outlay from the future net income from operating the revenue property. Conversely, the formula will help you determine the maximum price an investor would be prepared to pay for the property.

Net operating income (NOI) is a frequently used term in investment real estate. It is basically income produced by the property after all operating expenses and allowances for vacancies have been removed, but before mortgage payments.

For example, if you apply an NIM of 10 as your investment formula, and the NOI of a property is $30,000, you would place a maximum value that you would pay of $300,000 for the property. The formula is:

$$MV = NIM \times NOI$$
$$MV = 10 \times \$30,000 = \$300,000$$

The NOI formula is more accurate because all the variables in the building operation, such as rental income, vacancies, and operating expenses, have been accounted for. The only variable that has not been accounted for—because it varies, of course—is the cost of mortgage financing. This is the one factor that can affect the accuracy of the NIM rule of thumb, in terms of the bottom-line income. For example, what may appear to be a good investment because of the NOI would not be so attractive if there is a high-interest long-term closed mortgage with a large penalty clause. That is why you have to consider the limitations of the NOI multiplier formula and make allowances for it.

The basic formula for determining the NIM is as follows:

$$\text{Net income multiplier} = \text{Market value} \div \text{Net operating income or NIM} = MV \div NOI$$

For example, if an investment property has a purchase price of $600,000 and the net operating income is $60,000, the NIM multiplier would be 10. This number is also used for payback calculation purposes; for example, it would take 10 years to recover the total investment cost if all the net operating income was applied for that purpose. Conversely, the overall capitalization rate is the recipro-cal of the NIM (10)—that is, 10%. In other words, you would be receiving a return of 10% on your initial purchase price outlay relative to the NOI.

Internal Rate of Return

The internal rate of return, sometimes referred to as the IRR, is a calculation that some investors use to determine how much they will make annually on their investment. There are many factors that have to be taken into account to increase the accuracy of the results; e.g., mortgage principal reduction, antici-pated property appreciation, anticipated inflation, and after-tax cash flow.

Realistically, when you are projecting your final return on your investment upon sale, that is your true net profit. You also have to take into account such additional factors as the amount of capital gains tax on sale of the property, closing costs on sale, legal fees, real estate commissions, and mortgage penalty if there is a closed mortgage at the time of the sale. In addition, you have to calculate any projected interest you might be able to earn on the excess cash flow, if it is a positive cash flow. Such factors as your projected personal income tax rate also have to be estimated. This can vary, of course, but for projection purposes you have to make certain assumptions, such as percentage of appre-ciation and inflation.

Most IRR calculations are done on a computer spreadsheet program. At the bottom of the printout you will see the IRR percentage. For example, the IRR might show an annual return of 25%. You might intend to keep the invest-ment for five years and sell it, assuming the market conditions are favourable. Normally, the IRR figure would initially exclude the inflation factor. You will also want a calculation with inflation projected to make sure that your intended investment, in real value of money terms over time, exceeded inflation as much as possible. It does have some limitations as well, in terms of assumptions. As the IRR calculation is initially based on estimates, the IRR itself is only an esti-mate of the expected return on your investment capital. Your professional tax adviser can tell you more.

This section has covered some of the most common types of techniques for establishing the value of a property purchase. There are many others that expe-rienced or sophisticated investors may use in addition to the ones noted. Some of the techniques described are easier to calculate than others. Some are more accurate and reliable than others. Some require computer spreadsheet analysis.

The important point is to understand the basic concepts and to know when to apply them, to know their limitations, and to use several different formulas to provide some balance when comparing other properties as well as the property itself. The key benefit of these methods is that they can often be quickly calculated to determine if the owner is asking too much, if a property meets your personal investment criteria, or to determine if the property is a bargain. Remember, the rules of thumb are guidelines only. The calculations could also provide you with negotiating leverage to have the purchase price reduced. You will, of course, want to consider other factors before making your final decision.

Also keep in mind that the values are estimates only. You may not be prepared to pay the estimated price for various reasons, including the following:

√ the price is more than you can afford

√ the price is higher than your comfort level in terms of risk

√ the market is starting to decline

√ there is an economic turndown

√ you are waiting for more attractive property to invest in.

Conversely, you might be prepared to pay more than the estimates suggest. Here are some of the factors that might lead you to pay more than the estimates indicate:

Confidential Information

You might be aware of a possible zoning change, subdivision potential, or proposed development nearby.

Financing

You might be able to obtain favourable financial terms, e.g., a low-interest, vendor-take-back mortgage or high-ratio financing.

Potential for Income

The property could have a basement suite.

Attractive Closing Date

You could get a long closing date, enabling you to get funds that you are expecting from various sources, or to get access to higher mortgage financing by closing, or to sell the agreement of purchase and sale to someone else (almost like having an option).

Your Income Tax Bracket

Depending on your personal situation, you may be able to offset a negative cash flow against your other income and thus buy the property at a discount price because of the negative cash flow. You would then be relying on the factor of appreciation and a capital gain over time. You might also have a lower return on investment benchmark.

Web Sites of Interest

Here are some Web sites to assist you in researching information and contacts. Most of the professional associations provide names of accredited members in your geographic area.

Appraisal Institute of Canada:	www.aicanada.ca
Canadian Association of Home and Property Inspectors:	www.cahpi.ca
Canadian Home Builders' Association:	www.chbi.ca
Canadian Mortgage and Housing Corporation:	www.cmhc-schl.gc.ca
Canadian Real Estate Association:	www.crea.ca
The Royal Architectural Institute of Canada:	www.raic.org
Royal LePage Survey of Canadian Houses Prices:	www.royallepage.ca
Statistics Canada:	www.statcan.ca

Summary

This chapter discussed the many factors to consider when selecting a property, as well as where to find a property for sale. The various methods and formulas for determining the value of a property were explained. Finally, helpful Web sites were given, along with where to find other key research information. Now that you know the type of property that interests you and how to evaluate it, it's time to introduce you to the team of professionals you will need.

CHAPTER 4

Selecting Your Advisory Team

When starting out in real estate investment, whether you are purchasing a principal residence or an investment property, it is important to have a team of experts and professionals to assist you in achieving your goals. The team should consist of a realtor, lawyer, accountant, lender, financial planner, mortgage broker, building inspector, and insurance broker. Common selection criteria for each will be covered first, followed by specific selection criteria. At the end of this chapter is a list of various Web sites of interest.

Common Selection Criteria

You should be very selective in your screening process. The right selection will enhance your prospects for profit and growth; the wrong selection will be costly in terms of time, money, and stress.

There are many factors you should consider when selecting advisers. For example, the person's professional qualifications, experience in real estate investment, and the fee for services are factors you will want to consider. It is helpful to prepare a list of such questions, plus others relating to your specific needs, and pose these to each of the prospective advisers. Some people may feel awkward discussing fees and qualifications with a lawyer, for instance, but it is important to establish these matters at the outset before you make a decision to use that person's services. The most common selection criteria include qualifications, experience, compatible personality, confidence and competence in the area concerned, and fees. Having a comparison of at least three interviews or conversations is the ideal approach before you select the one suitable for your needs.

Qualifications

Before you entrust an adviser with your work, you will want to know that he or she has the appropriate qualifications. These may include a professional degree in the case of a lawyer or accountant, or some other professional training or qualifications relative to the area of work.

Experience

It is very important to assess the adviser's experience in the area where you need assistance. Such factors as the degree of expertise, the number of years of experience, and the percentage of time spent offering a service in that area are critically important. The amount of reliance you will place on a lawyer's advice and insights, for example, is obviously related to the degree of experience the lawyer has in the area. For example, the fact that a lawyer might have been practising law for 10 years does not necessarily mean that the lawyer has a high degree of expertise in the area of real estate. Perhaps only 10% of the practice has been spent in that specific area. An accountant who has had 15 years of experience in small-business accounting and tax advice will certainly provide you with a depth of expertise about small business in general. If that accountant has experience in the real estate investment area, this is an important factor. Inquire about the adviser's degree of expertise and length of experience in in real estate deals. If you don't ask the question, you won't be given the answer, which may make the difference between mediocre and in-depth advice.

Compatible Personality

When selecting an adviser, make certain that you feel comfortable with the individual's personality. If you are going to have an ongoing relationship with the adviser, it is important that you feel comfortable with the person's degree of communication, attitude, approach, candour, and commitment to your real estate investment. A healthy respect and rapport will put you more at ease when discussing business matters and thereby enhance your further understanding.

Confidence

You must have confidence in your adviser if you are going to rely on his or her advice to enhance the quality of your decision making and minimize your risk. After considering the person's qualifications, experience, and personality style, you may have considerable confidence in the individual. If you do not, don't use the person as an adviser because there is a very good chance that you will not use him or her as extensively as you should or when you need to. This in itself could have a serious negative impact on your decision making.

Good Communication Skills

You want an adviser who is a good listener, who elicits your responses, and provides feedback in understandable layperson's terms. Any issues and options should be fully disclosed, with pros, cons, and recommendations.

Your adviser should return your phone calls promptly and keep you regularly informed in writing. Some people and situations require more frequent communication than others do.

Accessibility

If your adviser becomes too busy for you, reconsider the relationship. Your needs should be a priority. If you are shunted to a junior adviser against your wishes, your original adviser may be culling clientele to concentrate on more lucrative clients.

Objectivity

If advice is tainted in any way by bias or personal financial benefit, obviously it is unreliable and self-serving. Get a minimum of three opinions on your particular situation before carefully deciding which professionals to select.

Trust

Whether the person is a lawyer, accountant, financial planner, or other adviser, if you don't intuitively trust the advice as being solely in your best interests, never use that person again. You have far too much to lose, in terms of your financial security and peace of mind, to have any doubts whatsoever. You cannot risk the chance that advice is governed primarily by the adviser's financial self-interest, with your interests as a secondary consideration.

Integrity

Your adviser should have a high standard of personal and professional integrity. The adviser's reputation with other professional colleagues is one reference point. Maintaining the confidentiality of information is another.

Depending on the nature of the advisory relationship, you may disclose your personal needs, wants, hopes, and dreams, as well as concerns. This puts you in a potentially vulnerable position.

References

References and word-of-mouth referrals are particularly important when selecting any adviser who will be taking an overall holistic approach to your financial affairs. Ask for professional references and then contact those professionals and ask about the adviser's strong attributes and any professional weak points. Also, ask how long they have been dealing with each other. Don't feel embarrassed to ask the tough questions—candid feedback can provide you with a revealing reality check.

Don't ask for or expect an adviser to provide you with a list of clients as this would normally breach confidentiality.

Fees

It is important to feel comfortable with the fee being charged and the payment terms. Are they fair, competitive, and affordable? Do they match the person's qualifications and experience? For instance, if you need a good tax accountant to advise you on minimizing taxes, you may have to pay a higher hourly rate for the quality of advice that will save you several thousands of dollars. On the other hand, if what you require is the preparation of annual financial statements, perhaps a junior accountant can do the job competently at a more affordable rate. You may want to hire a bookkeeper to do your books, or do them yourself. There are some excellent accounting software programs to manage your real estate investments. (This is covered in Chapter 10: Managing Your Property.) Be certain the rate is within your budget, or you may not fully use the adviser effectively because of the expense. Not using available professional advice when you need it is poor management. Ask about the estimated fee at the outset.

Comparison

It is a good rule of thumb to see at least three advisers before deciding which one is right for you. The more exacting you are in your selection criteria, the more likely it will be that you will find a good match and the more beneficial that adviser will be to your real estate investment goals. It is a competitive market in the advisory business, and you can afford to be extremely selective when choosing advisers to complement your real estate team.

Selecting a Realtor

There are distinct advantages to having a realtor act on your behalf when buying or selling a property. As in any profession, there is a range of competence among the many real estate salespeople throughout Canada, but with careful due diligence you can minimize the risk and benefit greatly from the skills of a knowledgeable and sincere realtor.

When buying or selling real estate relating to your business, the right realtor will make all the difference in ensuring a positive purchase or sale experience.

Over the past several years, a new relationship structure, sometimes referred to as agency disclosure, has replaced the old system. Many people assumed that if they found a realtor and the house was listed on the Multiple Listing Service (MLS), for example, the realtor would represent their interests exclusively when an offer was presented and through negotiation.

The new system spells out the respective roles and responsibilities of each realtor involved. The seller still pays the real estate commission, which is shared with any other realtor involved. All disclosure of who is acting for whom is spelled out in the agreement of purchase and sale. Some agents working with the buyer may also enter into a buyer agency contract. In other words, each realtor is acting exclusively for the benefit of the buyer or seller. However, if the listing realtor is also the selling realtor (double-end deal), the agent has to enter into a limited dual agency agreement. This is agreed upon and signed by both the buyer and seller. The agent modifies his or her exclusive obligations to both the buyer and the seller by limiting it primarily to confidentiality as to each party's motivation and personal information.

You can get more information from any real estate agent, real estate company, or your local real estate board.

Qualifications

Real estate agents are regulated by provincial government real estate legislation. Agents have to successfully complete an approved real estate agent licensing course and renew their licence annually.

How to Select a Realtor

There are a number of approaches to finding a good real estate agent:

√ Ask friends, neighbours, and relatives for the names of agents they have dealt with, and why they would recommend them.

√ Go to open houses for an opportunity to meet realtors.

√ Check newspaper ads that list the names and phone numbers of agents who are active in your area.

√ Check "For Sale" signs for agents' names and phone numbers.

√ Check the Internet.

√ Contact real estate firms in your area; speak to an agent who specializes or deals with the type of property you want and is an experienced salesperson.

After you have met several agents who could potentially meet your needs, there are a number of guidelines to assist you with your selection:

√ Favour an agent who is familiar with the neighbourhood you are interested in. Such an agent will be on top of the available listings, will know comparable market prices, and can target the types of property that meet your needs as you have explained them.

√ Favour an agent who is particularly familiar with the buying and selling of residential and revenue properties.

√ Favour an agent who is experienced and knowledgeable in the real estate industry.

√ Look for an agent who is prepared to prescreen properties so that you are informed only of those that conform to your guidelines for viewing purposes.

√ Look for an agent who is familiar with the various conventional and creative methods of financing, including the effective use of mortgage brokers.

√ Look for an agent to be thorough on properties you are interested in, in terms of background information such as length of time on the market, reason for sale, and price comparisons among similar properties. An agent who is familiar with the MLS can find out a great amount of information in a short time, assuming the property is listed on the MLS.

√ Look for an agent who will be candid with you in suggesting a real estate offer price and explain the reasons for the recommendation.

√ Look for an agent who has effective negotiating skills to ensure that your wishes are presented as clearly and persuasively as possible.

√ Favour an agent who is working on a full-time basis, not dabbling part-time.

√ Look for an agent who attempts to upgrade professional skills and expertise.

√ Look for an agent who is good with numbers; in other words, one who is familiar with the use of financial calculations and can therefore assist in clarifying the revenue property analysis aspects.

√ Look for an agent who uses the Internet highly effectively when acting for a vendor or purchaser.

You should give the agent your exclusive business if you have confidence in him or her because the agent will devote considerable time and energy to your needs. Keep the agent informed of any open houses in which you are interested. Advise any other agents that you have one working for you. Review the section called "the listing agreement" in Chapter 6: Understanding the Legal Aspects. Focus clearly on your needs and provide the agent with a written outline of your specific criteria to assist in shortlisting potential prospects. If for any reason you are dissatisfied with the agent who is assisting you, find another agent as quickly as possible.

Benefits of a Realtor to the Purchaser

There are obvious benefits to the buyer of using a realtor as outlined in the previous points. One of the key benefits is that the realtor can act as an intermediary between you and the listing broker. That way, the listing broker may never have an opportunity to meet you and therefore cannot exert any influence on you with aggressive salesmanship, or otherwise make an assessment of you that could compromise your negotiating position. The agent who has the listing agreement with the vendor would know you only through discussions with the realtor you are dealing with and through any offer that you might present. This arm's-length negotiating position is an important strategic tactic that will benefit you. This is discussed further in Chapter 9: Negotiating Strategies.

Another advantage to a buyer is the opportunity for the realtor to access a multiple listing service, which can provide instant, thorough, and accurate information on properties that might interest you. Without an agent searching for you, you seriously minimize your range of selection and the prospect of concluding the deal at a price that is attractive to you.

Benefits of a Realtor to the Vendor

There are extensive benefits to listing your property with a realtor rather than attempting to sell it on your own. Some of the key benefits include the following:

- √ Realtors can list your property on the multiple listing service as well as the Internet, which provides extensive exposure throughout and beyond your market area.
- √ Realtors can prequalify and prescreen potential homebuyers so that only serious buyers who have the interest and financial resources present an offer.
- √ Realtors can provide information to the purchaser on matters such as financing and other assistance programs that could facilitate the sale of your property.
- √ Realtors can suggest methods of improving the appearance of your property in order to maximize the positive impression and therefore the potential buyer's interest and sale price.
- √ Realtors can explain the real estate market in your area, and can provide you with MLS computer printouts of comparable listings or sales patterns in your area; they can also supply other facts and figures to assist you in realistically establishing a market price.
- √ Realtors free up your own time, using all their contacts and marketing techniques in order to effect the sale of your property.
- √ As is the case for purchasers, realtors negotiate an agreement on your behalf and according to your instructions, and you remain at arm's length from the one-on-one negotiating. This improves your negotiating position.

How Realtors Are Compensated

Traditionally the vendor pays the realtor a commission, which is negotiable. Some are fixed percentages and some are variable, depending on the price involved. Some commissions are a negotiated flat rate, regardless of the sale price. There are different commission structures for residential and commercial properties.

If there is more than one realtor involved, for example, a listing broker and a selling broker, then the commission is normally split based on an agreed formula, e.g., 55% to the listing broker because he or she incurs more expenses to sell the property, and 45% to the selling broker.

Resolving Disputes

If you have a dispute with a realtor, keep a record of all your correspondence outlining the complaint. Speak to the realtor first, followed by his or her manager, then the regional, provincial, and national managers. If the complaint is more serious, complain to the local real estate board or provincial agency that licenses realtors.

Selecting a Lawyer

Whether you are the buyer or the seller of real estate, it is essential that you obtain a lawyer to represent your interests—a standard precaution with any real estate transaction. As you will realize by the time you have finished reading this book, there are many potential legal pitfalls for the unwary when buying real estate. The agreement for purchase and sale and related documents are complex. For most people, the purchase of a home or other investment property is the largest investment of their life, and the agreement for purchase and sale is the most important legal contract they will ever sign.

The Selection Process

There are a number of ways to select the right lawyer for your needs:

√ Ask friends who have purchased real estate which lawyer they used, whether they were satisfied with the lawyer, and why.

√ Contact the lawyer referral service in your community. Under this service, sponsored by the provincial law society or a provincial division of the Canadian Bar Association, you can have a half-hour consultation with a lawyer for a nominal fee (usually $10), which lawyers generally waive to facilitate bookkeeping and PR. To obtain contact information for the lawyer referral service in your province, look in your phone book or check the Internet. Go to www.google.ca and then type in the key words "lawyer referral service" and then the name of your province. Make sure you specify that you want a lawyer who specializes in real estate. Contact the law society in your province for further information.

√ Look in the Yellow Pages under "Lawyers" and check the box ads, which outline the areas of expertise.

√ Check the Internet for specialty lawyers in your area. For example, do a google.ca search.

√ If you are obtaining a mortgage, speak to the lawyer who is preparing the mortgage documents on behalf of the lender. If the lawyer you choose is also preparing the mortgage documents, you could save on some duplicated disbursement costs and negotiate a package price. Be cautious, though, to avoid conflict; ensure that the lawyer provides you with a full explanation of the mortgage terms and conditions that might affect your interests. Keep in mind that the mortgage is being prepared on behalf of the bank, but at your expense. If you have any concerns in this area, retain a separate lawyer to do the non-mortgage legal work and explain the contents of the mortgage to you. Alternatively, ask the lender to let you see a lawyer of your choice from the lender's list of approved lawyers.

You may have heard the term "notary public" and assumed that it means the same as "lawyers." This is not necessarily so. In most provinces a lawyer is also automatically a notary public, but a notary public is not necessarily a lawyer. Make sure you know the difference. A notary public is not formally trained, qualified, or permitted by law to provide a legal opinion on any subject. He or she can only prepare the required transfer of title documentation, necessary affidavit material, and other related documentary material, and file the documents in the land registry office. In other words, the services provided are primarily technical and procedural. Thus, the buyer or seller of a property is advised to consult a lawyer. In matters relating to properties, you need a lawyer to avoid the potential risk and pitfalls involved, and to deal with the matter for you if a legal problem occurs.

In the province of Quebec, lawyers are referred to as "notaries" (non-courtroom lawyers) or "advocates" (courtroom lawyers). Therefore, in Quebec you would use a "notary" for your property purchase or sale transaction.

Once you have contacted the lawyer over the phone, ask about the areas of his or her real estate interest and expertise. Tell the lawyer that you are looking for a person with expert knowledge in property law. If the lawyer cannot offer this, ask for a recommendation.

If you did not obtain the referral through the lawyer referral service, ask the lawyer over the phone what a half-hour initial consultation would cost. (In many cases it is free.)

Have all your questions and concerns prepared in writing so that you won't forget any. If you wish to make an offer to purchase, bring your offer-to-purchase document with you, and the details about the new, resale, or revenue project you are considering. Ask about anticipated fee and disbursement costs. If you are not pleased with the outcome of the interview for any reason, move on to another lawyer.

Legal Fee Arrangements

Here are the most common fee arrangements and the types of costs you might encounter.

Hourly Fee

A lawyer bills a fixed rate per hour for all work done. The fee could range between $100 and $300 or more per hour, depending on specialty expertise, experience, and so on.

Fixed Fee

If you hire a lawyer to provide a routine service such as a conveyance (transfer of property to your name) or a will, the lawyer may be able to quote a flat fee, regardless of how much work might be involved. For example, a simple will may cost from $200 to $300. A straightforward conveyance could start at $500. Fees can vary based on geographic location, size of community, and so on.

Percentage Fee

Sometimes fees are calculated as a percentage of the value of the subject matter. This approach is often used when probating an estate. Most provinces have legislation that limits the maximum percentage that can be charged, regardless of the time spent.

Contingency Fee

Many provinces allow lawyers to charge on a contingency fee basis, that is, for a percentage of the total amount awarded if the case is won. This is negotiable, but can vary from 25% to 50% depending on the nature of what is being done. For example, let's say that you have a strong case, but do not have the funds to pay your lawyer at the outset. Your lawyer may agree to act for you and charge a percentage of the amount that you eventually receive, either at trial or settlement. If you lose or the matter is not settled, the lawyer gets nothing for the time spent. You would be responsible for paying the lawyer's disbursements, however.

Factors that Affect Legal Fees

Some of the factors that a lawyer considers when setting fees are as follows:

- √ the lawyer's degree of specialization in the specific area
- √ the number of years that the lawyer has been practising law
- √ the amount of time the lawyer spends on your behalf
- √ the legal complexity of the matter dealt with
- √ the monetary value of the matter at issue
- √ the lawyer's degree of responsibility
- √ the importance of the matter to the client
- √ the degree of difficulty in dealing with the issue
- √ the lawyer's degree of skill and competence
- √ the results the lawyer obtains on the client's behalf
- √ the client's ability to pay.

In many cases the legal fee structure is based on what other lawyers are charging. Although competition in the legal profession is obviously a factor in keeping fees competitive, there are many circumstances when two lawyers will charge a different fee for performing the same routine or specialized service. Always clarify the fee arrangement in writing in advance.

As in any other business relationship, in order to maintain an effective rapport with your legal adviser, good communication is essential. Be certain that you and your lawyer keep each other informed of matters of importance, so neither is operating without complete information. If you are in doubt about the particular advice you are being given, you may prefer to get a second opinion. This is reassurance that you are following the best advice for your business.

Resolving Disputes

Misunderstandings on fees or other matters should be immediately clarified to prevent them from becoming serious problems. You may decide at any time to have the working file transferred to a new lawyer. If you have serious doubts about a lawyer's invoice, you can have it "taxed" or reviewed by a court registrar. This is an informal procedure and results in the fee being upheld or reduced. Your local court office will be able to provide further information.

If you feel that the lawyer acted improperly or incompetently, you have other forms of recourse. All provincial law societies require that their members have a certain minimum coverage for professional liability insurance to cover negligence suits. Individual law firms could have additional coverage. If trust funds go missing, the Law Society allocates funds to cover that situation. Suing your lawyer is an option, but certainly the last resort.

If you have complaints such as possible conflict of interest, poor advice, or other forms of professional misconduct or incompetence, you can file a formal complaint with the provincial law society. The complaints committee has many forms of discipline.

In summary, make sure that you select a lawyer, and consult with that lawyer before you commit yourself to any final agreement for purchase and sale.

Selecting an Accountant

An accountant's chief role is to monitor the financial health of your investment and reduce the subsequent risks and tax payable. Along with your lawyer, your accountant will complement your real estate team to ensure that your real estate investment decisions are based on sound advice and good planning. Some accountants have also obtained their CFP (certified financial planner) certification, in order to offer their clients a more comprehensive consulting advice. Refer to the section on "Selecting a Financial Planner."

An accountant can help you right from the pre-real estate investment phase. The services that can be provided are wide ranging and include the following:

√ setting up a manual or computerized bookkeeping system that both the investor and accountant can work with efficiently

√ setting up a customized software program for real estate investment and management of the properties

√ setting up systems for the control of cash and the handling of funds

√ preparing or evaluating budgets, forecasts, and investment plans

√ assessing your break-even point and improving your profitability

√ preparing and interpreting financial statements

√ providing tax- and financial-planning advice

√ preparing corporate and individual tax returns.

Qualifications

In Canada, anyone can call himself or herself an accountant. One can also adopt the title "public accountant" without any qualifications, experience, regulations, or accountability to a professional association. That is why you have to be very careful when selecting the appropriate accountant for your needs. There are three main designations of qualified professional accountants in Canada: chartered accountant (CA), certified general accountant (CGA), and certified management accountant (CMA). Accountants with the above designations are governed by provincial statutes. The conduct, professional standards, training, qualifications, professional development, and discipline of these professionals are regulated by their respective institutes or associations. Rely on the advice of an accountant, therefore, only after you have satisfied yourself that the accountant meets the professional qualifications that you require for your real estate investment needs.

There are differences in the educational requirements, training, experience, and nature of practice of the accounting designations mentioned above. Some accountants, such as CAs and CGAs, pursue careers in public practice, e.g., serving the needs of the real estate investor. Other accountants work in industry, education, or government, or specialize in the areas of management, cost, financial, or tax accounting. For further information, contact the professional institution or association for the specific accounting designation and request an explanatory brochure. You can obtain the contact phone number from the Yellow Pages under "Accountants," from the Internet, or from your local library. The professional governing bodies are the Institute of Chartered Accountants, the Certified General Accountants' Association, and the Society of Management Accountants.

How to Find an Accountant

√ *Referrals:* Often a banker, lawyer, or other business associate will be pleased to recommend an accountant who has expertise in real estate investment. Such referrals are valuable since these individuals are probably aware of your area of interest and would recommend an accountant only if they felt he or she was well qualified and had a good track record in assisting real estate investors.

√ *Professional Associations:* The professional institute that governs CAs, CGAs, and CMAs may be a source of leads. You can telephone or write the institute or association with a request for the names of three accountants who provide public accounting services to real estate investors within your geographic area. Also, check out the provincial association Web sites. Often an initial consultation is free of charge. Always find out before you confirm the appointment.

√ *The Yellow Pages:* In the Yellow Pages, under the heading "Accountants," you will find listings under the categories "Chartered," "Registered," "Certified General," and "Management."

√ *Searching the Internet:* Do a google.ca search, for example.

Preparing for the Meeting

Prior to a meeting with your accountant, make a written list of your questions and concerns in order of priority. As noted earlier, you will want to know the person's qualifications, areas of expertise, and method of record keeping, e.g., what type of computerized system is used. Ask the accountant what his or her range of experience is in your type of investment: tax, business management advice, accessing financing, and so on. Ask about fees, how they are determined, how accounts are rendered, and what retainer may be required. Ask who will be working on your file—the accountant, a junior accountant, or a bookkeeper. It is common for accountants to delegate routine work to junior staff and keep more complex matters for their own review.

Understanding Fees and Costs

Accountants' fees vary according to experience, specialty, type of service provided, size of firm, and other considerations. They can range from $40 to $150 or more per hour. A highly skilled tax accountant could charge considerably more. It is common for an accountant to have different charge-out rates for the various activities performed: bookkeeping, preparation of financial statements, tax consultation, and advice. For example, if an accountant is doing bookkeeping, it will be at a lower rate scale; complex tax advice is charged at the high end of the range. Accountants generally charge for their time plus additional costs for a bookkeeper, secretary, etc. The bill-out rates for these staff members vary and you should ask in advance exactly what you will be charged.

As with your lawyer, a good level of rapport and communication with your accountant will enhance the quality of advice and the effectiveness of your use of that advice. Openly discuss your concerns and questions with your accountant. You may from time to time wish to seek a second opinion on advice you have been given. If you are not satisfied with your accountant for any reason, you should promptly find another accountant who could better meet your needs.

Resolving Disputes

If you have complaints about fees, service, or conduct, attempt to resolve the dispute directly with the accountant concerned. If that doesn't work, complain to the manager of the firm. Depending on the issues, you can also complain to the provincial professional accounting association. The association can investigate and discipline members. In addition, these provincial professional associations will have a basic insurance package to cover professional liability for negligence or incompetence, as well as missing trust funds. Individual accounting firms may have supplemental professional liability insurance coverage.

Selecting a Lender

When deciding which bank, credit union, or trust company to deal with for your real estate investment affairs, it is advisable to shop around, especially if you need bank financing. Services and rates vary among branches of the same bank. It is helpful to have a lender who has had experience in the area of real estate investment. As a lender's loan-approval limit will vary from branch to branch, you will ideally want a lender who has a loan-approval level greater than the amount of money that you need to borrow. (More information on dealing with lenders is given in Chapter 5: Understanding the Financing Aspects.)

Selecting a Financial Planner

Everyone's financial planning needs are different. The process should take into account all the psychological and financial factors that affect your financial goals and objectives and provide a short-term and long-term strategy. Some financial planners liaise with other professionals—for example, with lawyers, accountants, and insurance brokers—to make sure that the overall plan is integrated. (Refer to Chapter 12: Understanding Financial and Estate Planning.)

Qualifications

Anyone can call himself or herself a financial planner; there are no federal, provincial (except in Quebec), or local laws that require certain qualifications, such as those imposed upon lawyers. However, several associations grant credentials that signify a planner's level of education, although criteria can change from time to time, so check with the association. These are some of the most commonly recognized designations:

Certified Financial Planner (CFP)

CFP is an internationally recognized designation first introduced into Canada by the Financial Planners Standards Council of Canada (FPSCC). Their Web site is www.cfp-ca.org.

Chartered Life Underwriter (CLU)

A Chartered Life Underwriter is a financial advisor with advanced knowledge in life and health insurance and estate planning. An advisor with a CLU specializes in advice on insurance and related tax and estate planning integration. The CLU designation is awarded by the Financial Advisors Association of Canada. For more information, refer to their website: www.advoicis.ca.

How to Find a Financial Planner

Referral by Friend, Accountant, or Lawyer

If using word-of-mouth referral, ask why your contact recommends a particular person. Does the person making the referral currently use the planner's services? How long has he or she known the person professionally? What are the planner's strengths and weaknesses?

Financial Planning Standards Council of Canada

The Financial Planners Standards Council of Canada's (FPSCC) Web site at www.cfp-ca.org has the names of those having a CFP designation in your area.

Advocis

This is the name of the Financial Advisors Association of Canada. This association is a merger of the Canadian Association of Financial Planners and the Canadian Association of Insurance and Financial Advisors. Their Web site is www.advocis.ca from which you can obtain names of Advocis members in your area.

How to Select a Financial Planner

Once you've made the decision to seek the services of a financial planner, you may have many more questions: Which professional is right for me? How do I identify a competent financial planner who can coordinate all aspects of my financial life?

Just as when you select a lawyer or accountant, base your decision on a number of factors—education, qualifications, experience, and reputation.

When selecting your financial planner, choose one you can work with confidently. It is your responsibility and right to fully inquire about the practitioner's background, number of years in practice, credentials, client references, and other relevant information. Meet with the practitioner to determine compatibility and financial-planning style. Meet with at least three planners before you make your final selection. To work together effectively, it's important to find someone with whom you feel completely comfortable.

How a Financial Planner Is Compensated

It is important to understand, and be comfortable with, the way your financial planner gets paid. Financial advisers are compensated in one of four ways: solely by fees, a combination of fees and commissions, solely by commissions, or through a salary paid by an organization that receives fees. In some cases, financial advisers may offer more than one payment option. Here's how these different methods work.

Fee Only

Many lawyers, accountants, and fee-only financial planners charge an hourly rate, including time spent in research, reviewing the plan with you, and discussing implementation options. Others charge a flat amount, but usually offer a no-cost, no-obligation initial consultation. Some will do a computerized profile and assessment of your situation for a fee that can range from $200 to $500 or more.

Fee-only financial advisers typically advise you on investments, insurance, and other financial vehicles, but do not benefit from commissions. The planner has no vested interest in having you buy one financial services product over another. Some fee-only financial planners will help you follow through on their recommendations using mutual funds and other investments. Otherwise, you will have to take your own initiative.

Commission Only

Some financial advisers are compensated solely through commissions earned by selling investments and insurance, including life insurance, annuities, or mutual funds. A commission-only adviser will develop recommendations for your situation and goals, review the recommendations with you, and discuss implementation.

In some cases, commissions are clearly disclosed, for example, a percentage front-end load commission on a mutual fund. In other cases, the fees are lumped into the general expenses of the product, as with life insurance, so you won't know how much your planner makes unless you ask. When you interview potential candidates, ask about the relative percentages of commission revenues from annuities, insurance products, mutual funds, stocks and bonds, and other products. The candidates answers will give you a sense of the kind of advice the firm usually gives.

You could also pay ongoing charges that apply as long as you hold an investment. Some insurance companies pay planners trailer fees for each year a client pays premiums. In other situations, you must pay a fee if you sell a product before a set period of time has elapsed. These surrender charges, a percentage of your investment, reimburse the insurer for the commissions it has paid your planner. Some mutual funds require a back-end load fee on early sale. These are usually applied on a sliding scale. After the set time period, you will not be charged. Some companies entice commission-motivated planners with free travel, merchandise, or investment research if their sales of a particular product reach a target level. Your planner might not like your questioning of his or her cash payment and perks. However, it is your right to know whether the products you buy generate direct fees and indirect benefits for the planner in order to decide whether the advice is self-serving or objective.

Fee Plus Commission

Some planners charge a fee for assessing your financial situation and making recommendations, and also earn a commission on the sale of some of those products.

Some planners are "captives" of one company, so they recommend only its product line. Others are independent and can recommend the mutual funds or insurance policies of any company with which they affiliate.

Another form of compensation, called fee offset, involves a reduction in fees for every product purchased. If you buy so many products that your entire fee is covered, request a refund of the fee you paid for your basic plan.

Salary

In most instances, the staff financial advisers at many banks, trust companies, and credit unions are paid by salary, and earn neither fees nor commissions. Of course, there could be other monetary incentives based on the volume and value of the business done or quotas. Career advancement could also be tied to sales performance.

If an adviser helps you select and monitor the purchase of investments or insurance, there will be some cost to you and/or payment to the adviser. This could be in the form of a commission, redemption fees, trailer fees, or asset management fees.

Also, many investments charge annual management and transaction fees. For example, if you open an RRSP, the company that serves as trustee may charge an annual custodial fee for the service. Weekly comparisons of the management-expense ratios of various funds are available in newspapers. These costs will be in addition to the fee for advice.

What to Know about a Financial Planner

Compensation is just one important element that you should consider when hiring a financial adviser. Be sure that the planner you choose has a defined financial-planning process, that addresses your current situation, sets goals, identifies alternatives, selects and implements a course of action, and calls for periodical reviews. It should be a client-centred process. Education, credentials, references, trust, and rapport are also important.

Choose the compensation method that best meets your needs. As a smart consumer, you want to know what you're buying and how much you're paying for it and you're entitled to that information. Do not consider hiring a financial planner who is reluctant to disclose how he or she is compensated.

Research shows that consumers rate "trust" and "ethics" as the most important elements in their relationship with financial advisers. In fact, survey respondents gave this response twice as often as they mentioned good advice and expertise.

Resolving Disputes

If you have any complaints about fees, service, or conduct, first attempt to deal directly with the person concerned. If that does not resolve the matter, you can complain to management, the professional association that the adviser may belong to, the national industry association, the provincial regulatory association, and the provincial securities commission with which the adviser may be registered. Avoid potential advisory problems by pre-empting them through careful selection.

Selecting a Mortgage Broker

Mortgage lending has become very complex, with constantly changing rates, terms, and conditions. Each lending institution has its own criteria that apply to potential borrowers. Some insist on a particular type of property as security, while others require a certain type of applicant. In this latter case, factors such as type of employment, job stability, income, and credit background are weighed. Lending institutions have a broad range of philosophies and policies on the issue of security and applicant qualifications in order for a lender to advance mortgage funds. (For further information, refer to Chapter 5: Understanding the Financing Aspects.)

Other factors also affect mortgage approval. Availability or shortage of funds, past experience in a specific area, perceived resale market for a particular property, and the attitude of the lending committee (e.g., if it is a credit union) are all factors that could affect approval of a mortgage.

Mortgage brokers make it their business to know all the various plans and lending policies, as well as the lender's attitude on various aspects of mortgage security and covenants. A mortgage broker is in effect a matchmaker, attempting to introduce the appropriate lender to the purchaser.

Mortgage brokers have access to numerous sources of funds, including the following:

√ conventional lenders such as banks and trust companies

√ credit unions

√ Canada Mortgage and Housing Corporation (CMHC)

√ GE Mortgage Insurance

√ private pension funds

√ union pension funds

√ real estate syndication funds

√ foreign bank subsidiaries

√ insurance companies

√ private lenders.

The broker knows all the lenders' objectives; the broker is therefore capable of matching the applicant and his or her property with the appropriate plan and lender. Alternatively, the broker can provide a series of mortgage plans from which the borrower may select the one that best suits his or her needs.

Mortgage brokers basically offer two types of services:

√ They arrange a simple mortgage that will get automatic approval in your particular circumstance, which saves you a lot of time searching. The broker generally receives a commission directly from the lender as a "finder" or "referral" fee. You don't pay any extra money or higher interest. Lenders do this because the mortgage market is so competitive.

√ They arrange a more complex mortgage that would not be automatically approved. This takes more time, skill, and persuasion on the part of the broker to source out a lender or number of lenders who will provide the funds you need. For example, if you did not have the normal amount of down payment required, had a negative credit rating, were highly leveraged already, or did not have the normal income required, you would probably be turned down by a conventional lender such as a bank, credit union, or trust company.

If a mortgage broker succeeds in arranging your complex mortgage financing, given the above types of factors, you would pay a commission. The commission could be from 1% to 5% or more of the amount of the mortgage arranged, depending on the degree of difficulty, the urgency of the need for funds, etc.

To find a mortgage broker, look in the Yellow Pages of your telephone directory, check the Internet, or ask your real estate lawyer or your realtor. You can also obtain names of mortgage brokers from their provincial association, the Canadian Institute of Mortgage Brokers and Lenders (www.cimbl.ca).

Selecting a Building or Home Inspector

Qualifications

One of the most important aspects of purchasing your principal residence or investment property is to know the condition of the property in advance. It is a small expense for peace of mind. You don't want to have problems after you buy that will cost you money to repair. You could lose all your potential profit and put your investment at risk otherwise.

Make sure when you obtain an inspection that the person doing it is qualified and independent. Ask what association he or she belongs to, if any, and, if not, why not. One of the main associations in Canada is the Canadian Association of Home and Property Inspectors (CAHPI), with various provincial chapters. To become a member of CAHPI, an inspector must meet various professional and educational requirements, successfully complete a training course and write exams, and practise professionally for a trial period before being considered by the association. In addition, there are annual continuing education requirements to ensure that their industry knowledge is kept current. You can check out the CAHPI Web site (www.cahpi.ca) to get names of members in your area.

The terms "home inspector" and "building inspector" are frequently used interchangeably in terms of independent fee-for-service inspections. These services are different from municipal building inspectors, who approve various stages of a new home construction or renovation as staff of the local government.

Services Provided by a Building Inspector

A home inspector is an objective expert who examines the home and gives you a written opinion of its condition and, ideally, the approximate range of costs to repair the problems. Home inspectors look at all the key parts of the building, such as condition of the roof, siding, foundation, basement, flooring, walls, windows, doors, garage, drainage, electrical, heating, cooling, ventilation, plumbing, insulation, and so on. They should also look for signs of wood rot, mould, and insects.

The older the building, the more potential problems, but new buildings can have serious problems as well. If the new building is covered by a New Home Warranty Program, then you have some protection. However, that program does have some exclusions, and you don't need the hassle of rectifying a problem. If a new home is not covered by the New Home Warranty Program, or is not a new property, you definitely want a home inspection; otherwise, you might have to pay to repair the problem if the builder refuses to do so or goes out of business. You can have an inspection done of a house, townhouse, or apartment condominium, or any type of residential type of building.

Older homes present a more challenging inspection process, for example, to check for aluminum wiring, asbestos, urea formaldehyde foam insulation (UFFI), lead paint, and termites or carpenter ants.

Quite apart from avoiding expensive surprises, using a home inspector has another potential benefit. If the report shows problems with a quantifiable cost to rectify it, you could use that information to negotiate a reduction in the property's price to reflect the estimated cost of repair. You may not want to buy the home, even if problems can be rectified. At least the report gives some objective professional's opinion on the condition of the home to discuss with the vendor.

Make sure that you put a condition in your offer that says "subject to purchaser obtaining a home inspection satisfactory to the purchaser within X days of acceptance of the offer." This way it will be your discretion as to whether you want to complete the deal or not. In addition to the need for a home inspection, you might also be able to obtain a "vendor's disclosure statement." Real estate boards in some provinces have prepared such a form for vendors to sign, disclosing any known problems with the home. As this is a voluntary program in many cases, ask for the reasons if a vendor refuses to complete the form. Have a professional home inspection done anyway, for obvious reasons. The owner may honestly not be aware of serious problems with the home if they are not visible or obvious.

How to Select a Building or Home Inspector

It is important to obtain a qualified and independent inspector. (See section on "Qualifications.") Avoid someone who has a contractor business on the side and may hope to get the repair business from you. Their advice could be self-serving and biased. Apply the same selection criteria discussed earlier in this chapter. Look in the Yellow pages of your telephone directory under "Building Inspection Services." You can also ask friends, relatives, neighbours, or your real estate agent for names of inspection companies they know and recommend. Call several inspectors in your area and interview them. Check with your local Better Business Bureau to see if there have been any complaints against the company that you are considering. Ask for references and check out the references.

Home inspection fees range from approximately $200 to $400 or more depending on the expertise required and the nature of the inspection, the size of the home, its age and condition, your geographic area, the nature of inspection services requested, and other variables. It normally takes a minimum of three hours to do a thorough inspection.

Here are the questions that you should ask when deciding which inspection company to select:

√ What does the inspection include? Inspections should include the areas previously discussed under "Services Provided by a Building Inspector." Always make sure that you get a written report and ask for a sample of a report and what will be covered.

√ How much will it cost? Determine the fees up front.

√ How long will the inspection take?

√ Does the inspector encourage the client to attend the inspection? This is a valuable educational opportunity. You will have a chance to see the problems first-hand. You will also learn various helpful maintenance tips. If an inspector refuses to have you attend the inspection, this should raise a red flag.

√ How long has the inspector been in the business as a home-inspection firm and what type of work was the inspector doing before inspecting homes?

√ Is the inspector specifically experienced in residential construction?

√ What and where was the inspector's training? Does the inspector participate in continuing education programs to keep his or her expertise up to date?

√ Does the company offer to do any repairs or improvements based on its inspection? This might cause a conflict of interest.

√ Does the inspector carry errors and omission insurance? This means that if the inspector makes a mistake in the inspection and you have to pay to rectify the problem, the insurance will cover it. How much insurance does the inspector have and are there any restrictions or exceptions? Will the inspector confirm all that in writing before you make a decision to have the inspection done?

√ Does the inspector belong to an association that will investigate any consumer complaint? This is an important point and was covered earlier under "Qualifications."

Selecting an Insurance Broker

An insurance broker is not committed to any particular company and therefore can compare and contrast the different policies, coverage, and premiums from a wide range of companies that relate to the type of insurance coverage that you are looking for. Also, insurance brokers can obtain a premium quotation for you and coverage availability from insurance company underwriters if the particular investment you have is unique or difficult to cover by other existing policies. Insurance brokers generally have a wide range of types of insurance available. Ensure that the broker is affiliated with a reputable firm.

When selecting an insurance broker, you should ask about the person's professional credentials, expertise, and experience. It is important to have confidence in the broker's background and skills.

Every real estate investment building needs insurance. Creditors such as banks often require insurance. Ask the insurance broker for brochures describing the main type of insurance and an explanation of each. (The main categories and types of insurance that you should consider and discuss with your insurance broker are discussed in Chapter 8: Understanding the Insurance Aspects.)

Qualifications

Insurance agents are licensed and regulated by the provincial governments. Some agents are tied to a particular insurance company, and will sell only the insurance products offered by that company. However, it has become far more common for property or life insurance agents to operate as brokers and to deal with any number of insurance companies, although officially licensed by one company. If you want a broker for property insurance, make sure they are a member of the Insurance Brokers Association of Canada. If you want life or health insurance, make sure they are members of the Financial Advisors Association of Canada.

How to Find an Insurance Broker

There are several ways to find an insurance broker:

√ Look in the Yellow Pages under "insurance brokers."

√ Ask your accountant, lawyer, business associates, and friends for a recommendation.

√ Ask your business, trade, or professional association whom they would recommend.

√ Search the Internet.

√ Check with the Insurance Brokers Association of Canada (www.ibac.ca) for names of members in your area.

√ Check with the Financial Advisors Association of Canada (www.advocis.ca) for names of members in your area.

How to Select an Insurance Broker

Choose an agent you can trust, one who will take the time to listen to you and understand your needs. Ask the agent how long he or she has been in the business, and consider asking for references or a recommendation from one of the agent's other clients.

Your insurance agent should be willing to work with your accountant, lawyer, investment adviser, and tax adviser to develop the optimum estate-planning strategy. Check with your business association, local Chamber of Commerce, and provincial retail merchants association for special rates.

How Insurance Brokers Are Compensated

Insurance agents earn their income in commissions on the insurance policies they sell. Commission rates vary from company to company, and from one life insurance product to another, and recommendations should be evaluated as objectively as possible.

However, despite this apparent built-in lack of objectivity, most life insurance agents are people of integrity who will not recommend the purchase of life insurance unless it is clearly warranted under particular circumstances. They know that their recommendations must be able to withstand scrutiny by the client's accountant or financial adviser, and their reputations are at stake.

Resolving Disputes

If you have a problem with an insurance broker, deal with it directly, assertively, and candidly. Put your concerns in writing so that there is a record. If this approach does not work, talk to the manager, the regional or provincial manager, and even the national head office if necessary. Always keep copies of your correspondence.

Web Sites of Interest

Here are some Web sites of professional and other organizations that will provide helpful information. Also, most the professional associations provide names of accredited professionals in your area. The names of the associations are self-explanatory, unless otherwise described.

Appraisal Institute of Canada:	www.aicanada.ca
Canadian Association of Home and Property Inspectors:	www.cahpi.ca
Canadian Bar Association:	www.cba.org
Canadian Institute of Chartered Accountants:	www.cica.ca
Canadian Institute of Mortgage Brokers and Lenders:	www.cimbl.ca

Canadian Real Estate Association: www.crea.ca
The Association represents all real estate agents
in Canada.

Certified General Accountants Association of Canada: www.cga-canada.org

Certified Management Accountants of Canada: www.cma-canada.org

Financial Advisors Association of Canada: www.advocis.ca
The membership of this organization is the result of
a merger of the Canadian Association of Financial
Planners and the Canadian Association of Insurance
and Financial Advisors.

Financial Planners Standards Council of Canada: www.cfp-ca.org
This organization licenses financial planners with
the certified financial planner (CFP) designation.

Insurance Brokers Association of Canada: www.ibac.ca

Summary

You need to have a minimum benchmark comparison of three advisers in each area of your interest before you can make a reasonable decision in selecting one (if any) of them. As expert advice is critical to your personal, investment, and financial well-being, the selection process has to be thorough. This process will also greatly accelerate your learning curve, and raise your confidence level, and quality of decision making.

Now that you know how to select your team, it's time to learn about the ins and outs of financing a purchase.

CHAPTER 5

Understanding the Financing Aspects

If you have been considering the purchase of a house, condominium, or real estate investment for some time, you probably have some savings already set aside for a down payment. In order to be realistic in your search, it is important to ascertain the size of a mortgage for which you qualify. You also want to determine your personal financial needs. (See also Chapter 1: Understanding Real Estate Investment.) This information, along with knowing how much money you can raise personally and the demands of your investment strategy, will provide you with an affordable range for your new property.

This chapter covers many issues that you need to consider when obtaining property financing. It will help you understand the jargon and concepts to assist your financing selection process.

Topics to be discussed include the types and sources of financing, how to calculate the amount of your mortgage eligibility, applying for a mortgage, costs of a mortgage, and what happens if you default on a mortgage. In addition, this chapter explains creative financing and how to deal with negative cash flow, and provides negotiating tips. Web sites of interest are provided for your further research.

What Is a Mortgage?

A mortgage is a contract between one party who wants to borrow money and another party who wants to lend money. The borrower is referred to as the mortgagor, and the lender is referred to as the mortgagee. These terms can sometimes be confusing. The terms "borrower" and "lender" are also used. The mortgage agreement states that in exchange for the money that the lender provides, the borrower will provide security to the lender in the form of a mortgage document to be filed against the property. For the purposes of this book, the term "property" will refer to the purchase you are considering, whether it is a condominium, house, multi-unit dwelling (such as duplex, fourplex, apartment), or raw land. The mortgage document specifies the rights that the lender has to the property in the event the borrower defaults on the terms of the mortgage. The types of remedies that the mortgagee has against the mortgagor are covered later in this chapter.

A mortgage document filed against the title of the property in the appropriate provincial land registry provides security to the mortgagee against other creditors that the mortgagor may have. If a first mortgage is filed against the property and there are no other encumbrances or charges against the property, then the amount outstanding on the first mortgage takes priority over any and all other creditors, e.g., it is paid off first from the sale of the property on default. Additional loans could be obtained by the mortgagor that take the form of second and third mortgages, which are also filed against the property.

Each more recent loan ranks lower in priority than the previous one, as the date of registration is the criterion that determines priority. Because of the increasing risk involved for subsequent mortgages, higher interest rates are charged. For example, the first mortgage interest rate may be 6%, the second 8%, the third 12%, and the fourth 18%. The first mortgage would be paid out in full from any proceeds of sale, followed by the second mortgage, and so on. It is possible that the price that a home would sell for would cover only the first and second mortgages, leaving no funds available to pay off the third and fourth mortgages.

Mortgages are regulated by federal and provincial law. Although the laws may differ from one province to another, the description of a mortgage outlined in this book applies to most mortgages. The methods of mortgage registration and the enforcement laws vary among provinces. Some of the common clauses in a mortgage are discussed later in this chapter.

The difference between the amount the property could be sold for (less all costs) and the amount owed on the property's mortgage is referred to as the equity in the property.

Types of Mortgages

There are several varieties of mortgages available from banks, credit unions, trust companies, mortgage companies, private lenders, government, and the vendor. Although most residential property borrowers obtain financing through a conventional mortgage, it is useful to be aware of other alternatives. The following is a brief discussion of the main types of mortgages.

Conventional Mortgage

The conventional mortgage is the most common type of financing for principal residence or residential investment property. It is fairly standard in its terms and conditions, although there can be variations. In this type of mortgage, the loan generally cannot exceed 75% of the appraised value or purchase price of the property, whichever is the lesser of the two. Under the Bank Act, the federal government requires all first mortgages greater than 75% to be insured against loss in the event of default. High-ratio insurance is designed to protect the lender and encourage lenders to provide money when the potential risk might otherwise be considered too great. As a matter of public policy, the federal government wants to encourage people to buy homes and provides incentives to lenders to provide the mortgage money. That is why the NHA (National Housing Act) was established, with CMHC as the high-ratio financing insurance vehicle. The purchaser is responsible for raising the other 25% of the funds necessary, either through a down payment or through other means such as a second mortgage or vendor-back mortgage.

Conventional mortgages are available through most financial institutions, including banks and credit unions. In most cases, these mortgages do not have to be insured, but occasionally a lender may require it. For example, if the property is older or is smaller than is normally required by the lender's policy, or if it is located in a rural or rundown area, then the mortgage may be required to be insured with the Canada Mortgage and Housing Corporation (CMHC) or GE Mortgage Insurance Canada (GEM). CMHC is a federal Crown corporation; its Web site is (www.cmhc-schl.gc.ca). GEM is the largest private mortgage insurer in Canada; its Web site is (www.gemortgage.ca).

High-Ratio/Insured Mortgage

If you are unable to raise the necessary 25% funding to complete the purchase of the property, then a high-ratio mortgage may be available to you. These are conventional mortgages that exceed the 75% referred to earlier. By law, these mortgages must be insured, and they are available only through approved lenders that are accepted by CMHC or GEM. Both these organizations have specific guidelines for qualifying, but the administration is done through the bank, trust company, or credit union.

High-ratio mortgages are available for up to 90% of the purchase price or of the appraisal, whichever is lower, and in some cases 95%. In other cases, a homebuyer can get up to 100% high-ratio financing. The percentage for which you would be eligible depends on various circumstances; for example, whether the purchase is for a principal residence or real estate investment. There are also restrictions on the purchase price of the home that may be involved. Obtain further information from your realtor, banker, mortgage broker, or GEM or CMHC directly.

Collateral Mortgage

In a collateral mortgage, the mortgage security is secondary, or collateral, to some other main form of security taken by the lender. This main security may take the form of a promissory note, personal guarantee, or assignment of some other form of security that the lender may require. A collateral mortgage is therefore a backup protection of the loan that is filed against the property. The payment requirements on the loan are covered in the promissory note, and once the promissory note has been paid off in full, the collateral mortgage will automatically be paid off. You would then be entitled to have the collateral mortgage discharged from the title of the property.

One of the main differences between a collateral mortgage and a conventional mortgage is that a conventional mortgage may be assumed, whereas a collateral mortgage, of course, cannot be, as it is subject to some other form of security between the parties. Otherwise, the terms of the collateral mortgage could be very similar to the terms of a conventional mortgage. The money borrowed on a collateral mortgage could be used for the purchase of the property itself, or for other purposes such as home improvements or other real estate investments.

Government-Assisted Mortgage

National Housing Act (NHA) mortgages are loans granted under the provisions of this federal act. The loans are administered through CMHC. You can apply for an NHA loan at any chartered bank, trust company, or credit union. Borrowers must pay an application fee to CMHC that usually includes the cost of a property appraisal and an insurance fee. The latter is usually added to the principal amount of the mortgage, though it may be paid at the time of closing. Contact CMHC or your financial institution for the most current information on borrowing requirements.

In addition, some provinces have second mortgage funding or funding guarantees available for principal residence home purchases. Generally there is a limit on the amount of the purchase price of the home and a ceiling on the amount of the mortgage. Obtain further information from your realtor or lending institution.

Secondary Financing

Secondary financing generally consists of a second mortgage and possibly a third. You may wish to take out a second mortgage because the existing first mortgage (which you plan to assume) has an attractive interest rate or other desirable features, and because there will be a shortfall between the amount of your available down payment and the amount of the first mortgage. You therefore need to obtain funds. Chartered banks will usually provide money for second mortgages up to a limit of 75% of the lower of the purchase price or appraised value. You can also obtain second mortgages through mortgage brokers or other sources that could go as high as 90%, or sometimes higher, of the lower of the purchase price or appraised value. If the second mortgage has a term that is longer than that of the first mortgage you assume, make sure you have a postponement clause put into the second mortgage. With this clause, you would be able to automatically renew or replace the first mortgage when it becomes due without having to obtain permission from the second mortgage lender to do so. In other words, if you renewed the first mortgage or obtained a replacement first mortgage, that mortgage would still be in first position, ahead of the second mortgage. Your lawyer will advise you.

Assumed Mortgage

In the case of an assumed mortgage, the lender qualifies you to assume an existing mortgage on the property. In some instances mortgages can be assumed without qualifications. If you assume the existing mortgage, it will save you the cost of legal fees and disbursements for registering the mortgage, obtaining an appraisal, and other expenses. Whenever you are assuming an existing mortgage, it is important that your lawyer obtain a mortgage assumption statement showing the principal balance outstanding, the method of paying taxes, the remaining term on the mortgage, and a copy of the mortgage that shows other features such as prepayment privileges, and other details.

If you are a seller of the property, you should be very cautious about someone assuming your mortgage unless you obtain a release in writing from the lender that you will not be liable under the mortgage, in the event that the person assuming it defaults on his or her obligations. In the event of default, the lender would be entitled to go after the original mortgagor, as well as the person who assumed the mortgage, for the full amount of the debt outstanding or any mortgage shortfall after sale of the property due to mortgage default. Make sure that you obtain legal advice before permitting any buyer to assume your mortgage.

Builder's Mortgage

If purchasing a new house or building, you may be able to assume the builder's mortgage. Make sure that you obtain legal advice before signing any such mortgage to ensure that the provisions in the mortgage are acceptable to you. If you are building the house, the lender may approve a mortgage for construction purposes, but will advance mortgage draws based on the various stages of construction, e.g., foundation, framing, roofing. There could be three or more stages. It depends on the nature of the construction and the policy of the lender.

Discounted Mortgage

Another possibility is that the vendor will offer you a discounted mortgage. In other words, to make the house price attractive, the mortgage rate might be reduced to 2%, for example, whereas the prevailing interest rate for a first mortgage could be 5%. (The interest rates given in the examples throughout this book will obviously vary depending on the marketplace at any given time.) The builder is able to "buy down" a mortgage from a lender at an attractive rate by paying a discount—the difference in financial terms between what the lender would make on a 2% mortgage and what he would make on a 5% mortgage. However, vendors frequently add this discount onto the purchase price of the home; you could be paying a lower interest rate because you are paying a higher price for the property than you would otherwise pay. Another factor to be aware of is that the discounted mortgage may last only for a short time, e.g., six months or a year. After that period you will have to obtain your own mortgage at the prevailing rate. Thus, although a discounted mortgage could initially appear attractive, over the long term it could be a false economy.

Vendor Mortgage

A vendor mortgage is sometimes referred to as a vendor-back or vendor take-back mortgage. Here, the vendor encourages the sale of the property by giving the purchaser a loan on the purchase of the property. For example, if the purchaser is able to get 75% conventional financing, but does not have sufficient funds for a down payment of 25%, the vendor may be prepared to give, in effect, a second mortgage for 15% of the purchase price. That way, the purchaser would need to come up with only a 10% down payment. The purchaser would then make mortgage payments to the vendor as if a normal commercial lender held the second mortgage. If you are the purchaser, it is fairly common for the vendor not to conduct a credit check or any other financial assessment of you. On the other hand, if you are the vendor, for obvious reasons you should make sure that there is a provision in the offer to purchase, and that you can do a thorough credit check of the purchaser before deciding on granting the second mortgage. When doing a credit check, either of yourself or a prospective tenant if you are a landlord, you can obtain that credit report information from Equifax over the Internet. For more information, check out their site at www.equifax.ca.

Sometimes the vendor makes arrangements through a mortgage broker for the second mortgage to be sold at a discount as soon as the transaction is completed. This way, the vendor gets cash immediately, minus, of course, the cost required to discount the mortgage and the broker's fee. Generally speaking the mortgage has to have a fixed and not a floating rate if it is to be sold; the terms should be at least a year to be attractive to a purchaser of the mortgage; and the mortgage is generally not assumable. If the vendor intends to sell the vendor-back mortgage, there is usually a precondition in it that the purchaser will cooperate with any credit checks and will agree to the mortgage being assigned. Also, that acceptance of the offer to purchase is based on a commitment from a mortgage broker that there is a purchaser for the second mortgage as soon as the sale is completed.

If you are considering providing a vendor-take-back mortgage, again it is important to be cautious and obtain legal advice in advance. There is a risk that the purchaser will refuse to pay on the second mortgage if there appears to be any problem with the condition of the property after the sale. Naturally the vendor or the assignee of the vendor's second mortgage could commence foreclosure or order for sale proceedings, but in practical terms it is possible that the purchaser could attempt to raise defences. Discussion in any detail of these types of problems is outside the scope of this book. They are raised merely to alert you to the need for competent legal advice in these unique situations.

Blanket Mortgage

A blanket mortgage is a type of mortgage registered over two or more properties. The purpose behind the mortgage is to provide the lender with additional property as security. It is normally used where a borrower wants more money than the lender is prepared to provide on the basis of one property alone. That property may not have sufficient equity and, for example, the amount of money that is being requested could constitute 90% or 95% of the value of the first property. If the second property has attractive equity, the lender may be prepared to advance the funds to the borrower, but have one mortgage filed against both properties. In the event of default, the lender could proceed against one or both of the properties in order to get sufficient proceeds from the sale to satisfy the outstanding debt.

Blanket mortgages are very common in cases when someone invests in or owns several properties. They are also common in real estate development. The developer normally has a blanket mortgage over all the properties. As soon as a property is sold, the lender releases the portion of the blanket mortgage that was filed on that property in order for the purchaser of the property to place his own mortgage. The developer normally has a requirement with its lender that all or a portion (for example, 50% or 75%) of the purchase price of the property has to be paid to the lender to reduce the blanket mortgage as a condition for the lender's releasing the encumbrance on the individual property.

Leasehold Mortgage

A leasehold mortgage is a mortgage on a house, condominium, or other property where the land is leased rather than owned. The mortgage must be amortized over a period that is shorter than the length of the land lease. Normally a lender will not grant a mortgage on leasehold property unless the duration of the lease is of sufficient length that the risk is fairly minimal to the lender. For example, if a condominium is on leasehold land with a 99-year lease and there are 85 years left on the lease, then there is relatively little risk to the lender. On the other hand, if the leasehold is for a 30-year period and there are five years left on the lease, the lender will consider the risk too high, because at the end of the five-year period, the lease will expire and therefore there will be no right or entitlement to the leasehold interest. This would mean that the condominium would have no value to a potential purchaser after five years in the above example. The main lease would revert back to the lessor, e.g., the original owner of the land. (Refer to Chapter 6: Understanding the Legal Aspects for a discussion on leasehold interest in property.)

Condominium Mortgage

In many cases condominium mortgages are identical to any of the other mortgages discussed in terms of the provisions, except for a few special provisions because of the unique nature of a condominium. Although a purchaser of a condominium receives a legal title to one individual unit, the purchaser also has an undivided interest in the common elements of the development.

Some of the special clauses contained in most condominium mortgages that distinguish this type of mortgage from a conventional house mortgage are as follows:

√ The lender has the right to use the unit owner's vote or consent in the condominium corporation. In other words, the lender has a proxy to vote in place of the borrower. In practical terms, the lender does not usually vote on any and all decisions in normal circumstances. The lender, though, can require that the borrower provide notice of all condominium corporation meetings, including special or extraordinary meetings announced by the condominium corporation, and receive copies of minutes and information.

√ The lender requires the borrower to comply with all the terms of the bylaws, rules, and regulations of the condominium corporation. Any default on the borrower's part will constitute default under the mortgage.

√ The lender requires the borrower to pay the appropriate portion of maintenance costs of the common elements. In the event the borrower fails to do so, the lender is entitled to pay the costs on behalf of the borrower and add these onto the principal amount outstanding on the mortgage, with interest charged to this amount.

Agreement for Sale

An agreement for sale is not actually a mortgage, but another way of financing a sale. It should not be confused with an agreement for purchase and sale. An agreement for sale is normally used in a situation when the buyer of the property does not have sufficient funds for a down payment and the vendor wishes to dispose of the property. In an agreement for sale, the vendor finances the purchase of the property in a fashion similar to that of a vendor-take-back mortgage. The purchaser, though, does not become the legal owner of the property until the agreement for sale has been paid in full. At that time, the purchaser is legally entitled to have the conveyance of the legal interest of the property transferred over to the purchaser. In the meantime, the vendor remains the registered owner on title of the property. The purchaser has the legal right of possession and makes regular payments to the vendor under the terms of the agreement between the vendor and the purchaser. The purchaser has a legal "right to purchase" that is registered against the title of the property in the provincial land registry office.

The terms of an agreement for sale are in many ways very similar to the terms of a mortgage. The agreement for sale may have a five-year term, for example, after which time the full amount is due and payable. At that time either the purchaser has to arrange conventional mortgage financing or other form of financing to pay off the vendor, or else make an agreement with the vendor for an extension of the agreement for sale for another term. Agreements for sale are frequently used where the purchaser cannot qualify to assume the existing mortgage or to obtain a new mortgage; in effect, the purchaser assumes a mortgage that would otherwise be unassumable. The purchaser pays the vendor and the vendor maintains payments on the underlying mortgage.

Sources of Mortgages

It is important to keep in mind that the competition for mortgage lending is extremely intense. There are numerous lenders of mortgage funds and they are all attempting to attract the customer to use their services. You should therefore do thorough research before deciding on which mortgage lender to use. Major city newspapers tend to publish a comparison of the prevailing mortgage rates by institution in the real estate section of the weekend newspaper. This will save you a lot of research time.

You can also find prevailing mortgage rates on the Web sites of banks, credit unions, on-line banks, mortgage companies, and mortgage brokers. Also check with mortgage brokers in your community. They frequently publish a list of current comparative rates and will generally send a copy to you free upon request. A list of mortgage brokers can be found in the Yellow Pages of your telephone directory, through the Internet search engines, or from the Canadian Institute of Mortgage Brokers and Lenders at www.cimbl.ca. By doing a search through www.google.ca under "mortgages Canada" (or your province or city) or "mortgage brokers Canada" (or your province or city), you will see many listings of interest. You can also obtain mortgage approvals directly over the Internet through many lenders and mortgage brokers.

You can also find mortgage calculators on the Internet, as will be discussed in the next section.

These are the main sources of mortgage funds available for residential or investment purchases that you may wish to consider:

√ banks

√ trust companies

√ credit unions

√ government (As mentioned earlier, the federal government, through CMHC, provides mortgage funds if you qualify.)

√ a vendor-take-back mortgage

√ assumption of an existing mortgage

√ obtaining funds from personal sources such as family, relatives, friends, or business associates

√ mortgage companies

√ real estate companies

√ mortgage brokers (A discussion of the benefits of using a mortgage broker and how to locate them is covered in Chapter 4: Selecting Your Advisory Team.)

√ on-line banks, credit unions, mortgage companies, and mortgage brokers.

Key Factors to Consider When Selecting a Mortgage

There are many factors you will have to consider before finalizing your mortgage decision. The key factors are amortization, term of the mortgage, open or closed mortgage, interest rate, payment schedules, prepayment privilege, and assumability. A brief explanation of each of these concepts follows, as well as where to find mortgage calculators on the Internet.

Amortization

Amortization is the length of time over which the regular (usually monthly) payments have been calculated, on the assumption that the mortgage will be fully paid over that period. The usual amortization period is 25 years, although there is a wide range of options available in 5-, 7-, 10-, 15-, and 20-year periods as well. Naturally, the shorter the amortization period, the more money you save on interest (see Chart 5 in the Appendix).

Term of the Mortgage

The term of the mortgage is the length of time the mortgagee will lend you the money for. Terms may vary from 6 months to 10 years. If the amortization period was 25 years, that would mean that you would have several different mortgages, possibly 10 to 20 separate terms, before you have completely paid off the loan. In reality, many people sell their principal residence or investment property after 5 to 10 years of ownership, depending on needs and circumstances; for example, illness, death, divorce, job loss or a new job, increasing or decreasing size of family.

At the end of each term, the principal and unpaid interest of the mortgage become due and payable. Unless you are able to repay the entire mortgage at this time, you would normally either renew the mortgage with the same lender on the same terms; renegotiate the mortgage; depending on the options available to you at that time; or refinance the mortgage through a different lending institution. If you renew with a different mortgage lender, there could be extra administrative charges involved. As there is considerable competition among lenders, often there is no administrative fee if you are transferring a mortgage to another institution. In some cases the other institution will absorb the legal fees and costs and still offer an inducement for you to take the business away from a competitive lender and bring it to them.

Some people take out short-term mortgages (e.g., six months), anticipating that interest rates will go down and that at the end of that term there will be a lower interest rate. The problem is that if rates have gone up instead of down at the end of the six months, your monthly mortgage payment will increase and you may not be able to afford, or want to pay, the higher rates. The other option you have is to negotiate a long-term mortgage (e.g., five years) so that you can budget for the future over a five-year period with certainty about the interest rates. The lender is not obliged to renew the mortgage at the end of a term, but in practical terms will do so as long as you have met your payment terms. If the lender decides to renew, an administration fee of $100 to $250 is often charged.

Interest Rate

There are various ways to calculate the interest: the fixed rate, which means the interest rate remains fixed for the term of the mortgage (e.g., one year); and the variable rate, which means that the interest rate varies every month according to the premium interest rate set by the lender every month. In this latter case, although the actual monthly payments that you would make would usually stay the same, the interest charge proportion of that monthly payment of principal and interest will vary with that month's rate.

How often interest is compounded—in other words, the interest charged on interest—will determine the total amount of interest that you actually pay on your mortgage. Obviously, the more frequent the compounding of interest, the more interest you will pay. The lender can charge any rate of interest, within the law, and compound that at any frequency desired. That is why it is important for you to check on the nature of the compounding of interest.

By law, mortgages have to contain a statement showing the basis on which the rate of interest is calculated. Mortgage interest has traditionally been compounded on a half-yearly basis. If a mortgage is calculated on the basis of straight interest, there is no compounding, but just the running total of the interest outstanding at any point in time. Some mortgages, such as variable-rate mortgages, may be compounded monthly. The initial rate quoted for a mortgage is called a *nominal rate*, whereas the real interest rate for a mortgage compounded semi-annually, for instance, is called the effective rate. As an example, a mortgage that quotes a nominal rate of 10% has an *effective rate* of interest of 10% when compounded yearly, 10.25% when compounded half-yearly, and 10.47% when compounded monthly.

Interest Averaging

If you are considering assuming an existing first mortgage because the rate and term are attractive, but concerned about the current interest rate of second mortgage financing, do an interest averaging calculation. You might find the average interest rate to be less than the prevailing first mortgage rate. Here is an example of how you calculate it:

First mortgage: $60,000 × 5% = $3,000

Second mortgage: $30,000 × 8% = $2,400

$90,000 × X% = $5,400

Average interest rate X% = $5,400 ÷ $90,000 = 6%

Open or Closed Mortgage

An open mortgage allows you to increase the payment of the amount of the principal at any time. You could pay off the mortgage in full at any time before the term is over without any penalty or extra charges. Because of this flexibility, open mortgages cost more than standard closed mortgages.

A closed mortgage locks you in for the term of the mortgage. There is a penalty fee for any advance payment. A straight closed mortgage will normally have a provision that if it is prepaid because the property is sold, a three-month interest penalty will be applied, or the penalty will be waived entirely if the new purchaser of the property takes out a new mortgage with the lending institution. Most closed mortgages have a prepayment feature. This is discussed shortly.

Payment Schedules

As to payment schedules, there are many options available in the marketplace, including weekly, biweekly (every two weeks), monthly, semi-annually, annually, and other variations. Naturally, the more frequently you make payments, the lower the amount of interest that you will pay (see Chart 5 in the Appendix).

Depending on your negotiations with the lender, you may make payments on interest only or have a graduated payment schedule. This would mean that at the beginning of the term of the mortgage, your payments are lower and increase over time, so that at the end of the term the payments will be considerably higher. The reason for this type of arrangement is that the borrower's ability to make the payment may increase over time, and the payment schedules are graduated to accommodate that. This could be an advantage with revenue real estate purchases.

Usually payments made on the mortgage are a blend of principal and interest. These have traditionally been amortized assuming a monthly payment basis.

Prepayment Privilege

This is a very important feature to have in your mortgage if it is a fixed mortgage. If it is an open mortgage, you can pay the balance outstanding on the mortgage in part or in full at any time without penalty. If, on the other hand, you have a closed mortgage that does not have any prepayment privileges, you are locked in for the term of the mortgage (e.g., three years) without the privilege of prepaying without penalty.

You may therefore wish to have a mortgage that, though called a closed mortgage, is in fact partly open and partly closed, permitting prepayment at certain stages and in a certain manner, but not at other times. For example, you may be permitted to make a prepayment of between 10% and 20% annually on the principal amount outstanding. This could be made once a year at the end of each year of the mortgage, or at your choice any time within the year.

Another variation would also give you the option of increasing the amount of your monthly payment by 10% to 20% once a year. The results are impressive in terms of saving interest costs and reducing the amortization period. Every time a prepayment is made, or every time you increase your monthly payments, the balance owing and thus the monthly cost of interest is reduced. (For a graphic illustration, see Chart 5 in the Appendix.) The net effect is that a larger portion of each payment is applied toward the principal, since monthly (or other agreed-upon regular) payments usually remain the same. Make sure you completely understand your prepayment options, as they could save you a lot of money.

Assumability

Assumability means that the buyer takes over the obligation and payments under the vendor's mortgage. Most mortgage contracts deal with the issue of assumability very clearly. The lender can agree to full assumability without qualifications, assumability with qualifications, or no assumability. For example, if a vendor reluctantly gave a vendor-back second mortgage for $50,000 for a period of two years, the vendor (the lender) may not want to have that mortgage assumed by anyone else because the vendor would prefer to be paid out in full in the event that the property is sold, rather than carry the mortgage any longer.

The issue of assumability is an important one to consider. You would have a wider range of potential purchasers interested in buying your property if purchasers who may not otherwise qualify for your mortgage would be able to assume it without qualifications. Most mortgages, though, generally have a clause that says the mortgage is assumable with qualification by the lender. While a negotiable item, lenders typically check out the creditworthiness and debt-servicing capabilty of the new owner.

Also, there is a risk if someone assumes your mortgage and you are still on the mortgage document. For example, what if the new owner defaults on the mortgage and the lender has to foreclose? Your name would be added onto the court documents. That is why you don't want to have anyone assume your mortgage unless you obtain a release of any liability from the lender at the same time. It would be prudent to get your lawyer's assistance to ensure that your interests are properly protected.

Portability

Some lenders offer a feature called portability. This means that if you sell one home and buy another during the term of your mortgage, you can transfer the mortgage from one property to the other. In practical terms, you could save money if interest rates have gone up during the term of your present mortgage. Thus you would not have to take out a new mortgage for your new home at current, higher mortgage rates, thereby decreasing the amount of mortgage money available to you. Remember, the higher the interest rate, the lower the mortgage amount that you can qualify for. Conversely, if mortgage rates have gone down since your current mortgage took effect, you would probably not be at all interested in continuing your existing mortgage. You must take into consideration the costs of early termination of a mortgage.

General Contents of a Mortgage

Most mortgage documents are in fine print and are fairly detailed. There are no "standard" clauses in a mortgage. The only way you can fully understand your mortgage is to have a competent and experienced real estate lawyer review it and explain the key areas to you. In addition to differences in mortgage contracts, the laws change constantly. Many people sign mortgages without having any idea of what is in them. The purpose of this section is to outline some terms that you should be familiar with, so that you will be better prepared when discussing the matter with a lawyer.

In any mortgage, there are these basic provisions: the date of the mortgage, the names of the parties who are signing, a legal description of the property, the amount of the loan, the payment terms including interest and frequency, the respective obligations of the lender and the borrower, and the signatures of all the parties. Fifteen common clauses that you may find in the mortgage are discussed below.

Personal Liability

Under a mortgage, the borrower is personally liable for the debt to the lender, assuming the mortgage is in an individual's name rather than a corporate name. In the event of default, the lender can sue the borrower for the full amount of the mortgage. While the lender *is not obliged* to commence foreclosure or power of sale proceedings, and take over or sell the property, the lender usually commences a form of foreclosure or power of sale action to protect its interest, in addition to suing the borrower personally. If the property is sold, then the borrower would be responsible for the shortfall, plus all the associated legal and other costs that the lender has incurred.

If there is a co-covenantor on the mortgage—someone else who covenants or promises that he or she will meet all the obligations of the mortgage—the lender can sue both the borrower and the co-covenantor for the debt under the mortgage. (Sometimes the term "guarantor" is used instead of co-covenantor. In practical terms, they are interchangeable.)

The lender may refuse to give funds covered by a mortgage without extra security protection by means of an additional guarantor or co-covenantor. If you are married and are purchasing the property under your personal name, the lender will almost always insist that your spouse sign as a guarantor or co-covenantor, regardless of your creditworthiness. This is to protect the lender under the matrimonial or family relations legislation of the province in the event that a separation or divorce occurs. The lender does not want its property security to be compromised by a marital dispute.

If you have an incorporated company to purchase real estate and take out a mortgage in that name, in most cases the lender will ask you for a personal guarantee of the corporate mortgage. This makes you personally liable, of course.

Insurance

This clause requires that the mortgagor insure the building against fire. The insurance policy must show that the mortgagee is entitled to be paid first (if a first mortgage) from the mortgage proceeds in the event of a claim on the policy.

There is also a provision in the mortgage that sets out the amount of the insurance (replacement). It states that if you fail to pay the premium, the mortgagee can do so, or if you fail to get sufficient insurance, the mortgagee can do so. Also, all the additional premium costs can be added on to the principal amount of debt of your mortgage.

Requirement to Pay Taxes

This clause states that you are obliged to pay all property taxes when they come due, and that if you do not do so, the lender is entitled to pay the taxes. The lender would then add the amount paid in taxes to the principal amount of the mortgage. Some lenders attempt to avoid any problem with taxes by having a separate tax account set up at the time you take out the mortgage. This means that you pay an extra amount every month on your payment to the bank for a tax portion that goes into that account, and once a year the lender pays the property taxes directly. Attempt to negotiate your way out of this prepayment provision and look after the taxes yourself. Some lenders require proof that taxes are current and have been paid every year.

Maintain Property

This clause in the mortgage states that you are required to keep the property in good repair. The reason for this provision is that the lender obviously does not want the property to deteriorate through neglect and therefore reduce its property value, compromising the value of the security.

Requirement to Keep Any Subsequent Mortgages in Good Standing

This provision states that you must maintain all your financial obligations on the second and third mortgages so that they do not go into default. If they do go into default, foreclosure proceedings could occur. If the property were sold, the first mortgage would be paid off first, followed by the second and the third, etc.

No Urea Formaldehyde Foam Insulation (UFFI)

Many mortgages state that no UFFI is permitted in the premises at the time the mortgage is granted or subsequently. Urea formaldehyde foam insulation is considered hazardous to public health as it has been shown to cause breathing problems and has potential cancer-causing properties. For these reasons, lenders do not want to be sued, so they will refuse to provide financing if there is any UFFI in the property.

Prohibition against Renting Out Premises

Some mortgage documents state very clearly that the premises cannot he rented out, but can only be used as your principal residence. This can occur with some residential mortgages that are granted for the benefit of the owner-occupier and not for investment or rental purposes.

Having said this, almost all lenders permit "mortgage helper" rental suites in your home. In fact, most lenders will include the revenue you receive from your rental suite as part of your overall personal income for calculating the maximum amount of mortgage that you are eligible for.

Due to the realities of the competitive mortgage marketplace and demand, you can readily get mortgages for properties used for rental purposes.

Assignment of Rents

If you are purchasing a revenue house or building, the lender may request that you sign a document entitled "Assignment of Rents." In the event that you fail to make your monthly payments to the lender, the lender can formally notify the tenants that you have assigned the rent payments directly to the lender.

Must Comply with All Laws

This provision would advise that all federal, provincial, and municipal laws concerning the use and occupancy of the property must be fully complied with. This is an important provision if you intend to rent out the property. Although there may not be a strict prohibition against rentals, there could be one indirectly if municipal zoning bylaws prohibit rental of residential premises. In practical terms, most mortgage companies don't care if you rent out part of your home as a "mortgage helper," even though it does not technically comply with existing municipal bylaws. On the other hand, there is a trend in many municipalities to permit "illegal" suites, as it is serving a community and social need.

Quiet Possession

This provision states that unless the mortgagor defaults, the mortgagee will not interfere in any way with the peaceful enjoyment of the property by the mortgagor. In practical terms, this means that the mortgagee cannot enter the premises.

Prepayment Privileges

It is important that the prepayment privileges are set out clearly in the agreement. The various types of prepayment privileges have been previously discussed.

Assumption of Mortgage Privileges

Assumption of mortgage privileges should be set out clearly in the mortgage document. This subject also has been discussed earlier.

Special Clauses Relating to a Condominium Purchase

These have been covered under the section on "Types of Mortgages."

Acceleration Clause

This clause states that if the mortgagor defaults on any of the terms of the mortgage agreement, then at the option of the mortgagee, the full amount outstanding on the principal of the mortgage plus interest is immediately due and payable. In some provinces, legislation restricts the mortgagee from exercising the right of acceleration, even though it may be in the mortgage document.

Default

This section of the mortgage deals with the type of matters that could place the mortgage in default of the mortgage agreement, and sets out the rights of the mortgagee in the event of default. This is discussed later.

Refer to Checklist 2 in the Appendix when negotiating with a lender. Again, have your lawyer advise you on the contents of the mortgage before signing it.

Determining the Amount of Mortgage Available

Different lenders have different criteria for approving the amount of mortgage funds available. There is considerable flexibility with many lenders and it is important to compare or have a mortgage broker do so on your behalf in order to get the maximum amount of mortgage funds possible in your situation. Lenders use the gross debt-service ratio and total debt-service ratio as standard formulas for determining mortgage qualification. There are other calculations that you may want to utilize to determine the data relating to mortgages.

In calculating matters of principal and interest relating to mortgages and other factors, such as different pay periods and options, there are various sources of information. This will be covered at the end of this section.

Gross Debt-Service (GDS) Ratio

The GDS ratio is used to calculate the amount you can afford to spend for mortgage principal (P) and interest (I) payments. Some lenders also include property taxes (T) as part of this formula, and possibly heating costs (H) as well. All these expenses are added together. Under the GDS ratio, payments generally should not exceed 30% of your income. There is flexibility in lending criteria, though, as some lenders will go up to 32% and in some cases 35% or more of your income and only include P and I rather than PIT or PITH. Refer to Form 3 in the Appendix to calculate your own mortgage eligibility.

Total Debt-Service (TDS) Ratio

Many people have monthly financial obligations other than mortgage and taxes, which lenders want to know about in order to determine ability to debt service the mortgage. Using the TDS ratio, the bank would want to know your fixed monthly debts such as credit card payments, car payments, other loans, and condominium maintenance fees. In general terms, no more than 40% of your gross family income can be used when calculating the amount you can afford to pay for principal interest and taxes, plus your fixed monthly debts. The lender is naturally concerned about minimizing the risk that you will be unable to meet your financial obligations relating to the mortgage if the ratio is too high. Refer to Form 4 in the Appendix.

It is important to consider all your monthly obligations (e.g., insurance and electricity costs), some of which may not be taken into account by the lender, so that you get a good sense of your financial standing. Complete your personal cost-of-living budget (Form 1 in the Appendix). This should give you some idea, net after tax, of what your monthly income is and what your monthly debt-servicing charges will be on the mortgage, plus other expenses.

Obtaining Mortgage Amortization Tables

There are different ways that you can access information to obtain free amortization tables customized for your needs:

√ Contact any mortgage lender or mortgage broker and ask for a free copy of a mortgage amortization schedule based on your needs. They will e-mail it to you to print out, or you can pick it up, without any obligation on your part.

√ Research the mortgage sites of lenders or mortgage brokers.

√ Check on-line mortgage calculators that you can personalize based on various variables and options, and then print out the results to review. Two sites in particular that have a range of different types of mortgage and borrowing calculators are GE Mortgage Insurance Canada site (www.gemortgage.ca) and the *MoneySense* Magazine site (www.moneysense.ca).

√ Amortization or mortgage interest books, which you can buy at most bookstores or obtain from your local library.

Refer to Chart 6 in the Appendix, which is a sample mortgage amortization schedule, and Chart 7, which shows monthly mortgage payments. These examples illustrate the point. The information you get from the sources noted above will give you more customized and accurate information.

Applying for a Mortgage

In applying for a mortgage there are various steps you should follow to make sure you obtain the funds you need on the terms and conditions you want. If you go through a mortgage broker, some of these steps may not be required.

Preparing to Obtain a Mortgage at the Best Rate

Here is a summary of the steps that you should follow prior to an interview with a lender:

√ Complete your comparison shopping of all the types of lending institutions from which you could obtain mortgages. Check competing interest rates for different types of mortgages by contacting a mortgage broker to obtain a current schedule. Refer to your local newspaper for comparative mortgage rates. The mortgage market is highly competitive, and there are often incentives—for example, free legal fees, free appraisal, free home inspection, etc.—from lenders.

√ Understand the jargon. This book should help you to understand what you want from a mortgage, and therefore negotiate the package that is suited to your purposes.

√ Decide what you want to ask the lender and, using Checklist 2 in the Appendix as a guide, think of other questions you may want to ask.

√ You may want to do a personal credit check, especially if you think your past credit history might show any cause for concern for the lender. Alternatively, you might just be curious, and want to know what others know, or just see that the information is accurate, and nothing negative exists on your record. Your are entitled to know this information, and can generally obtain it from the Internet. Check with your local credit bureau, if you have one. In addition, there is a credit-reporting company that lenders frequently use, called Equifax (www.equifax.ca).

√ Plan your strategy to be a tough negotiator. For example, you could ask: "What incentives do you have to offer me to get my business?" Also, "What is the best discount that you can give me on the 'posted' [printed out or displayed or on the Internet] rate for the mortgage I want?" You should try to obtain at least a 1% discount off the posted rate. In most cases you will get it just by asking for it! You can also say that you are comparing various lenders and want the best rate. Another option is to say that you have been a customer of the lender for many years and have other products with them (e.g., personal loan, RRSPs). That would give them the discretion to give you a better deal. Also, check out mortgage brokers. As discussed in other sections, including Chapter 4: Selecting Your Advisory Team, mortgage brokers frequently get the best discounted rates from lenders on your behalf, due to their volume leverage.

√ Determine your financial needs. Complete the cost-of-living budget (Form 1 in the Appendix) as well as the mortgage checklist.

√ Calculate the maximum amount of mortgage available that you might be able to expect from a lender (refer to the previous section that provides the necessary formulas). Remember, these are guides only.

√ Check out the Web sites that have mortgage calculators to get a sense of the options available, the benefits, and the probable maximum amount that might be available to you. This, however, can depend on the lender. Some are more generous in their criteria and formulas than others. The last part of this section discusses the sites that provide free on-line mortgage calculators.

√ Obtain a letter of confirmation of employment from your employer (if you are employed). This letter should confirm your salary, and position, and the length of time you have been with that employer. If you are self-employed, you will be required to produce copies of recent financial statements and/or income tax returns (usually the last three years). Because so many people are self-employed and because of the competitive marketplace, lenders are generally more accommodating and understanding of the variable income cycles of self-employment, and therefore are more flexible than they have been in the past.

√ Prepare a statement of your assets and liabilities and net worth (refer to Form 2 in the Appendix).

√ Complete the details on the amount of the down payment that you will be providing and where the funds are coming from. This last step could include savings accounts, term deposits, Canada Savings Bonds, RRSPs, a family loan, an inheritance, a divorce settlement, proceeds from the sale of a house, or other sources.

√ Obtain a copy of the agreement of purchase and sale.

The Mortgage Application Process

There are various ways of obtaining a mortgage, as mentioned earlier, for example, the "traditional way" of speaking with your existing lender, comparing various lenders to get the best deal, applying on-line, or by using the services of a mortgage broker. The following overview describes the usual approval-process protocols.

The steps to this process are as follows:

√ You could go to a lending institution, generally with your spouse or partner, and any co-applicant or guarantor. The process from this point on is basically the same as it would be if you apply for a mortgage on-line or through a mortgage broker.

√ A formal mortgage application is completed. The application is typically divided into three main sections: description of the property, financial details relating to the purchase of the property, and personal financial information.

Processing the application normally takes between one and five business days. During that time the lender will:

√ Check your credit references and credit rating.

√ Verify the financial information you have given.

√ Have the property appraised (at your cost or their cost).

√ Assess your application within the lender's approval guidelines.

√ Issue a formal commitment of approval in writing.

Guidelines for Assessing Mortgage Applications

Different lenders have different guidelines when assessing mortgage applications, but generally there are three main criteria: character, capacity, and collateral.

Character

The lender will assess your credit history, and other factors as well, to predict how you will meet your obligations. For example, do you regularly pay your bills on time? What is your credit rating in terms of your credit history in previous loans that you have had? (How to obtain a copy of your own credit report was discussed in "Preparing to Obtain a Mortgage at the Best Rate.") Do you seem to be dependable in terms of the length of employment? Or have you had a different job every three or four months?

Capacity

The lender is concerned about your ability to meet your financial obligation and will be concerned about the following questions:

√ Does your GDS ratio come within their guidelines?

√ What are your other debts and obligations?

√ Is your income sufficient to handle the mortgage payments?

√ Is your income stable and does it appear as though it will continue to be so?

√ Is there a "mortgage helper" rental suite in the home?

√ Are you self-employed and for how long and in what type of industry?

Collateral

Lenders want to know that the security that has been provided for a loan is sufficient to cover the loan if it is not repaid. That is why they use their own appraisers to assess the value of a property; generally they want to have a conservative appraisal of the property as an extra precaution. The lender wants to be satisfied that the property being offered as security could be readily sold if necessary. When making an appraisal and therefore determining the value of the security that is being pledged as collateral, the following factors are considered: location, price, zoning, condition of the housing unit, quality of neighbourhood, size, appearance, municipal services available, and comparative sales in the same area.

Pre-approved Mortgage

The pre-approved mortgage is fairly popular with most conventional lending institutions and with trust companies and credit unions. The purpose is to give you a precise amount of money on which you can rely for mortgage purposes when you are out searching to buy a property and negotiating a purchase. You are given a fixed amount of mortgage for a period of time, for example, $100,000 with an interest rate that would be guaranteed for 60 to 120 days, depending on the relative stability of mortgage rates at the time. There is always a condition, of course, that the lender must approve the actual property being purchased before you can enact a final contractual offer to purchase. This provides the lender with an opportunity to make sure that the security is suitable.

Loan Approval

When the lender is in the process of approving the loan, the amount requested is an important consideration. As discussed earlier, if the loan exceeds 75% of the appraised value or the purchase price, whichever is lower, the mortgage normally has to be insured as a high-ratio mortgage.

Once the lender has granted approval for the mortgage, the lender will generally appoint its own lawyer to protect its interests by checking on the title of the property to make sure that it is clear, and to perform any necessary duties, including filing the mortgage. Alternatively, the lender may allow the borrower's lawyer to perform the mortgage work. In either case, the borrower customarily pays all the legal fees and disbursements. If you are required, or prefer, to use the lender's lawyer for preparing the mortgage documents, obtain independent legal advice about the provisions of the mortgage to make sure that the document sets out your intended deal. (Other legal aspects relating to the transfer of title of the property and the filing of a mortgage are covered in Chapter 6: Understanding the Legal Aspects.)

Cost of Obtaining a Mortgage

There are numerous direct and indirect expenses related to obtaining a mortgage. Not all the following expenses will be applicable in your case, but it is helpful to be aware of them. There are also additional expenses that are not covered in this chapter as they relate to purchasing a property and having the title of the property transferred over to your name. Expenses in this category include legal fees and disbursements, provincial land-transfer filing fees, and property-purchase tax. (These will be discussed in Chapter 6: Understanding the Legal Aspects.) Other expenses that may be involved include new home warranty fee, condominium-maintenance fee adjustment, utility connection charges, cost of repairs required prior to occupancy, and moving expenses (see Checklist 3, Real Estate Purchase Expenses, in the Appendix).

Costs will vary considerably from one lender to another. The type of financing that you obtain will be a factor. The following sections discuss some of the most common expenses that you should consider and, if necessary, budget for.

Appraisal Fee

The lender will obtain its own appraiser to determine the value of the security for mortgage purposes. The necessary fee is either paid by the borrower to the lender (generally in advance) at the time of application or is taken from the mortgage proceeds by the lender. In any event, the borrower generally pays the cost of the appraisal. Lenders usually will not give you a copy of the appraisal, although you should attempt to get it by requesting it in advance. In a competitive marketplace, ask the lender to assume the cost of the appraisal. This is a fairly common request, as part of your negotiation. The lender will automatically assume the cost. If you use the services of a mortgage broker, the broker will know which lenders are providing incentives, including assumption of the appraisal fee.

You might save on the appraisal fee under certain circumstances. For example, if a vendor or purchaser has already arranged for a professional appraiser to evaluate the property, and the appraisal is not over 60 to 90 days old, the lender may be prepared to accept the appraisal if it approves of the appraiser, and if property values have remained the same or increased since the appraisal was made.

Mortgage Application Fee

Some lenders charge a processing fee or set-up fee for their administrative expenses to process your mortgage application. Avoid paying this type of fee if at all possible. Due to the highly competitive nature of the mortgage industry, many lenders do not charge any application fee for residential mortgage purposes. If you are borrowing money for real estate investment, this type of fee is fairly common because of the extra work required to assess the loan application. Normally, though, when purchasing a single-family dwelling for rental purposes, such as a house or condominium, the mortgage application fee is waived.

Standby Fee

Some lenders charge a fee to the borrower for setting aside and reserving the money that the borrower requires until the money is advanced. The rationale behind this fee is that the mortgage company will lose revenue on this money in the interim. This is not a common fee for principal residence mortgage purposes and should be applied in this case. It is not, however, an uncommon fee on money committed for real estate investment purposes or for new construction.

Credit Investigation Report Fee

The lender may charge this fee to the borrower for the expense the lender incurs for doing credit investigation on the borrower. The fee may be either a separate fee or included in the mortgage application fee. Many institutions do not charge this fee and absorb it as a cost of doing business, as they hope to make money from you on the interest that you pay on your mortgage.

Survey Fee

You will generally be required to obtain a property survey before the mortgage funds are paid out. A qualified professional surveyor will do the survey to make sure that the lender knows the exact dimensions of the property that it is using as security. The lender may also want to be satisfied that the building meets the requirements for setbacks as required by the municipal bylaws, or that any additions to the building have complied with the bylaws. The cost of the survey would be deducted from the mortgage funds that have been advanced to you, or you would pay for it directly. Your lawyer normally arranges for this survey for you. Sometimes this expense is negotiable with the lender, who might absorb that cost to obtain your business. If you don't ask for concessions, you don't automatically get them. This negotiating attitude and style should be an automatic part of your approach to business or real estate investment.

Mortgage Broker Fee

If you use a mortgage broker to obtain financing, you may have to pay a fee, normally 1% to 2% or more of the amount of mortgage that was raised for you. This is paid at the time of closing. Alternatively you may not have to pay any fee. There is generally no fee charged for principal residence purposes, and a small fee for investment real estate that is more complex or difficult to obtain. (This was discussed in Chapter 4: Selecting Your Advisory Team.) Most mortgage brokers will require an advance fee from you for appraisal costs and out-of-pocket costs incurred in advance. This is not the same as an application fee or administration fee, but could be included within such fees if they are charged.

Mortgage Insurance Fees (CMHC or GE Mortgage Insurance)

If you are obtaining a high-ratio mortgage or the lender requires you to obtain mortgage insurance for other reasons, then you will pay a mortgage insurance premium fee, which ranges between 0.5%–4.25% of the amount of the mortgage that is being insured. The premium depends upon various risk factors and whether the home is a new purchase or being re-financed. It is either added onto the mortgage total or paid by you in a lump sum at the time of closing the mortgage transaction. Mortgage insurance was discussed earlier under "High-Ratio/Insured Mortgages."

Mortgage Life Insurance Premiums

Mortgage life insurance is not the same as mortgage insurance. Many lending institutions provide an option for you to purchase insurance that will pay off the mortgage in the event of your death, the premium for which is generally loaded into your monthly payments. You should compare the cost with term insurance from private insurance carriers to see if the rates are competitive. Generally term insurance is cheaper.

As an option you may prefer to protect yourself by taking out your own term insurance, which would be payable to your estate in the event of your death. Your estate would then have sufficient proceeds to pay off the mortgage. An additional benefit of this option is that the insurance policy is portable, e.g., you (not the lender) would have control over it. You can obtain competitive term life insurance rates from an insurance broker. You can get names of insurance brokers from a mortgage broker, your accountant or financial planner, or from the Yellow Pages of the phone book. The Canadian Life and Health Insurance Association has a Web site with excellent consumer information and member brokers in your area (www.clhia.ca). (Refer to Chapter 4: Selecting Your Advisory Team for the process of selecting an insurance broker. Also, see Chapter 8: Understanding the Insurance Aspects.)

In certain circumstances a lender may require, as a condition of mortgage approval, that you take out mortgage life insurance. Usually this would only be if the lender considered your health to be a risk factor. Again, you could purchase your own term insurance or other type of life insurance and verify to the lender that you had such insurance. The lender may require it to be shown on the insurance policy as being paid first from the proceeds, but this would be an unusual request for a principal residence deal. It might be more common if you were borrowing money for real estate investment purposes.

Home Fire Insurance Premium

Lenders require borrowers on a mortgage to carry sufficient fire insurance to cover the amount of the mortgage, and that they be paid off first. The second mortgage lenders would want the same type of coverage and have it shown that they would be paid off second, and so on. It is necessary for the borrower to purchase sufficient replacement insurance. The borrower is responsible for making insurance arrangements and paying the costs of the insurance policy.

The policy would show that the lender would be paid first or second, as the case may be. This must be provided to the lender's lawyer before any mortgage funds are advanced.

Property Tax-Adjustment Holdback

This concept is related to the previous topic. If the lender requires you to pay a portion of the property taxes every month, and if you purchase the property on April 1 with property taxes due in July, obviously there will be a shortfall in the tax account. In other words, if the property taxes are due and payable in full on July 1 and you have made payments each month of one-twelfth of the projected annual tax, then by July 1 the tax account set up by the lender will be short by nine-twelfths of the amount required to pay the taxes. The lender may require that you pay nine-twelfths of the projected annual tax into the tax account at the time of closing the mortgage transaction. Either you would have to come up with these additional funds or the lender would subtract that amount of money from the mortgage proceeds being made available to you. Alternatively you may be required to pay four-twelfths of the projected property tax to the lender for each of the three months of April, May, and June prior to the tax payment deadline of July 1.

Contribution to Property Tax Account

Some lenders require that you pay one-twelfth of the projected annual taxes each month. This payment would be built into your monthly mortgage obligations, and the lender would set up a separate tax account and remit the funds directly to the municipality at the appropriate time each year. Normally taxes are payable in June or July every year, although they are calculated on the calendar year, i.e., January 1 to December 31. Some municipalities require an advance part-payment in February of each year and the balance in July of that year. If the lender makes the automatic monthly property tax payment a condition of mortgage approval, ask whether interest will be paid on your tax account to your credit and, if so, what the interest rate would be. The interest paid is normally lower than the interest paid on deposit accounts. The reason that some lenders require monthly payments is to minimize the risk that you will not have sufficient funds to pay the taxes every year. If this happened, the property could conceivably be put up for tax sale and jeopardize the lender's security.

In most cases lenders will give you the option to be responsible for paying your own taxes directly once a year. Try to negotiate this option. If you are paying a portion of the projected property tax every month, you will have to build that expense into the costs related to your mortgage.

Interest Adjustment

When you pay rent, you are paying in advance. When you are paying mortgage payments to the lender for principal and interest, you are paying in arrears. In other words, if you make a mortgage payment on March 1, it is to cover the use of the funds and the interest on those funds for the month of February.

Because the lender's internal system runs on a monthly payment basis, assuming that it is a fixed interest rate, the lender will want to be paid in advance for the use of the funds from February 15 to March 1. This interest adjustment is then advanced from the mortgage funds provided to you on February 15 so that the interest is prepaid up to March 1. When your normal mortgage payment is made on April 1, it would cover the one-month interest for the month of March, plus a small repayment of the principal. Not all lenders require this arrangement, but you should know in advance so that you are aware of the net proceeds that you will receive on the mortgage.

Interest

Interest is, of course, the cost of having the funds paid to you under a mortgage. What you will have to pay to the lender in interest, and the steps you should go through to obtain the most attractive interest rate, have been discussed.

Provincial Mortgage Filing Tax

Most provinces charge a tax or a fee for filing a mortgage in the land registry.

Provincial Property Purchase Tax Fee

Some provinces charge a tax for transferring title in property. The tax formula varies, depending on the province.

Legal Fees and Disbursements

You are responsible for paying the lawyer's legal fees as well as out-of-pocket disbursements that the lawyer incurs relating to the preparation and filing of the mortgage documentation. Disbursements would cover such things as: property search, photocopy expenses, courier costs, and other costs associated with the preparation and registration of the mortgage. The disbursement costs would normally include the provincial mortgage filing tax or fee referred to earlier. It is usual for lawyers to deduct the legal fees and disbursements directly from the money to be advanced under the mortgage.

Sometimes lenders require that you use a particular law firm. Alternatively, they might provide you with a list of approved law firms and you can select which firm you would prefer to deal with. At other times the lender will permit you to use a lawyer of your choice. In all cases you are responsible for the legal fees and disbursements. Due to the competitive nature of the marketplace, some lenders will offer to pay all your legal costs and disbursements related to the mortgage, and sometimes the transfer of title as well.

Defaulting on Your Mortgage

As long as you meet the payments and the terms as agreed with the mortgage company, the mortgage company cannot commence any action to foreclose on the property or obtain an order for sale. On the other hand, if you have difficulty with your payments or breach any terms of the mortgage, the lender can resort to severe measures to protect its security. Defaulting on a mortgage has potentially serious consequences. If you are consistently late, this could affect your credit rating, and also your ability to renew your mortgage or obtain other mortgages in the future.

This section will cover factors that constitute default, the borrower's (mortgagor's) options, and the lender's (mortgagee's) options. It is not within the scope of this book to go into any more detail on mortgage default or foreclosure other than to give an overview of the issues to consider.

Factors that Constitute Default under a Mortgage

The mortgage agreement sets out in considerable detail what is required of the borrower. Some of the most common clauses were discussed in a previous section. The main areas of default would be:

√ failure to make your mortgage payments

√ failure to pay your taxes

√ failure to have insurance, or sufficient insurance

√ failure to obey municipal, provincial, or federal law as it relates to the premises that you have mortgaged

√ failure to maintain the premises in a habitable condition

√ failure to keep the premises in proper repair

√ deliberately damaging the property that secures the mortgage.

Borrower's Options on Default

If a mortgagor is having difficulty maintaining payments under the mortgage, there are many options to consider. You can do the following:

√ Make arrangements with the lender for a waiver of payments for a period of time (e.g., three or six months) or arrange for partial payments to be made, which is normally done if the borrower is sick, injured, laid off, or has a reduced monthly income to debt service the mortgage due to a marital separation, a spouse who has been laid off, or other such factors.

√ Reschedule the debt and make new payment arrangements.

√ Refinance the mortgage with another lender on terms that are more flexible and appropriate in the circumstances.

√ Provide additional security to the lender in order to negotiate concessions.

√ Put the property up for sale.

√ Transfer the property to the lender. This is not always feasible or desirable from the owner's or the lender's perspective.

√ Exercise your right of redemption. You are generally entitled to this by law. This means you pay the arrears outstanding under the mortgage, which generally prevents the mortgagee from commencing or from continuing foreclosure or power of sale proceedings. An exception is that if there is an acceleration clause, which many mortgages have, the lender is entitled to deem the full amount of the mortgage immediately due and payable. In that event you would have to pay the full amount of the mortgage in order to stop foreclosure proceedings.

Some provinces have legislation restricting the application of acceleration clauses. In many provinces you have a right of redemption of from one to six months in order to pay the lender, or the lender would be entitled to take over the property or sell it, among other measures.

√ Ask the court for more time. If you know that you will not be able to pay off the lender within the right-of-redemption period, you are entitled to ask the court for an extension of time. Whether the court grants an extension depends on the circumstances.

For example, it is in your favour if you had previously lost your job and you are now employed, you are expecting proceeds from an inheritance, or you are having family members raise funds for you. All of these are factors that could show that the delay request is based on a realistic assessment of your ability to make the necessary payment. Having a substantial equity in the property would also assist you.

Mortgagee's (Lender's) Options on Default

If you are in default and, despite all your efforts, are unable to come to terms with the lender, the lender has various options. Generally the last thing lenders want to do is take over the property, as there are other options that are more appropriate, depending on the circumstances. The lender is required to go to court and get approval for most of the main measures available. That gives you an opportunity to present your side of the situation and reveal unique circumstances if you so wish.

Legislation governing the mortgage is provincial and can vary between the provinces. For the most part, though, the following measures would be available to the lender:

- √ Pay taxes, maintenance fees, or insurance premiums on your behalf. The lender then adds these payments onto your total mortgage debt and charges interest on the amount.

- √ Obtain an injunction from the court that you stop carrying on some improper or illegal activity. In addition, the order could require you to perform some specific obligation under the mortgage document to protect the mortgage security. You would have to pay the lender's costs of obtaining the injunction.

- √ Obtain a court order to appoint a receiver of the rents to pay the mortgage payments. This procedure is not often utilized except in serious situations involving revenue property. In reality, if you have borrowed money for revenue property, the lender will probably have asked you to sign an assignment of rents at the outset. The lender then can automatically notify all tenants to direct the rent payments to the lender if you default on the payment terms in the mortgage.

- √ Obtain a court order to put the property into receivership. In this case an independent party, called a receiver-manager or receiver, takes possession of the property on behalf of the lender and maintains it. This procedure is usually utilized in the case of revenue property if other remedies are not more efficient, and if the property is held in a corporate (rather than a personal) name, which has given the bank a debenture (a security document).

√ Accelerate the mortgage. The lender can either request the arrears under the mortgage, or deem the full amount of the balance outstanding on the mortgage as immediately due and payable. The lender cannot request this latter course unless there is an acceleration clause in the mortgage. Some provincial legislation restricts the use of acceleration clauses, as noted earlier.

√ Sell the property. The lender would be able to put your property up for sale and sell it if you are in default in your payments over a set period of time. The period of time depends on the province. In many cases the lender will go through the court to get a court order for a sale so that the court can monitor the sale price and therefore minimize the risk of a borrower's claim that the house was undersold. In other cases the lender does not have to go to court to list it for sale.

√ Sue the borrower personally for the debt outstanding. The borrower's liability under the terms of the mortgage remains an option for the lender whether or not the property has been sold. If it is sold, the borrower is responsible for any shortfall. If the property is being held in a corporate name, the lender usually requests a personal guarantee of the people behind the corporation. The lender is not required to commence other actions such as foreclosure or sale of the property.

√ Foreclose against the property. In a foreclosure, the lender requests that the court extinguish your property rights and transfer all legal interest that you have, including the right of possession and legal title, to the lender. In this situation the lender is entitled to all the equity in the property. The courts are generally involved in this procedure and your rights are protected in that regard. For example, the court would consider it unfair to you if you had considerable equity in the property. It would probably advise the lender that instead of foreclosure, there should be an order for sale. In that event, the equity in the mortgage property would be able to go to the mortgagor after all the costs associated with the sale had been paid off. These costs would include the sales commission, the lender's legal expenses and disbursements, plus any principal and interest outstanding. In practical terms, therefore, lenders foreclose probably less than 1% of the time. The most common method of recovery is sale of the property.

As you can see, there are many factors to consider if you are having financial difficulties with your mortgage. The circumstances of your default will make a difference in terms of what steps you wish to take. Contacting the lender and attempting to negotiate a resolution is clearly the first step toward resolving the problem. If that does not turn out to be a satisfactory procedure, it would be prudent to obtain advice from a lawyer specializing in foreclosure matters, so that you are fully aware of your available rights and options. Your lawyer could also negotiate with the bank on your behalf.

Creative Financing

Sometimes the only way to make a particular deal work is with creative financing. This simply means that financing is arranged legally but in non-traditional ways. The standard fixed-payment bank mortgage, for example, would be considered traditional financing. A regular payment is made monthly, with the interest due applied first and the balance to the reduction of the principal. Here are some alternative creative-financing techniques.

Interest Deferral

Interest is still calculated as usual, but payment of the interest is delayed. This is sometimes referred to as a balloon payment mortgage.

Equity Participation

In exchange for lending money with attractive terms, the lender shares in the price increase (equity) in the property.

Mortgage Assumption

Rather than taking out a new mortgage, the purchaser assumes the vendor's existing mortgage. The vendor should normally negotiate a full release of any future obligations under the mortgage.

Variable-Rate Mortgage

Interest rate is adjusted according to an index (e.g., Bank of Canada's prime rate), but at certain intervals and with a limit on the amount of interest. Terms and payment may be adjusted. Many lenders have the option that you can quickly convert your variable-rate mortgage into a fixed-term mortgage if you think interest rates are going to rise.

Reverse Mortgage

Owners of property with substantial equity can receive regular monthly payments that have to be repaid at a later time, generally at the time of the house's sale or the debtor's death. In effect, it is similar to an annuity. Retired people tend to find this an appealing program. A minimum age of 62 is generally required. There are drawbacks to a reverse mortgage, the main one being that the interest can rapidly add up, diluting considerable equity over time. As with any financial decision, you need to analyze the pros and cons. In some cases, it might be a better alternative to simply borrow money on a line of credit secured by your home.

Graduated Payment Mortgage

In this example, the payments start at a lower monthly amount and gradually increase over time. Over the term of the mortgage (e.g., five years), the monthly payments could average out. This mortgage is common for people who have investment property but don't want to have negative cash flow. The monthly payments therefore increase with the monthly cash flow over time.

The following section discusses negative cash flow.

Dealing with Negative Cash Flow

Negative cash flow has to be taken in perspective. It simply means that there is a shortfall every month in terms of monthly financial obligations.

You would normally have to subsidize the shortfall yourself. The negative cash flow could be temporary and, in relation to the potential of the property, could therefore be justified. Each situation is unique. There are different ways of avoiding or dealing with the issue of negative cash flow.

Rent with an Option to Buy

A renter pays an extra premium every month over the base rent, along with an option to purchase. The vendor would deem the overage to be a down payment on eventual sale. In the meantime, the vendor has eliminated the cash flow shortage. If the renter does not exercise the option, the overage is deemed a fee for the option and is not returned to the renter.

Equity Sharing

Equity sharing was discussed previously in Chapter 1: Understanding Real Estate Investment in the section on "Buying with Partners." Basically, it means the renter pays a monthly premium and shares in the equity buildup when the property is sold. Generally the renters also have a first option to buy.

Graduated Payment Mortgage

This was covered in the previous section, and is an effective way of dealing with negative cash flow.

Purchase Lower Priced Home

Obviously, one way of dealing with the problem is to reduce the amount of negative cash flow by having a lower monthly debt.

Rent Out the Basement Suite

If you have an investment property with a self-contained suite, rent it out separately.

Refinance the Property

If interest rates have dropped, you may be able to refinance the property. Even if you have to pay a penalty on a closed mortgage, you could still be further ahead over time in terms of the savings. Your calculations will tell you the cost/benefit. Also, consider locking in a long-term, fixed-rate mortgage (e.g., five years or more) if interest rates are at an attractive level.

Rent to Singles

You can probably generate considerably more revenue by renting a house to, say, six singles rather than a married couple with a family. The extra revenue could eliminate any negative cash flow. Of course there is potential for non-payment and wear and tear, especially if the singles are college or university students. Careful selection and monitoring should minimize the risk.

Obtain a Longer Amortization Period

As you know, the longer the amortization period, the lower the monthly rates. So a 30-year period will have lower payments than a 20-year period.

Reduce Expenses

Review all the expenses that are being incurred, and look for ways to reduce them. (Refer to the section on "Saving on Expenses" in Chapter 10: Managing Your Property.)

Increase Your Income

There are many ways of doing this. Refer to the section on "Increasing Revenue Property Income" in Chapter 10: Managing Your Property.

Negotiate a Lower Purchase Price

If you know in advance that you will have a shortfall (which you normally should, of course), use that as leverage to attempt a price reduction.

Pay a Larger Amount Down

Clearly, this will reduce the monthly debt servicing and reduce or eliminate the cash flow shortfall.

Web Sites of Interest

Here are several Web sites that should assist you in your information and education research. Many of these sites have been referred to throughout this chapter.

Appraisal Institute of Canada:	www.aicanada.ca
Bank of Canada:	www.bankofcanada.ca
Canada Mortgage and Housing Corporation (CMHC):	www.cmhc-schl.gc.ca
Canadian Institute of Mortgage Brokers and Lenders:	www.cimbl.ca
Canadian Life and Health Insurance Association:	www.clhia.ca
Equifax Canada:	www.equifax.ca
First Canadian Title Insurance:	www.firstcanadiantitle.com
GE Mortgage Insurance Canada:	www.gemortgage.ca
Google Internet Search:	www.google.ca
Insurance Brokers Association of Canada:	www.ibac.ca
MoneySense Magazine:	www.moneysense.ca

Summary

When you are considering financing a property, there are numerous options available. This chapter provided a detailed overview of locating, selecting, and negotiating mortgage financing. It covered the various types and sources of financing, and tips on determining your needs and successfully attaining your objectives. Pitfalls to avoid were also covered throughout the chapter.

Financing goes hand-in-hand with understanding the legal issues of property ownership, which are discussed next.

CHAPTER 6

Understanding the Legal Aspects

It is important to understand the legal issues and terminology in order to discuss the appropriate matters clearly with your lawyer and make the correct decisions. Every aspect of a real estate purchase for personal use or investment involves legal implications, so you want to avoid legal problems.

This chapter explains different kinds of property ownership, the legal documents involved in the purchase and sale of real estate, the implications of backing out of an agreement, services provided by a lawyer, types of listing agreements, and legal structures to hold revenue property.

Types of Ownership of Property

Types of Interest in Land

There are several types of legal interests in land, the most common being free-hold and leasehold.

Freehold

This type of ownership entitles the owner to use the land for an indefinite period and to deal with the land in any way desired, subject to legislation (e.g., municipal bylaws, hydro utility easements or rights of way, provincial mineral rights), contractual obligations (e.g., subdivision restrictive covenants), and any charges that encumber the title of the property and are filed in the provincial land titles office (e.g., mortgages, liens, judgements). Another term for freehold is "fee simple."

Leasehold Interest

In a leasehold interest, the holder of the interest in land has the right to use the land for a fixed period, e.g., 50 or 99 years. The owner of the property (landlord or lessor) signs an agreement with the owner of the leasehold interest (tenant or lessee) that sets out various terms and conditions of the relationship. The leasehold interest can be bought and sold, but the leaseholder can sell only the right to use the land for the time that is remaining in the lease, subject, of course, to any conditions contained in the original lease.

Both freehold interest and leasehold interest can be left in your will as an asset of your estate, or specifically bequeathed in your will.

Types of Joint Ownership in Property

You may wish to have shared ownership in the property with one or more other people. There are two main types of legal joint ownership: joint tenancy and tenancy in common. (Chapter 1: Understanding Real Estate Investment has a section on "Buying with Partners.")

Joint Tenancy

In a joint tenancy, an owner has an undivided but equal share with all the other owners. No one person has a part of the property that is specifically his or hers because all the property belongs to all of the owners. At the time of purchasing the property, all the people who are joint tenants will be listed on the title of the property equally and each of the joint tenants has the right in law to possession of the whole property. These are the essential conditions involved in joint tenancy, and if any of these conditions are not met, then the ownership is deemed to be a tenancy in common and not joint tenancy.

One of the main features of a joint tenancy is the right of survivorship. This means that if one of the joint tenants dies, the others automatically and immediately receive the deceased person's share, equally divided. In other words, the deceased person's share in the joint tenancy is not passed on as an asset of his or her estate to beneficiaries, whether or not a will exists. It is fairly common for a couple to hold the legal interest in the property by means of a joint tenancy. Thus, you should consider tenancy in common if you do not want to have your interest go automatically to other parties.

Tenancy in Common

In this form of ownership, the tenants can hold equal or unequal shares in the property. Each party owns an undivided share in the property and therefore is entitled to possession of the whole property. For example, there could be five people who are tenants in common, but four of them could own one-tenth of the property each, and the fifth person could own six-tenths of the property.

If the holder of a tenancy in common wishes to sell or mortgage his interest in the property, that can be done. If a buyer cannot be found and the tenant in common wants to get his money out of the property, he can go to court and, under a legal procedure called partition, request that the court order the property to be sold and that it distribute the net proceeds of sale proportionately.

Tenancy in common does not carry an automatic right of survivorship as joint tenancy does. In other words, if one of the tenants in common dies, the interest does not go to the other tenant(s), but to the estate of the deceased. If there is a will, the interest is distributed under the terms of the will. If the deceased person does not have a will, there is provincial legislation to deal with that type of situation, and the person's assets, which would include the tenancy interest, would be distributed to relatives according to the legislation.

There are various reasons why some people prefer tenancy in common to joint tenancy.

√ If you are purchasing property for investment purposes with people who are not relatives, you may not want them to automatically have your interest in the property in the event of your death.

√ If you have been previously married, have children from a previous relationship, and have since remarried, or are living in a common-law relationship, you may want to specify in your will that a certain portion of the value of the estate goes to those children individually or collectively. The only way this can be dealt with is in a tenancy-in-common situation because the interest would be deemed to be an asset of one's estate.

√ If you are putting unequal amounts of money in the property, a tenancy-in-common structure would reflect those different contributions in terms of the percentage interest in the property.

Written agreements should be signed by tenants in common, setting out the procedures if one of them wants to get out of the situation. This is a prudent procedure that can be accomplished by giving the others the first right of refusal on a proportional basis to buy out the interest, or there could be a clause requiring the consent of the other tenants in common in approving a potential purchaser, or there could be a provision requiring a certain period of notice to the other tenants before the property is sold. Another case when tenancy in common might be preferable would be when one of the owners of the property wishes to have the personal independence to raise money for other outside interests, e.g., a business. In many cases the tenancy-in-common portion could be mortgaged without the consent of the other parties.

Understanding the Purchase-and-Sale Agreement

The most important document you will sign will be the offer to purchase, which, if accepted, becomes the agreement of purchase and sale. It sets out the terms and conditions between the parties and, as in any contract, it is legally binding if there are no conditions in the contract that have to be met before it becomes binding. Of course, there can be verbal contracts, but all contracts dealing with land must be in writing to be enforceable. That includes a purchase-and-sale agreement or a lease, which, of course, is also a contract.

This section will cover the elements that make up a contract, legal implications of backing out of the agreement, and how to understand the contents of a purchase-and-sale agreement.

Elements of a Contract

Five main elements have to be present in order for a contract to be valid. These are mutual agreement, legal capacity, exchange of consideration, intention to be bound, and compliance with the law.

Mutual Agreement

There must be an offer and an acceptance. The terms and conditions of the bargain must be specific, complete, clear, and unambiguous. The parties to the contract must be sufficiently identifiable.

An offer may be withdrawn (revoked) any time before acceptance by either party as long as that revocation is transmitted to the other party—ideally in writing so you have proof. If the offer has already been accepted without condition and signed to that effect before receipt of the revocation, a binding contract has occurred.

Legal Capacity

The parties to a contract must have the capacity to enter into a legally binding contract, otherwise the contract cannot be enforced. Each party to a contract:

√ must be an adult, i.e., over the "age of majority," which varies from province to province but is usually 19 years or older

√ must not have impaired judgement, i.e., the party must understand the nature and quality of what is involved in signing the contract; if a person is impaired by drugs, alcohol, stroke, or mental infirmity (diminished capacity), that would invalidate the contract if it could be proven

√ must not be insane in medical and legal terms

√ must be able to act with free will, i.e., is not under duress or threat or intimidation.

Exchange of Consideration

This concept means that "something of value" must be exchanged by the parties in order to bind the contract. Usually money changes hands, but "consideration" could mean another property by exchange, something of value to the other side such as a service or product or other benefit, or a promise to do something in exchange for a promise to do something.

Intention to Be Bound

The parties must have the intention of being bound by the agreement and its commitments, and they must expect that it will be a bargain that could be enforced by the courts.

Compliance with the Law

A contract, to be enforceable, must be legal in its purpose and intent. The courts will not enforce a contract that is intended to, or has the effect of, breaching federal, provincial, or municipal legislation.

Legal Options and Implications of Getting Out of a Signed Contract

There are instances where either the vendor or the purchaser may wish to back out of an agreement. You have to be careful because legal problems can result in litigation, and litigation is expensive, time-consuming, stressful, protracted, and uncertain in outcome. Get legal advice before you act. Some examples are discussed below.

Rescission

In several provinces and states there is a "cooling-off" or rescission period, whereby the purchaser of a new property has a period of time (usually from 3 days to 30 days) to back out of the contract by giving notice to the vendor in writing before the deadline. The vendor is obliged to pay back without penalty all the money that the purchaser has placed on deposit. In cases where legislation does not give an automatic right to rescission, the documents that are a part of the property package may have a rescission period built in. If you do not have a statutory (by law) right to rescission and it is not part of the documents relating to the purchase of a new property, then you may want to make it a condition of your offer.

Specific Performance

If the vendor or purchaser refuses to go through with a purchase-and-sale agreement when there are no unfulfilled conditions attached to the agreement, the other party is entitled to go to court and request the court to order that the breaching party specifically perform the terms of the agreement, e.g., complete the transaction. The party who succeeds in obtaining the court order would be entitled to ask for the costs of the application from the court. Generally, court costs awarded represent about 25% to 40% of the actual legal costs incurred; therefore, those who win at court ultimately lose financially in terms of total cost recovery of legal costs expended.

Damages

If one party refuses to complete the agreement, instead of suing for specific performance of the terms of the agreement, the other party can sue for damages. Damages mean the financial losses that have been incurred because the other party failed to complete the bargain. There is a basic legal maxim that says "to get financial damages (compensation), you have to prove you have suffered financial damages." For example, if a vendor refused to complete the deal because he thought he could make $50,000 more on the sale of the house (if the price had gone up considerably), and if in fact it could be shown that he did sell it for $50,000 more after refusing to go through with your signed commitment, then you could claim $50,000 damages plus court costs. Your loss could be quantified, assuming that there were no other reasons that could explain the differential in price. Alternatively, if the purchaser fails to complete and the vendor can show that he was relying on those funds and therefore the purchase he had planned failed to occur, and so on down the line with various back-to-back purchases and sales that were all relying on the first, there could be considerable damages for which the purchaser may possibly be liable. These are called "consequential" and "foreseeable" damages. This is a complex area of law and skilled legal advice is critical.

If the house value has not gone up or down by the purchase date, and if, for example, another purchaser was found and no other losses occurred, the vendor (in this example) could attempt to claim the deposit funds as "liquidated damages." This is generally negotiable unless it states clearly in the agreement of purchase and sale that the deposit funds automatically and irrevocably go to the vendor.

Conditional Contract

If the vendor or purchaser has preliminary conditions built into the purchase-and-sale agreement ("subject to" clauses), and those conditions cannot be met, no valid binding contract exists and neither party is liable to the other.

Void Contracts

A contract is void and unenforceable if the required elements that make up a contract (discussed earlier) are not present, or if the contract is prohibited by statute (e.g., municipal, provincial, or federal law).

Voidable Contracts

If one of the parties has been induced to enter into the contract on the basis of misrepresentation—whether innocent, negligent, or fraudulent—that party may be entitled to void the contract. If the misrepresentation was innocent, generally only the contract can be cancelled and any money returned, and no damages can be recovered in court. If there is negligent or fraudulent misrepresentation, however, not only can the contract be cancelled, but damages can also be recovered in court. For example, if the vendor was going to provide vendor-back financing and relied on the purchaser's representations concerning his creditworthiness and ability to pay, but prior to completion of the transaction (by doing a credit check and/or other investigation) the vendor finds out that the purchaser is a terrible credit risk, then that could be deemed to be negligent or fraudulent misrepresentation. For that reason the contract could be cancelled. To give another example, if the purchaser finds out before completion that the representation of the vendor or the vendor's agent is grossly untrue (e.g., that zoning has been approved for subdivision purposes, and investigation shows that no application has been made for subdivision purposes), then the purchaser could get out of the contract and sue to recover damages, if any can be proven.

These are just some examples of things that could affect the validity or enforceability of a contract. Competent legal advice in advance from a skilled real estate lawyer is needed to minimize potential problems.

Understanding the Purchase-and-Sale Agreement

Most purchase-and-sale agreements come in standard formats, with standard clauses, and are drafted by the builder, the local real estate board, or commercial stationers. There are generally spaces throughout the agreement for additional, customized clauses. A contract prepared by a builder has distinctly different clauses from those of a standard form for resales, and there are considerable differences in the standard contract clauses among builders and among real estate boards.

There is a high risk that the standard clauses, or additional ones that you may choose to insert, will not be comprehensive enough for your needs; you may not even understand them, or their implications, and may sign the agreement nevertheless. That is why it is so important to have a lawyer review your offer to purchase before you sign it. Regrettably, only a small percentage of people do this, because they either don't realize they should, perceive it will be an unnecessary or costly legal expense, or are naive or too trusting. It would be a false economy to save on a legal consultation, as the costs to obtain a legal opinion are very reasonable relative to the risk involved in signing a bad contract. Alternatively, rather than seeing a lawyer before submitting an offer to purchase, some people may wish to insert a condition that states the offer is "subject to approval as to form and contents by the purchaser's solicitor; such approval to be communicated to vendor within X days of acceptance, or to be deemed to be withheld."

There are many common clauses and features contained in the purchase-and-sale agreement, many of which vary from contract to contract according to various circumstances—whether one is purchasing a new or a resale property, type of property, revenue property, etc. Here is a brief overview of some of the common features of the agreement for purchase and sale.

Amount of Deposit

A deposit serves various purposes. It is a partial payment on the purchase price, a good-faith indication of seriousness, and an assurance of performance if all the conditions in the offer to purchase have been fulfilled. The deposit is generally 5% to 10% of the purchase price. If there were conditions in the offer, and these conditions were not met, then the purchaser is entitled to receive a refund of the full amount of the deposit. This is one reason why it is important to have conditions or "subject to" clauses in the offer to protect one's interests fully.

Most agreements for purchase and sale have a provision that gives the vendor the option of keeping the deposit as "liquidated damages," in the event that the purchaser fails to complete the terms of the agreement and pay the balance of money on the closing date.

When making a deposit, it is very important to be careful to whom you pay the funds. If you are purchasing on a private sale and no realtor is involved, never pay the funds directly to the vendor; pay them to your own lawyer in trust. If a realtor is involved, the funds can be paid to the realtor's trust account or your own lawyer's trust account, as the situation dictates. If you are purchasing a new property from the builder, do not pay a deposit directly to the builder. The money should go to your lawyer's trust account, or some other system should be set up for your protection to ensure that your funds cannot be used except under certain conditions based on those that are clearly set out in the agreement. The risk is high in paying your money directly to a builder because if the builder does not complete the project and goes into bankruptcy, you could lose all your money and, in practical terms, could have great difficulty getting it back. Although several provincial governments have brought in legislation dealing with new property projects to protect the public on the issue of deposits—as well as many other property risk areas—legislation provides only partial protection.

Another matter you have to consider is interest. If you are paying a deposit, you want to ensure that interest at the appropriate rate or based on the appropriate formula is paid to your credit. In many cases, deposit monies can be tied up for many months, and that could represent considerable interest.

Conditions and Warranties

It is important to understand the distinction between conditions and warranties, as it is very critical to the wording that you would use in the agreement.

A condition is a requirement that is fundamental to the very existence of the offer. A breach of condition allows the buyer to get out of the contract and obtain a refund of the full amount of the deposit. A buyer's inability to meet the condition set by a vendor permits the vendor to get out of the contract.

A warranty is a minor promise that does not go to the heart of the contract. If there is a breach of warranty, the purchaser cannot cancel but must complete the contract and sue for damages. Therefore, if a particular requirement on your part is pivotal to your decision to purchase the property, it is important to frame your requirement as a condition rather than as a warranty. Both vendor and purchaser frequently insert conditions into the agreement. These conditions are also referred to as subject clauses and should:

√ Be precise and clearly detailed.

√ Have specific time allocated for conditions that have to be removed, e.g., within 2 days, 30 days. It is preferable to put in the precise date that a condition has to be removed, rather than merely refer to the number of days involved.

√ Have a clause that specifically says that the conditions are for the sole benefit of the vendor or purchaser, as the case may be, and that they can be waived at any time by the party requiring the condition. This is important because you may wish to remove a condition even though it has not been fulfilled, in order for the contract to be completed.

Here is just a sampling of some of the common subject clauses. There are many others possible that you or your lawyer may feel it appropriate to insert.

For Benefit of Purchaser

√ title being conveyed free and clear of any and all encumbrances or charges registered against the property on or before the closing date at the expense of the vendor, either from the proceeds of the sale or by solicitor's undertaking

√ inspection being satisfactory to purchaser by relative, spouse, partner, etc. (specify name)

√ inspection being satisfactory to purchaser by house inspector/contractor selected by purchaser

√ sale of purchaser's other property being made

√ confirmation of mortgage financing

√ deposit funds to be placed in an interest-bearing trust account with the interest to accrue to the benefit of the purchaser

√ approval of assumption of existing mortgage

√ granting of vendor-take-back mortgage or builder's mortgage

√ removal of existing tenancies (vacant possession) by completion date

√ existing tenancies conforming to prevailing municipal bylaws

√ interim occupancy payments being credited to purchase price

√ review and satisfactory approval by purchaser's lawyer of the contents of the agreement of purchase and sale

√ warranties, representations, promises, guarantees, and agreements shall survive the completion date

√ no urea formaldehyde foam insulation (UFFI) having ever been in the building

√ vendor's warranty that no work orders or deficiency notices are outstanding against the property or, if there are, that they will be complied with at the vendor's expense before closing.

Additional Clauses If Purchasing a Condominium

√ receipt and satisfactory review by purchaser (and/or purchaser's lawyer) of project documents, such as disclosure, declaration, articles, rules and regulations, financial statements, project budget, minutes of condominium corporation for past two years, management contract, estoppel certificate, etc.

√ confirmation by condominium corporation that the condominium unit being purchased will be able to be rented.

Additional Clauses If Purchasing a Revenue Property

√ review and satisfactory approval of financial statements, balance sheet, income and expense statement, list of chattels, list of inventory, names of tenants, amount of deposits and monthly rents, dates of occupancy, list of receivables and payables, list and dates of equipment safety inspections, list of repairs and dates, service contracts, leases, warranties, property plans, and surveys.

For Benefit of Vendor

√ removal of all subject clauses by purchaser within 72 hours upon notice in writing by vendor of a backup bona fide (legitimate) offer

√ confirmation of purchase of vendor-take-back mortgage through vendor's mortgage broker

√ satisfactory confirmation of purchaser's creditworthiness by vendor or vendor's mortgage broker

√ issuance of building permit

√ builder receiving confirmation of construction financing

√ registration of a subdivision plan

√ deposit funds non-refundable and to be released directly to the vendor
   once all conditions of the purchaser have been met

√ review and satisfactory approval by vendor's lawyer of the contents of
   the agreement of purchase and sale.

Risk and Insurance

It is important that the parties agree to an exact date when risk will pass from
the vendor to the purchaser. In some cases the agreement will state that the risk
will pass at the time that there is a firm, binding, unconditional purchase-and-
sale agreement. In other cases the contract states that the risk will pass on the
completion date or the possession date. In any event, make sure that you have
adequate insurance coverage taking effect as of and including the date that you
assume the risk. The vendor should wait until after the risk date before termi-
nating insurance.

Fixtures and Chattels

This is an area of potential dispute between the purchaser and vendor unless it
is sufficiently clarified. A fixture is technically something permanently affixed
to the property; therefore, when the property is conveyed, the fixtures are
conveyed with it. A chattel is an object that is moveable; in other words, it is
not permanently affixed. Common examples of chattels are washer and dryer,
refrigerator, stove, microwave, and drapes.

A problem can arise when there is a question of whether an item is a
fixture or a chattel. For example, an expensive chandelier hanging from the
dining room ceiling, gold-plated bathroom fixtures, drape racks, or television
satellite dish on the roof might be questionable items. One of the key tests is
whether the item was intended to be attached on a permanent basis to the
property and therefore should be transferred with the property, or whether
it was the vendor's intention to remove these items and/ or replace them with
cheaper versions before closing the real estate transaction.

In general legal terms, if it is a fixture and it is not mentioned in the
agreement, it is deemed to be included in the purchase price. On the other
hand, if it is not a fixture and no reference is made to it in the agreement, then it
would not be included in the purchase price. To eliminate conflict, most agreements for purchase and sale have standard clauses built into them stating
that all existing fixtures are included in the purchase price except those listed

specifically in the agreement. In addition, a clause should list any chattels specifically included in the purchase price, and they should be clearly described.

Adjustment Date

This is the date used for calculating and adjusting such factors as taxes, maintenance fees, rentals, and other such matters. As of the adjustment date, all expenses and benefits go to the purchaser. For example, if the vendor has paid the maintenance fee for the month of March and the purchaser takes over with an adjustment date as of March 15, there will be an adjustment on the closing documents showing that the purchaser owes half of the amount of the prepaid maintenance fee to the vendor for the month of March. (A discussion of adjustments for property tax is included in Chapter 5: Understanding the Financing Aspects.)

Completion Date

This is the date when all documentation is completed and filed in the appropriate registry and all monies are paid out. The normal custom is for all the closing funds to be paid to the purchaser's solicitor a few days prior to closing. As soon as all the documents have been filed in the land registry office and confirmation has been obtained that everything is in order, the purchaser's solicitor releases the funds to the vendor's solicitor. The steps taken by the lawyers for the vendor and purchaser relating to the closing date are further discussed later in this chapter. The adjustment date and the completion date are frequently the same.

Possession Date

This is the date on which you are legally entitled to move into the premises. It is usually the same date as the adjustment and completion date. Sometimes the possession date is a day later in order for the vendor to be able to move out; in practical terms, though, many purchasers prefer the adjustment, completion, and possession dates to be the same, and make prior arrangements in terms of the logistics, if it is possible. One of the reasons is that the risks of the purchaser take effect as of the completion date, and there is always a risk that the vendor could cause damage or create other problems in the premises if he remains there beyond the completion date. As soon as your lawyer has advised you that all the documents have been filed and money has changed hands, the realtor or lawyer with whom you have been dealing arranges for you to receive the keys to the premises.

Merger

This is a legal principle to the effect that if the agreement for purchase and sale is to be "merged" into a deed or other document, the real contract between the parties is in the document filed with the land registry. To protect you, it should be stated in the agreement for purchase and sale that the "warranties, representations, promises, guarantees, and agreements shall survive the completion date." There are exceptions to the document of merger in cases of mistake or fraud, technical areas that require your lawyer's opinion, but it is important to understand the concept.

Commissions

At the end of most purchase-and-sale agreements there is a section setting out the amount of the commission charged, which the vendor confirms when accepting an offer. The vendor should make sure the purchase-and-sale agreement states that, if the sale collapses, at the option of the vendor the deposit monies can be deemed liquidated damages and the full amount can go to the vendor. A discussion of the various types of agreements for listing and selling real estate through a realtor is given later in this chapter.

Services Provided by the Purchaser's Lawyer

There are many services provided by your lawyer at various stages—before the agreement is signed, after the agreement is signed, just before closing the transaction on the closing day, and after closing the transaction. What follows is a partial summary of some of the matters discussed and services performed in a typical real estate transaction. Each situation will vary according to the complexity and nature of the transaction.

Before the Agreement Is Signed

- √ Discuss the contents of the offer to purchase with your lawyer. If there is a counteroffer from the vendor, make sure that you continue your communication with your lawyer before accepting the counteroffer, unless it is simply a matter of the purchase price.
- √ Discuss with your lawyer the ways in which you intend to finance your purchase.

√ Enquire as to all the various legal fees and out-of-pocket disbursement costs that you will have to pay.

√ Ask your lawyer about all the other costs related to purchasing the property that you should be aware of. The most common expenses are shown in Checklist 3 in the Appendix.

√ Discuss matters such as your choice of closing date, inspection of the property before closing, and any requirements that you want the vendor to fulfill.

After the Agreement Is Signed

Once your lawyer has received a copy of the signed agreement, he or she will carry out a process of thorough investigation to ensure that all the terms of the contract are complied with and that you obtain clear title to the property without any problems. In other words, your lawyer will make sure that all your rights are protected and that you are getting what you contracted for. The types of areas that a lawyer will check generally include the items below.

Title of Property

An agreement for purchase and sale normally states that the vendor will provide title free and clear of all encumbrances. Therefore, your lawyer has to make sure that there are no claims or other filings against the property that could impair the title that you are purchasing. When searching the title, you will be able to discover the name of the registered owner, the legal description, the list of charges (matters affecting the property) registered against the property, and other documents that are filed against the property. The types of charges that may be shown against the property would include the following. Different provincial jurisdictions may have varying terminology, but the concepts are the same.

√ mortgage

√ right to purchase (agreement for sale)

√ restrictive covenant (discussed in Chapter 2)

√ builder's lien (claim for money owing)

√ easement (discussed in Chapter 2)

√ right of way (discussed in Chapter 2)

√ option to purchase

√ certificate under provincial family relations legislation, restricting any dealing with the property

√ judgement

√ caveat (formal notice that someone has an interest in the property and the nature of that interest)

√ lis pendens (an action pending relating to the property, e.g., foreclosure proceedings)

√ lease or sublease, or option to lease

√ the government's mineral rights

√ condominium project documents

√ condominium bylaws.

The following documents and items are also generally reviewed:

√ survey certificate

√ property taxes

√ outstanding utility accounts

√ zoning bylaws

√ status of mortgages being assumed or discharged

√ ensuring financing will be sufficient and in place on closing

√ compliance with restrictions, warranties, conditions, and agreements

√ fixtures and chattels that are included in the purchase price

√ documents prepared by solicitor acting for seller (if applicable)

√ survey certificate

√ all documents required relating to property purchase (e.g., building regulations, project documents, bylaws, rules and regulations, financial statements, disclosure statement, estoppel certificate, and other documents as required)

√ insurance obtained

√ mortgage reviewed

√ benefits of title insurance are considered.

Title Insurance

Your lawyer could also recommend the benefits of obtaining title insurance for your peace of mind. Sometimes lenders require it. This insurance protects you in the event that pre-existing property defects show up after you bought the property. You would be covered up to the amount of your policy for as long as you are still the property owner.

The types of risks that are usually covered include: claims due to fraud, forgery, or duress; work orders; zoning and setback non-compliance or deficiencies; survey irregularities; forced removal of existing structures, unregistered rights of way or easements; and lack of vehicular or pedestrian access to the property. Do your comparison-shopping of policy rates, features, and coverage. One of the largest title insurance companies in Canada is First Canadian Title Search (www.firstcanadiantitle.ca). The site has extensive consumer information.

Just Before Closing the Transaction

Just prior to closing, there are various steps that your lawyer will generally go through, including the following:

√ preparing documents relating to any sales tax for the chattels that you may be purchasing

√ preparing any mortgage documents necessary and making arrangements for depositing funding to the lawyer's trust account from the mortgage proceeds on filing

√ showing you a purchaser's statement of adjustments, which gives the balance outstanding that you must come up with before closing the transaction; you normally have to provide these funds to your lawyer two days or more beforehand

√ preparing the vendor's statement of adjustments

√ receiving for forwarding any postdated cheques required for the mortgage lender

√ preparing all documents for filing in the land registry office on the closing date; if a different lawyer is involved in preparing the mortgage, that has to be coordinated for concurrent registration.

On the Closing Day

On the date of closing the transaction, your lawyer will perform various services, including the following:

√ Checking on the search of title of the property to make sure that there are no last-minute claims or charges against the title.

√ Releasing funds held in trust after receipt of mortgage proceeds from the lender if applicable, and sending an amount to the vendor's lawyer based on the amount the vendor is entitled to as outlined in the purchaser's statement of adjustments.

√ Receiving a copy of the certificate of possession from the New Home Warranty Program, if applicable.

√ Paying any monies required on the date of closing as outlined in the purchaser's statement of adjustments, e.g., sales tax on chattels being purchased, land transfer tax as applicable, and balance of commission owing to the real estate company paid from the proceeds of the purchase funds due to the vendor, and as outlined in the purchaser's statement of adjustments.

√ Holding back any "non-resident withholding tax" if you purchased the property from a non-resident of Canada. The withholding tax is 25% of the purchase price. If you fail to have the appropriate funds held back from the purchase funds, Revenue Canada (CRA) could attempt to collect the appropriate taxes from you. The premise behind this requirement under the *Income Tax Act* is that if the vendor owes any taxes for capital gains from the sale of the property to you, Revenue Canada would have difficulty collecting those taxes if the vendor does not live in Canada and has no other real property assets in Canada. That is why the onus of responsibility for collection and remittance of the 25% of the sale price to Revenue Canada is shifted to you. Your lawyer can tell you more about this.

After Closing the Transaction

Once the purchase has been completed, your lawyer will confirm that fact to you. You can then make arrangements with the realtor to obtain the keys to your home, or your lawyer will arrange to get the keys for you. Your lawyer will also:

√ Send you a reporting letter with all the filed documents and all the other related documents attached for your records, including an account for fees and disbursements that have been taken from the funds that you provided to your lawyer in trust prior to closing.

√ Arrange to obtain and register the appropriate discharges of mortgages that were paid off from the funds you paid for the purchase, unless the vendor's lawyer is attending to this obligation.

√ Ensure that all the vendor's promises have been satisfied.

There are numerous costs involved in purchasing new property, as shown in Checklist 3 in the Appendix. As to legal fees, you should be able to calculate them accurately in advance by asking your lawyer, and budget for the costs. Most lawyers charge a fee based on a percentage of the purchase price. In the case of condominiums or revenue properties, there is a higher charge generally for the extra documentation and responsibility involved on the lawyer's part, due to the nature of a condominium or revenue property transaction. Although fees can vary from place to place because of market competition and other factors, between 3/4% and 1% of the purchase price is normal. This relates only to legal fees and not to disbursements, which can vary considerably according to the nature of your transaction. It helps to shop around for legal fee comparative quotes, as a flat rate quote could be given to you that will save you money, especially if the lawyer is doing both the transfer of title (conveyance) and the mortgage documentation preparation.

Services Provided by the Vendor's Lawyer

If you are a vendor, it is important that you obtain a lawyer to represent your interests in the sale transaction. Whereas it is customary for the purchaser's lawyer to be paid a percentage of the purchase price, it is customary for the vendor's lawyer to be paid on an hourly basis for time actually expended. In view of the fact that condominium and revenue property transactions are more complicated and therefore take longer, you can expect that they will be slightly more expensive than house purchases. The hourly bill-out rate would normally be between $100 and $200 or more, depending on the regional location and the lawyer's experience and expertise.

The lawyer acting for the vendor will perform a wide range of services, the extent of which depends on each transaction. Some of the services that will be performed at various stages are discussed below.

Before the Agreement Is Signed

Before you sign the agreement, you should have selected a lawyer to represent you, and discussed the contract with him or her to make sure that you are protecting your interests and not incurring any additional expense or unnecessary frustration. If you are presented with a written offer, there are basically three options open to you:

1. You can accept the offer in the form in which it is presented by signing the offer. In this event there is a binding contract between you and the purchaser, once all conditions have been removed.

2. You can alter the offer by making changes that are more suitable to you and having the offer resubmitted to the purchaser. By making changes to the purchaser's offer, you are in effect rejecting the offer and countering with a new offer. The purchaser can either accept your changes or make further changes and return the agreement to you, which would constitute a new offer.

3. You can ignore the offer completely if you feel that it is unrealistic or otherwise unsatisfactory to you.

After the Agreement Is Signed

Once the bargain has been reached in writing between the vendor and the purchaser, the vendor's lawyer will request various documents from the vendor in order to assist in completing the transaction. The type of material that you should obtain depends on what is customary in your area and on provincial jurisdiction. The documents may not all be easily obtained, but you should attempt to provide the following:

√ real estate tax bills

√ hydro or other utility bills

√ copies of any insurance policies

√ a survey, if you have one available

√ a copy of the deed to your home, if you are in a province that has such a system

√ a copy of any outstanding mortgages, with the address of the mortgage company and, if possible, the mortgage account number and amortization schedule

√ if an existing tenancy is being assigned, details on the tenancy and on any security deposits

√ any condominium-related documents, such as project documents, bylaws, rules and regulations, estoppel certificate, and others that may be required

√ any revenue property–related documents such as financial statements, income and expense statement, balance sheet, list of chattels, names of tenants, and so on.

Prior to completion of the transaction, you should make arrangements to notify the utility, cable television, Internet, and telephone companies that you want service disconnected from your address as of a certain date. Also, advise your insurance company to cancel the insurance policy on the day after the closing date.

Just Before Closing the Transaction

Your lawyer will prepare a deed or transfer document that you must sign before title can be passed to the purchaser. Your lawyer will also review the vendor's statement of adjustments. In most provinces or regions the custom is for the purchaser's lawyer to prepare the conveyance (property transfer) documents for the vendor to sign and prepare the vendor's and the purchaser's statements of adjustments. These would then be forwarded to the vendor's lawyer for review before the vendor signs.

If there is a mortgage on your home, it is the vendor's responsibility to discharge the mortgage so that clear title to the property can be transferred. Your lawyer, after obtaining a copy of the mortgage statement showing the balance outstanding as of the closing date, would then "undertake" (legally promise) to the purchaser's lawyer that the mortgage would be paid off first from the proceeds of the purchase.

If you are a non-resident of Canada, there is a withholding tax that will be kept back from the sale proceeds and remitted to Revenue Canada. This is because a non-resident could be making a profit or capital gain on the sale of the property, and is required to pay tax on that property, but Revenue Canada could have difficulty collecting from someone outside of the country. That problem is prevented by having funds paid to Revenue Canada directly from the sale proceeds. The withholding tax under the *Income Tax Act* is 25% of the sale price. Your lawyer will advise you as to the correct amount of withholding tax.

Title Insurance

Your lawyer could advise you to obtain title insurance coverage in case any defects with your property are discovered after the sale, and a claim is made against you. Title insurance would cover your liability up to the amount of your policy, and under the terms of the policy, as long as the risk existed as of the date of the policy. There are many different types of risks covered by title insurance, but you need to comparison shop for features, benefits, and costs. To obtain names of title insurance company Web sites in Canada, go to www.google.ca and type in key words such as "title insurance Canada."

On the Closing Day

On the date of closing, your lawyer or your lawyer's agent will meet the purchaser's lawyer or lawyer's agent at the land registry office so that the transfer documents can be filed, changing title.

After Closing the Transaction

After the transaction has been completed, and your lawyer has received the appropriate money based on the vendor's statement of adjustments, he or she will clear off any existing mortgages with those funds and have the mortgages discharged from the title of the property. You will then receive the balance of funds after the legal fees and disbursements have been deducted.

Finally, your lawyer will send you a reporting letter setting out the services that were performed and enclose any appropriate documents for your files.

The Listing Agreement

The real estate listing agreement is usually a partially pre-printed form with standard clauses and wording. The balance of the agreement, completed by the agent and the vendor, covers the specific information with respect to the property being offered for sale and the nature of the contractual bargain between the agent and vendor. Because the listing agreement is a binding legal contract, you should be very cautious about signing it without fully understanding the implications of what you are signing. If in doubt, get advice from your lawyer beforehand. The following section covers the general contents of, and the types of, listing agreements.

Contents of a Listing Agreement

A listing agreement performs two main functions. First, you are giving the real estate agent the authority to act on your behalf to find a purchaser for your property. The agreement sets out the terms and conditions of this agency relationship, including the commission rate or method of compensation for the agent's services, the length of time of the appointment, when and how the fee or commission is earned, and how and when it will be paid to the agent.

A second feature of the listing agreement sets out the details of the property being offered for sale. All pertinent details should be set out, including civic and legal address, list price, size of property, description of the type of property, number and size of rooms, number of bedrooms, type of heating system, main recreational features, and other amenities. Any chattels or extra features that are to be included in the list price should also be set out. For example, such things as appliances, draperies and drapery track, and carpeting.

You should also insert other particulars in the listing agreement relating to the property for sale, including details of existing financing, the balance on the mortgage, the amount of monthly payments, and the due date on the mortgage. Any other mortgages should be listed as well. Annual property taxes should be set out, as well as any liens, rights of way, easements, or other charges on the property.

Once you have come to an agreement on all the terms and you are satisfied with them, the agreement is signed and witnessed and you receive a copy.

Types of Listing Agreements

There are three basic types of agreements that you may wish to consider when listing your property with a real estate agent: open, exclusive, and multiple listing.

Open Listing

In an open listing, the real estate agent does not have an exclusive right to find a purchaser for the property; you can sign any number of open-listing agreements with as many different agents as you wish. Only the agent who sells the property earns a commission. The problem with an open listing is that many realtors don't spend a great deal of time on such a listing because of the lack of assurance that they will ever receive a commission on the sale of the property. This is because so many other realtors could also be looking for purchasers.

Open listings are more common in commercial sales than in residential sales, and in any event you should obtain legal advice on drafting an open-listing agreement if you are considering such an option. To protect yourself, make sure that the agreement is in writing and the terms clearly spelled out. Commission rates could be similar to the "exclusive listing" below.

Exclusive Listing

In this example, the vendor gives to the real estate agent an exclusive right to find a purchaser for the property. This right is given for a fixed period. The real estate agent is automatically entitled to receive a commission whether someone else sells the property, the vendor sells the property, or the property is sold at some future point to someone who was introduced to the property by the real estate agent during the listing period. The duration of an exclusive listing is normally 30, 60, or 90 days. In many ways the shorter the time period, the more energetically the realtor will have to work to achieve the sale. You can always extend the listing if you are satisfied with the realtor's performance and service. The range of commission is between 4% and 5% on the first $100,000, and 2.5% thereafter. If it is raw land, a 10% commission is common. Commissions can vary and are generally negotiable, depending on the circumstances.

Multiple Listing

With a multiple listing, a realtor is given an exclusive listing, in effect, for a fixed period of time, but also the right to list the property with the Multiple Listing Service (MLS). This is a highly sophisticated computerized database that is available to all members of the real estate boards who participate in the MLS. In practical terms, this constitutes almost all real estate companies; the entire real estate network becomes like a group of subagents for the sale of your property.

If another agent finds a buyer, the selling company and the listing company will split the commission equally. Multiple listings are generally offered for a minimum of 60 days, but this is negotiable. Commission rates vary between 5% and 7% on the first $100,000, and 2.5% thereafter. Commissions can vary and are negotiable, depending on the circumstances.

Forms of Legal Structure to Hold Investment Property

One of the first issues you have to consider when buying investment real estate is deciding the form of legal structure in which to hold your property. This will be necessary before you set up a bank account or purchase the property. Your main alternatives are sole proprietorship, partnership, and corporation. A general description of each of these follows, along with advantages and disadvantages of each.

The type of legal structure you choose will depend upon the type of real estate investments you wish to acquire, your potential risk and liability, the amount of money needed to start, what you expect to earn, whether you have partners, and the tax implications. (See also Chapter 1: Understanding Real Estate Investment in the section on "Buying with Partners.") If your risk and liability are high, the incorporation process will provide some protection. On the other hand, there may be tax advantages to having a sole proprietorship instead. Once you become familiar with the differences between each form, you should consult a lawyer and tax accountant. The decision is an important one.

Sole Proprietorship

A sole proprietorship refers to an individual who owns an investment in his or her personal name. The real estate investment income (if it is a revenue business) and the owner's personal income are considered the same for tax purposes. Therefore, business profits are reported on the owner's personal income tax return and are based on federal and provincial income or loss schedules. Business expenses and losses are deductible. It is advisable, though, to keep personal and business bank accounts separate. For instance, you may wish to pay yourself a salary from your business account and deposit it into your personal account for your personal needs—food, clothing, lodging, personal savings, etc.

Advantages:

√ There is minimal government regulation.

√ It is relatively easy to roll over into an incorporated company if necessary or desired at some later point.

√ There is total control by the owner, and all profits go to the owner.

√ It is easy to calculate the capital gain or loss from the investment.

Disadvantages:

√ The owner has unlimited liability; that is, he or she is personally liable for all debts and obligations of the business.

Partnership

A partnership is a proprietorship with two or more owners. The owners may not necessarily be 50/50 partners; they may have whatever percentage reflects their investment and contribution to the partnership. The partners share profits and losses in proportion to their respective percentage interest. While the partnership has to file a tax return, it does not pay any tax. Instead, the partners pay tax on the basis of their portion of the net profit or loss. In a partnership, each partner is personally liable for the full amount of the debts and liabilities of the business. Each of the individuals is authorized to act on behalf of the company, and each can bind the partnership legally, except if stated otherwise, in a partnership agreement. It is sound business advice not to enter into any partnership arrangement without a written agreement between the partners regarding responsibilities for financing the business, sharing the profits and losses, working in the business, specific duties, and other important considerations. Partnerships are governed by provincial partnership legislation.

Advantages:

√ There is minimal government regulation.

√ It is relatively easy to roll over into an incorporated company if necessary or desired at some later point.

√ There is joint responsibility; not everything rests on your shoulders.

√ There is greater access to money and skills.

√ You can easily apportion the capital gain or loss from the investment, depending on your percentage interest.

Disadvantages:

√ There is potential conflict of authority between partners.

√ There is unlimited liability; all the partners are individually and collectively liable for all the debts and liabilities of the business. Thus, if one person makes an error in judgement, all partners will be exposed.

√ Ownership and control must be shared, as well as the profits.

Corporation (Limited Liability Company)

A corporation is a business that is a legal entity separate from the owner or owners of the business. After being incorporated with the provincial or federal registry, a business must file annual reports, submit regular tax returns, and pay tax on its profits. The owners are called shareholders and have no personal liability for the company's debts unless they have signed a personal guarantee. The liability of the company is limited to the assets of the company. You can have a single-shareholder corporation. If there are two or more shareholders, make sure you have a shareholders' agreement. This is similar to a partnership agreement. The shareholders elect directors (usually the shareholders), who are responsible for managing the affairs of the corporation. Directors have some potential liability to statutory creditors (e.g., Revenue Canada, CRA) for the company's debts.

It is advisable to obtain legal and tax advice to assist with the preparation of the incorporation documents and shareholders' agreements.

Advantages:

√ The shareholders are not personally responsible for any of the debts or obligations of the corporation unless a shareholder has signed a personal guarantee.

√ The corporation continues regardless of whether a shareholder dies or retires.

√ There may be various business tax advantages not available to a proprietorship or partnership.

√ The tax rate could be lower than for a proprietorship, up to a certain level of income.

√ You should still be eligible for the personal lifetime capital gains tax exemption when the property is sold and you obtain a profit on your initial investment. Get your tax accountant's advice in advance to make sure the original deal is structured properly.

√ There is increased business stability, in that while shareholders may come and go, the business continues uninterrupted and all property of the corporation remains intact.

√ Share ownership interest is transferable.

√ A corporation is a separate legal entity from an individual. It may sue or be sued in its own name.

Disadvantages:

√ Corporations are regulated by each province or the federal government. The regulations are more complex than those of the partnership legislation.

√ The costs of incorporating are higher than costs relating to other business structures—approximately $400 to $700 plus the lawyer's out-of-pocket disbursements, which are approximately $300 to $400.

√ The operating losses and tax credits remain within the corporate entity; they are not available to individual shareholders if the corporation is unable to utilize them.

Other Legal Cautions and Protections to Consider

Limiting Your Personal Liability Exposure

If you are operating a small business, or consider your real estate investments as a business, you also want to protect yourself and your family from creditors. Here are some techniques to discuss with your lawyer.

√ Don't sign personal guarantees or limit them. There is no point in going to the effort of incorporating a company if you nullify the personal protection by signing a personal guarantee of the corporate debts. Don't sign personal guarantees at all, for example, to suppliers, trade creditors, landlords. Alternatively, only do so for a bank if absolutely necessary, and then limit the amount of liability. For example, if the company is borrowing $45,000, and there are three partners, agree to be liable for a maximum of one-third only. Get legal advice before you sign any personal guarantee to a lender. Remember that the marketplace is very competitive. Use that knowledge as leverage when choosing one creditor over another.

√ Never pledge personal security. Adopt a policy of not pledging any personal security—your personal car, house or life insurance policy—under any circumstances.

√ Transfer property and other assets to your spouse. You can transfer the ownership of your home and other personal assets, such as your car, to your spouse. That way, the assets are not in your personal name. In the event of a marital breakup, the matrimonial home is generally considered to be owned 50/50 in many situations anyway. Also, under family law legislation of most provinces, family assets are combined for calculation purposes and then divided in half. Speak to your lawyer about the laws in your province.

√ Be aware of director liability. If you are a director of a corporation, you do have liability risks, particularly under provincial and federal government legislation. For example, there could be potential liability for corporate tax, GST, provincial employment standards legislation, provincial sales tax, builder's lien legislation, etc. Therefore, if you are a director, consider not owning any personal assets of consequence to limit the potential risk.

√ Don't have your spouse as guarantor or director. To limit the family's risk, you don't want to ask your spouse to act as a director or guarantor.

√ Don't have joint accounts. If you have a joint account, and a creditor garnishees your bank account, they will seize all the funds in that account. By having separate accounts, you avoid that risk.

√ Consider spousal RRSPs. If your spouse is earning less than you are, you may wish to contribute to his or her RRSP as a spousal RRSP. You get the RRSP tax deduction, but your spouse gets the money in his or her RRSP account. Therefore, if a creditor tries to collect on your RRSP with a court judgement, there will be less money available. If an RRSP is collapsed to pay the creditor, there will only be the amount left after federal tax is taken off the RRSP amount. This fact gives room for your lawyer to negotiate with the creditor for some creative compromise settlement—for example, a maximum of 10 cents to 25 cents on the dollar, with flexible payment terms over time, interest-free. Your lawyer should be able to negotiate on your behalf, as most people do not have the skills or objectivity, and are too emotionally involved. Also, your lawyer should have experience in negotiating, and have more credibility in the eyes of the creditor.

√ Consider RRSPs with insurance companies. If you have an RRSP, RRIF, or non-registered investments with an insurance company, under certain circumstances, creditors are not able to collect on the RRSP. Check with your financial and tax adviser and lawyer.

√ Sign business documents as authorized signatory of corporation. In order to get the full protection of your corporation, always make it clear that you are signing on behalf of your corporation. That way, no one can try to claim that you were signing in your personal capacity.

√ Consider allocating CPP primarily in spouse's name. Another income-splitting option, which also has the effect of putting more money in your spouse's hands, is to apportion a certain percentage of your CPP to your spouse. You are entitled to start taking out your CPP at age 60, at a reduced amount. This approach means that there is less money available for creditors from your personal income. Get tax advice on the appropriateness of this option.

√ Lend money to your corporation and become a secured creditor. You could lend money as a creditor to the company and take back security, like any other creditor could. This could be in the form of registered general or specific security agreements, assignment of receivables, or mortgage filed against the property, and so on.

√ If your company wants to borrow money from a lender, and the lender does not want its security against your company's assets to rank in claim-priority after the security you have previously registered for any personal loans you have made, you do have an option. You can subordinate or postpone your claim; in other words, give priority to the lender's security. However, your security document remains registered against the property. You therefore, remain a secured creditor for any claim you make against the corporate assets, after the lender gets its money back.

√ Consider creating a personal management company for your services. Rather than drawing a salary as an employee of your own company, you may wish to have a management-consulting agreement with your own company as an independent contractor. You might consider a separate corporation as your personal management corporation. There are various tax and other considerations for this approach.

√ Make sure you have a will. The legal and financial nightmare your family will have to deal with if you don't have a will won't be the type of legacy you want to be remembered for. (Refer to Chapter 12: Understanding Financial and Estate Planning.)

√ If you are interested in a discussion on legal protections relating to small business, refer to *The Canadian Small Business Legal Advisor* by Douglas Gray and *The Complete Canadian Small Business Guide* by Douglas Gray and Diana Gray.

Limiting Your Estate Liability Exposure

What if you are currently running your own small business as a real estate investor when you die? Your business could cease to function, as you are the key person. If the business goes under, creditors will start looking for assets. If you are liable under a personal guarantee or as a director, then creditors could make claims against your estate.

Here are some options to discuss with your professional advisers to minimize the risk to your estate:

√ Make sure you have a will. A current will that has been drafted with your lawyer and accountant is the first step. (Refer to Chapter 12: Understanding Financial and Estate Planning.)

√ Make sure you have a shareholder's agreement with a buy-sell clause. This enables one owner to buy out the other's interest in certain situations while they are alive or from their estate.

√ Designate beneficiaries of your insurance policies. By designating beneficiaries in your insurance policies, the money bypasses the will completely and is therefore not part of your estate. It goes directly to your designated beneficiaries tax-free. Your personal creditors can claim only from assets in your estate.

√ Designate beneficiaries for your RRSPs and RRIFs. By designating a beneficiary for registered retirement plans, you bypass your will and your estate. The money goes directly to the beneficiary and is unavailable to creditors. You can also designate beneficiaries for your non-registered investments.

√ Consider the use of trusts. If you set up a living trust while you are alive, it bypasses your will and therefore your estate on your death. A testamentary trust is set up through your will, and takes effect after your death. Both types divert assets out of your estate, away from creditors of your estate.

√ For more information on will and estate planning, refer to the latest edition of the book *The Canadian Guide to Will and Estate Planning* by Douglas Gray and John Budd. Also refer to www.estateplanning.ca.

Keeping Peace in the Family When Asking for Loans or Investment Money

In a worst-case scenario, if you have a small business or real estate investment business and your business goes under, ensure that your relationships with your friends, family, and relatives survive the business ordeal. Here are some do's and don'ts.

√ Secure loans from family and friends. If you borrow money from friends and family, consider securing them with security registered against property, such as a mortgage or general or specific security agreement. That way they are a secured creditor, like any secured creditor.

√ Consider loans plus equity. You could structure your loans from family and friends to include an equity (share) feature in your business or real estate investment as a value-added incentive.

√ Consider a convertible option from loans to equity. You could give an option to your family or friends who are lending money to be able to convert those loans in part or in full to share equity if they wanted to do so later; that is, after the company has proven itself to be viable.

√ Don't ask family or friends to sign personal guarantees or co-sign. If you ask family, friends, or your spouse to act as a guarantor or to co-sign a loan, and the loan is called, you will regret it. The relationship may not survive the financial loss, depending on the amount and related circumstances.

√ Don't ask family or friends to act as directors. Being a director carries a lot of potential liability to a lot of different categories of creditors. Depending on the business, the risk could be very high. Directors don't generally appreciate being sued personally and having all their personal assets at risk. That process does not bode well for the continuation of a meaningful relationship.

√ Don't ask your spouse or partner to consent to a collateral mortgage on your house, no matter how immune you think you might be to the statistical reality of business failure. Ask yourself how the quality of your marital relationship will be affected in a business downside situation if the bank starts action to foreclose on the house.

√ Don't assign life insurance proceeds. If you assign your life insurance proceeds to secure a loan and you die, your creditor could get all the money, leaving nothing for your family. If a creditor insists on insurance and you have tried all alternatives, most banks will offer special loan insurance. A monthly insurance premium is added to your loan, and if you die, the loan is paid off in full.

Avoiding the Pitfalls of Litigation

At some point in your business or real estate investment career, you might be faced with a litigation issue as the plaintiff or defendant. As in any game, litigation is inherently an adversarial process; if you don't know how to play it well, or retain a lawyer who does, the odds of winning are not in your favour. No matter what debt, breach of contract, or negligence is causing you to consider suing, keep the following pitfalls and street-smart suggestions foremost in mind.

Avoid Lawsuits Based on Emotion

You might feel that you have been wronged and you are naturally very upset. Your decision to sue, however, should be based on hard-nosed business realities. Maybe there is not much money involved, but it is a matter of principle. Give yourself some time, maybe several months, to see if the intensity of your emotions subsides. The litigation process itself has enough negative emotion associated with it.

Have Realistic Expectations

Many people assume that if they are right, they will win at the end of the day. However, very few issues in law are black and white. The litigation process is inherently unpredictable. In addition, when you factor in legal fees, even if you win, the court costs you are awarded amount to only about 15% to 35% of your legal fees, so you still lose financially. And then you still have the challenge of attempting to collect on the judgement.

Assess the Defendants' Assets

You could win at trial, but still be a big-time loser. The defendant could have no assets in his or her name or have all the assets leveraged up with debt at the time you commence an action or by the time you get a judgement. A corporate entity could be a hollow shell without any net worth.

Do an objective risk assessment of the realistic potential of collecting on a judgement. You could be throwing good money after bad. The negative learning experience could be seen as a cost of doing business, and you could then commit to changing your business practices to pre-empt a recurrence.

Weighing Potential Gains vs. Losses

Realistically assess the relative pros and cons of litigation in terms of money and lost productivity. Can you afford the fight to the end? Have you obtained three written quotes as to the cost of the complete pretrial and trial process? Will it cost more than the amount you are claiming? What if you lose? You will be out not only legal fees, but court costs as well. What if the defendant counter-claims against you and wins?

Consider a Settlement

Settlements occur all the time. Only about 5% of lawsuits ever end up at trial, with the exception of small claims court. Even small claims court has a settlement hearing process before trial in many provinces. Settlements allow both parties to strike a deal and get on with life, saving a lot of court time. Because of the uncertainty of the trial process outcome, settling for 20%, 30%, 50%, or 70% of the original claim is better than the risk of getting nothing and being out legal fees as well.

Don't Sue Too Early

Don't commence your action before you have all the facts. Ideally, you want to have all your arguments included in your claim to show your opponent that you have done your homework.

Don't Sue Too Late

If you wait too long, you could miss a statutory time limit to commence your action. Different actions and different provinces have different time limits.

Get Expert Legal Advice

This is not a time to use your family lawyer whom you've known for a number of years. Instead, select a lawyer who specializes in the specific area of law or litigation if it will proceed to court. Before you make any decisions, have at least three lawyers give you objective feedback on your chances at trial, how long it will take, and how much it will cost. You need a benchmark for comparison and to make sure that the advice is consistent and, if not, why not. (Refer to Chapter 4: Selecting Your Advisory Team.) A few legal consultations will enhance your knowledge and increase your confidence in your final decision. Then, sleep on your dilemma for a few weeks or a month. See if you have the same opinion at the end of that time.

Alternative Dispute Resolution

Using the legal process to resolve a conflict should be a last resort. Apart from the time and costs involved, the relationship will probably be damaged beyond repair. If the parties get to the point where they communicate only through their respective lawyers, it is inevitable that there will be at best a winner and loser, or more likely two losers. It is doubtful that it will be a win-win situation, which is obviously the best outcome.

The first step to resolving a dispute is obviously for both parties to sit down together and attempt to work out a solution that is mutually acceptable. If a dispute cannot be resolved at this level, the alternative dispute-resolution (ADR) approach is gaining favour in many types of business conflicts. Trained professionals can provide mediation and arbitration services for business disputes, including mediating contract interpretation, disputes or negotiations, or provide a written opinion proposing a pragmatic, equitable, and reasonable resolution of conflict.

Mediation is an informal resolution facilitation service. Arbitration is more formal and is generally governed by the provincial arbitration legislation, which sets out procedures and protocols. Many lawyers are also accredited mediators and arbitrators.

As mentioned earlier, for a detailed discussion of legal matters relating to small business, refer to the most current editions of the books, *The Canadian Small Business Legal Advisor* by Douglas Gray, and *The Complete Canadian Small Business Guide* by Douglas Gray and Diana Gray.

Summary

As you can clearly see from reading this chapter, there are many legal issues, options, and implications to consider when buying, selling, or investing in real estate. Topics covered include the different kinds of property ownership, what types of legal documentation are involved when buying or selling real estate, and what services are provided by a lawyer. Also covered were the different types of listing agreements and legal structures to hold revenue or investment property.

Part of prudent legal strategic planning is to anticipate and avoid legal problems and related financial risks. This chapter discussed how to limit your personal liability exposure and that of your estate in the event of your death. Tips were given on how to avoid the pitfalls of litigation if a dispute occurs. Finally, if you decide to borrow money or ask for investment funds from family or friends, suggestions were given on how to avoid estrangement or conflict with the people you care about the most.

Hand-in-hand with the financial and legal issues of purchasing a house are the tax issues, which are discussed next.

CHAPTER 7

Understanding the Tax Aspects

As you can appreciate, this is a particularly important section, whether you are buying a principal residence or investment property. The information and tips suggested will save you money, or at least help you to understand the key options open to you to save money. As income tax provisions can change at any time, before making any real estate purchase plans for investment purposes, make sure you contact a tax accountant to obtain current income tax advice. (Chapter 1: Selecting Your Advisory Team gives guidelines on how to find a professional accountant.)

The following discussion highlights the main categories of local, provincial, and federal government taxes that could affect you. It also includes tax-planning strategies, tax-saving tips, ways of maximizing your deductions, and avoiding pitfalls.

Local/Regional Taxes

Municipalities assess taxes for various purposes. Some municipalities include all taxes within one assessment. Others separate out the taxes. The main taxes are as follows:

Property Taxes

These are generally due on an annual basis, with assessment of value determined within six months prior to the property taxation year. For residential property, a "mill rate" is generally determined annually and multiplied by the assessed value of the property, including the building on the property, to determine the actual tax due. In many provinces there is a homeowner's grant that is subtracted from the gross taxes assessed for your property to determine the net payable tax you owe. As you might assume, this annual grant is for a principal residence only, not an investment property. The grant amount can vary depending on the age of the homeowner.

If you believe your property taxes are unfair because they are based on an artificially high assessment of property value, you can appeal the assessment notice. For example, when a real estate market has gone down, it is not uncommon for property assessment appeals to go up because of the lag time before the assessment reflects the reduction in value. Make sure you don't miss the appeal deadline, as the time window can be tight.

Property taxes are generally assessed for municipally supplied services such as schools, education, roads, and hospitals.

Utility Taxes

These taxes tend to be for services such as water, sewer, and garbage pickup.

Further Information

To obtain further information about the taxes noted above, and other taxes, contact your lawyer, City Hall, or regional assessment authority.

Provincial Taxes

Many provincial governments charge a property purchase tax when purchasing a property. This is the main form of provincial tax dealing with property.

Property Purchase Tax

Basically this tax is assessed and paid at the time of purchase based on the purchase price of the property. The formula for determining the amount payable varies between provinces.

Further Information

To obtain further information about provincial taxes, contact your lawyer or the local branch of your provincial government land titles office.

Federal Taxes

There are two main federal taxes: the goods and services tax (GST) and income tax.

Goods and Services Tax

The GST applies to every "supply" of real property, both residential and commercial, unless the "supply" can fit within one of the exemptions set out in the legislation.

The term "supply" has broad meaning. It includes not only sales and leases of real property but also transfers, exchanges, barters, and gifts. Most services dealing with the real estate transaction are also covered by the GST. In other words, whenever you consume a "good," e.g., buy a product or use a service, you will be required, in most cases, to pay the 7% tax.

The following overview discusses how certain types of real estate purchases are affected by or exempted from the GST, and how the GST rebate system operates. Check with your accountant to make that you are aware of any changes. Governments tend to modify legislation over time.

How the GST System Works

The purchaser pays the GST to the vendor at the time of purchase. The vendor then remits the tax to what is colloquially and historically referred to as Revenue Canada. It is now technically referred to as the Canada Revenue Agency (CRA). (In this book, the term "Revenue Canada" is used, as it familiar to everyone.) Sometimes the vendor includes the GST within the purchase price, and other times it may be added on separately. There are also several categories of GST exemptions relating to real estate. Although the basic rate of the GST is currently 7%, that could be changed at any time, of course. Historically, most countries that have brought in a GST counterpart have increased the percentage over time.

If you are the purchaser who has to pay GST, you may be able to receive a partial or full rebate or offset the GST tax paid against GST tax received. It depends on whether you purchased the property as a principal residence, for investment purposes, or are in the business of buying and selling properties.

Resale Home or Other Residential Dwelling

If you buy a used residential property as a principal residence, there is no GST payable on the purchase price. In other words, it is exempt. Revenue Canada defines "used residential property" to include an owner-occupied house, condominium, duplex, apartment building, vacation property, summer cottage, or non-commercial hobby farm.

The "used" property definition requires that the vendor must not be a "builder" as defined in the legislation. A builder is someone who builds or substantially renovates the property as a business. Used property can also mean a recently built house that is substantially complete and has been sold at least once before you buy it.

If you purchase a resale home that includes a room used as an office, and you are self-employed, the entire house still qualifies for the GST exemption if you use it primarily as your residence. However, if you purchase a home that is used primarily for commercial business purposes, and it is zoned for that type of operation, at the time of purchase you would be GST exempt only for the portion that you would reside in.

When purchasing a resale home, you can request that the vendor provide you with a certificate stating that the property qualifies as "used" for GST purposes.

New Home

When you purchase a newly constructed home from a builder as a principal residence for yourself or a relative, the entire purchase price, including land, is taxable. The word "home" refers to a residential dwelling and includes a single family house, condominium (apartment or townhouse format), or mobile home. If the home will be your principal residence, it may qualify for a partial GST rebate, depending upon the sale price.

Purchasers of homes priced up to $350,000 will qualify for the maximum rebate of $8,750, or 36% of the GST paid on the purchase price, whichever is less. Since the $8,750 amount is 2.5% of $350,000, a purchaser is really paying the GST at a rate of 4.5% on a $350,000 home instead of 7%.

If you are purchasing a home priced at more than $350,000 but less than $450,000, the rebate is gradually reduced, in other words declines to zero on a proportional basis. On a home priced at $450,000 for example, the full GST of $31,500 is payable without rebate. There is no rebate for homes selling for $450,000 or more.

If you are purchasing the home for investment purposes and you intend to rent out the property to tenants, the full 7% GST is charged on the purchase price and no rebate is available. If you are purchasing the home through a limited company, a rebate is not allowed.

Here are some examples of how the rebate is calculated if you are buying for a principal residence. The term "purchase price" refers to the price paid to the builder for the home and lot before the GST is calculated, and does not include any associated realty or legal fees.

Example 1: Formula used for homes selling for $350,000 or less:

If you buy a new home for $150,000, you would calculate the rebate like this:

GST paid (7% of $150,000) = $10,500

Amount of GST rebate ($8,750 or 36% of $10,500; the smaller amount must be claimed) = $3,780

Net amount paid in GST (GST paid minus rebate) = $6,720

Example 2: Formula used for home selling for more than $350,000 but less than $450,000

If you buy a new home for $400,000 you would calculate the rebate like this:

GST paid (7% of $400,000) = $28,000

Step 1 of rebate calculation ($8,750 is the amount because 36% of $28,000 is $10,080 and you must use the smaller amount)

Step 2 of rebate calculation ($8,750 [Step 1] × [$450,000 – $400,000 purchase price] ÷ $100,000 = $ 4,375

Amount of GST rebate = $4,375

Net amount paid in GST (GST paid minus rebate) = $23,635

Example 3: Sample new home rebates

Purchase Price	GST Paid	GST Rebate	Net GST Paid
$100,000	$ 7,000	$2,520	$ 4,480
150,000	10,500	2,780	6,720
200,000	14,000	5,040	8,960
250,000	17,500	6,300	11,200
300,000	21,000	7,560	13,440
350,000	24,500	8,750	15,750
400,000	28,000	4,375	23,625
450,000	31,500	no rebate	31,500

When the home is purchased, the builder can either pay the rebate directly to you or deduct it from the GST you owe on the purchase price. You have to complete a form called "GST New Housing Rebate." You can obtain the form from real estate agents, builders, or the Revenue Canada office. Also, check out the Revenue Canada (CRA) Web site at www.cra-arc.gc.ca.

Owner-Built Home

If you build your own home or hire someone to build or substantially reno-vate a home for you as a principal residence for yourself or a relative, you will qualify for a GST rebate if any of the following applies:

√ You paid the GST on construction materials and contracting services.

√ You or a relative are the first occupants of the home.

√ You sell the home and ownership is transferred to the purchaser before it is occupied as a place of residence.

The amount of the rebate will depend on the fair market value (FMV) of the home and whether or not the GST was paid on the acquisition of the land. FMV must be under $450,000. If you owned the land when the GST started, you will not have paid the GST on this purchase.

To determine the FMV of the home you build, you can have it appraised or compare it to similar homes in your neighbourhood. If the FMV of your property is close to or more than $350,000 but less than $450,000, you may be required to obtain a formal appraisal to validate your rebate claim.

When you acquired the land for your new home, if you paid GST, the rebate is calculated in the same way as the new home rebate formula for homes purchased from a builder, e.g., on the land and home. This formula was discussed above under the "New Home" section.

If you did not pay the GST when you acquired the land, the rebate is reduced for homes valued up to $350,000 to a maximum of $1,720 or 10% of the GST paid, whichever is less. For homes valued at more than $350,000 but less than $450,000, the rebate is gradually reduced. There is no rebate for homes valued at $450,000 or more.

Here are some formulas to show how to calculate the rebate on an owner-built home when the GST has and has not been paid on the land. Remember, FMV stands for "Fair Market Value."

GST Paid on Land

Example 1: If the FMV of the home, including land, is $350,000 or less, the rebate calculation is $8,750 or 36% of the GST paid on the land, building, contracting services, and building materials, whichever is less.

Refer to the previous "New Home" Example 1 for a similar calculation example.

Example 2: If the FMV of the home, including land, is more than $350,000 but less than $450,000, the rebate calculation is based on the following formula:

A × ($450,000 − B) ÷ $100,000

A = $8,750 or 36% of the GST paid on the land, building, contracting services, and building materials, whichever is less

B = the fair market value of the home

Refer to the previous "New Home" Example 2 for a similar calculation.

GST Not Paid on Land

Example 1:

If the FMV of the home, including land, is $350,000 or less, the rebate calculation is $1,720 or 10% of the GST paid on the building, contracting services, and building materials, whichever is less.

Example 2:

If the FMV of the home, including land, is more than $350,000 but less than $450,000, the rebate calculation is based on the following formula:

A × ($450,000 − B) ÷ $100,000

A = $1,720 or 10% of the GST paid on the building, contracting services, and building materials, whichever is less

B = the fair market value of the home

Renovated Home

Under the GST, sales of substantially renovated homes are treated in the same way as sales of new housing. "Substantial renovations" mean that all, or substantially all, of the house except the foundation, external walls, interior supporting walls, floor, roof, and staircases are removed or replaced.

For example, if a person in the renovation business buys an older home, there is no GST on the purchase price as the GST does not apply to resale homes. The person then completely guts and replaces the interior with new walls, railings, floor, kitchen, wiring, and plumbing. At least 90% of the items on the Revenue Canada (CRA) guidelines must be removed to constitute a substantial renovation. For GST purposes, this substantially renovated home, when sold, will be treated like a new home. If you purchase this substantially renovated home, you will pay the GST on the purchase price and be entitled to claim the GST new housing rebate if the price is under $450,000. Refer to the "New Home" section discussed earlier.

If there are other renovations or improvements to a home, such as replacing a kitchen or building an addition, these are not considered substantial renovations. If you buy an older home that has only been partially renovated, such as a remodelled bathroom, an additional bedroom, or a new roof, you will not have to pay the GST on the home.

You can see the importance of making sure that the renovations do not fall under the "substantial renovation" category if possible when you buy a home from a builder in the business of renovating older homes. It will mean you pay less for the house at the outset if you can avoid the GST on a resale home.

A substantially renovated home is considered a resale home if the renovator owns it and lives in it, even for a short time. That is an important point to keep in mind, especially if you are buying from another homeowner or renovating it yourself, and in both instances the renovations are substantial. You should be able to get more money on resale if the purchaser does not have to pay GST.

Land

There is no GST on the sale of vacant land or recreational property, such as a hobby farm owned by an individual or by a trust for the benefit of individuals. Certain sales and uses of farmland are also exempt.

If you paid GST on the land because the previous use of the land was such that GST was applicable, the rebate would be the same as for a new home. See the "New Home" section.

If you build on the land and sell it, refer to the GST discussion in the "Owner-Built Home" section.

Real Estate Transaction Expenses

GST is applicable to most of the services associated with completing a real estate transaction. For example, GST is applied to the commission that a real estate agent charges for facilitating a sale. The tax is paid by the person responsible for paying the commission, usually the vendor. Real estate commissions are GST taxable, even if the total GST owed is reduced by a rebate or the sale is exempt from GST. For example, if you sell a used home, the sale price is exempt from GST, but the real estate commission is still taxable.

Other real estate related services on which GST is charged include fees for surveys, inspections, appraisals, and legal and tax advice. GST is charged on these fees regardless of whether the house you purchase is exempt from the tax. All moving charges are taxed.

There are several exemptions from GST, however. Mortgage broker fees are not taxed if the fees are charged separately from any taxable real estate commissions. Also, mortgages and interest on mortgages are exempt from GST.

Rent

Most residential rents are exempt from GST. A renter of residential premises will not be required to pay GST on rent paid to the landlord, provided the renter occupies the premises for at least one month.

The landlord will be required, of course, to pay GST charges on all services necessary to keep the property in good repair. Rather than underwriting this additional cost, the landlord will generally increase rents. If you are the landlord, you will want to make sure you recover the additional cost.

If you employ a realtor or property management company to find and arrange a tenant for your rental property, GST applies to the fees and commissions charged for providing this service. All repair and maintenance services charge GST.

Condominium Maintenance Fees

If you own a condominium, the monthly fee charged by the condominium corporation is not subject to GST. However, the condominium corporation will be charged GST on all services employed to maintain the building and grounds. These additional GST costs will obviously be passed on to the condominium owners in the form of increased monthly fees.

Homeowner Expenses

Any service you employ around the house, such as gardening, plumbing, carpentry, etc., will carry a 7% charge. You will already have noted a GST charge on your cable, hydro, and telephone bills.

Income Tax

There are many tax considerations you should be aware of when buying real estate for personal use or for investment purposes. The following discussion highlights only the common areas to consider. It is not intended to be complete or go into detail. As cautioned before, it is important that you obtain advice from a professional tax accountant familiar with real estate issues before you make a decision on real estate investment. Laws and regulations dealing with taxation matters are complex and constantly changing. Also, you need specific advice based on your personal circumstances. In addition, there are forms, guides, information criteria, and interpretation bulletins available from Canada Revenue Agency (CRA). Make sure you obtain the *Rental Income Guide* for further tax details. Look in the Blue Pages of your telephone directory under "Government of Canada" departments. Check the Web site of the Canada Revenue Agency for information, and forms, at www.cra-arc.gc.ca.

Principal Residence

Most people start their first real estate investment by purchasing their own home to live in. Your principal residence may be a house, apartment, condominium, duplex, trailer, mobile home, or a houseboat.

A property will qualify as a principal residence if it meets various conditions:

√ It is a housing unit, a leasehold interest in a housing unit, or a share of the capital stock of a co-operative housing corporation.

√ You must own the property solely or jointly with another person.

√ You, your spouse, your former spouse, or one of your children ordinarily inhabit it at some point during the year.

√ You consider the property your principal residence.

Tax Benefits of a Principal Residence

One of the key benefits is that the gain you will realize on the sale of your principal residence is not usually subject to tax. For example, if you bought the property originally for $50,000 and sell it for $250,000, you would not pay tax on this increase in value of $200,000.

Renting Out Part of the Principal Residence

It is not uncommon for people to rent out part of their principal residence as an income source or "mortgage helper." Sometimes these rental suites are referred to as "illegal suites." This term refers to the fact that the suite or room rented to someone who is not a relative may contravene existing municipal zoning bylaws in the community in which you reside. The zoning for your home might be "single family," so renting to a tenant, in effect, means that you are arbitrarily converting your home into a multi-family dwelling. The important point to keep in mind is that the federal government does not care whether your rental space contravenes municipal zoning bylaws or not. Municipal bylaws and Revenue Canada tax regulations relate to two separate levels of government. All Revenue Canada cares about is whether you are reporting the income or not in your tax returns.

In practical terms, many municipalities do not enforce the bylaw regulations relating to "illegal suites" if there is a shortage of rental accommodation in the community unless a neighbour complains. In most cases you have a right to appeal if your municipality requests that the tenant vacate your premises. Each situation can vary. If in doubt, contact your lawyer for advice.

If you are renting out one or two rooms of your house to a boarder, it will not interfere with its principal residence status as long as you do not claim capital cost allowance (CCA) on the rental portion. Essentially, CCA means depreciating a portion of the value of the home, excluding land, and deducting that portion as an expense from your income. (CCA is described in more detail in the next section on "Real Estate Investment Property.") In addition, the rental portion is supposed to be minor in relation to the whole house, although in some cases this can be up to 50% or more. You are not supposed to make major structural changes to your house to accommodate tenants. In normal circumstances, you should have nothing to concern yourself about. For peace of mind, speak to your tax accountant if you have any doubts.

If you do claim CCA, a change in use occurs. That rental portion will no longer qualify as a principal residence, and you might have a taxable capital gain on that rental portion. The "change in use" aspect is discussed shortly, and an explanation of capital gains is discussed in the next section on "Real Estate Investment Property."

If you do rent out part of your principal residence, you can deduct many types of expenses from your income. The net effect might be that your expenses (excluding CCA of course) exceed or equal the income, meaning that you have no tax payable to Revenue Canada. The normal expenses would be for things such as interest on your mortgage, property taxes, maintenance and repairs, insurance premiums, light, heat and water, and advertising. Expenses specifically related to the rented part of the building may be claimed in full. However, expenses that relate to the whole property must be apportioned between rental and personal use. You may base the apportionment on square feet/metres or the number of rooms rented in the building, as long as it is done on a reasonable basis. For example, if you rent 4 rooms of your 10-room house, you may deduct the following:

√ 100% of expenses specifically related to the rented rooms, such as the repairs and maintenance of the rooms

√ 40% (4 out of 10 rooms) of expenses that cannot be attributed specifically to the four rented rooms, such as mortgage interest, property taxes, insurance, utilities, and maintenance.

You are supposed to fill out a "Statement of Real Estate Rentals" and included in it with your personal income tax. This form, along with examples, is included in the *Rental Income Guide* referred to earlier. More discussion of types of rental expenses is covered in the description of operating a business out of the home, and in the next section on "Real Estate Investment Property."

Change in Use to or from a Rental Operation

If you were living in your home as a principal residence and then decided to leave and rent out the home, the day you begin to use your residence as a rental property you are deemed to have:

√ disposed of it for proceeds equal to its fair market value at that time, and

√ immediately reacquired it for the same amount.

If your property had qualified as your principal residence every year since you acquired it, any gain you realized on the deemed disposition will be exempt from tax. For example, if you bought the property originally for $75,000 and lived in it and then subsequently decided to rent it out (and not reside in any part of it), and at that time the value was $275,000, you do not have to pay any tax on the capital gain of $200,000. If you sell the property a few years later for $325,000, you would have a taxable capital gain on the difference between $275,000 and $325,000 (e.g., $50,000), minus any appropriate deductions, of course.

There are several ways that you could avoid paying tax on this capital gain, however. First, there is a provision in the income tax legislation that allows you to claim that you have not converted your principal residence to a rental property if you report your rental income, in certain circumstances. You may deduct any allowable expenses incurred, but not claim any CCA on the residence. The effect is that you don't pay any tax when the property is eventually sold.

Generally, the above provision is for a four-year maximum period and due to your leaving for various reasons, such as job relocation. Your intention should be to eventually return to the house. There are special provisions where you can extend that four-year limitation period indefinitely, such as:

√ Your absence results from a relocation required by your employer or your spouse's employer.

√ You and your spouse are not related to the employer.

√ You return to the original house while still with the same employer or within one taxation year after leaving that employer.

√ The original house is located at least 40 kilometres (25 miles) farther from your (or your spouse's) new place of employment than your temporary residence.

Check with your tax accountant to make sure that you make decisions that comply with Revenue Canada regulations. You don't want Revenue Canada to disallow your claim to retain your principal residence status. Tax laws and regulations are always in a state of flux.

If you acquire a property for rental purposes and later begin to use it as your principal residence, you are deemed to have disposed of the property for an amount equal to its fair market value at the time you ceased to use it for rental purposes. However, you may elect to postpone the recognition of any capital gain until you actually dispose of the property. This is assuming you have not claimed CCA. Speak to your tax accountant to get proper advice in advance.

Operating a Business Out of Your Home

Many people, at some point, intend to start part-time or full-time businesses out of their homes. There is a growing trend in this area for various reasons, including eliminating the daily commute to work, lifestyle choice (e.g., to raise a family), retirement opportunity, supplementing salaried income, testing a business idea, or saving on business overhead and thereby reducing financial risk by writing off house-related expenses. There are many different types of home-based businesses. One of them could be managing your real estate investment property, including doing the bookkeeping, etc.

It is important to keep in mind that you need competent tax and legal advice before you start up. Also, you may want to obtain a GST number if you have over $30,000 in income in your business, or are paying GST on items you purchase and want to set off against GST you are charging. Check with your accountant and closest Revenue Canada office.

Revenue Canada allows you to have a business at home without affecting the principal residence status, as long as you don't claim CCA on your home as part of your business operation. You can claim CCA on other non-home business capital expenditures, according to the CCA class. The percentages range from 4% to 100% depreciation in a year. This is explained shortly.

There are numerous categories of expenses that can be deducted depending on the nature of your business. An expense is deductible if its purpose is to earn income, it is not a capital nature (e.g., depreciated over time by using CCA), and is reasonable in the circumstances. Your accountant will advise you as to which are deductible and which are not. Also, if some of the expenses are related to personal use, you are required to deduct that portion from the business expense. Reasonable salaries paid to a spouse and/or children for services rendered to the business are also deductible. The "Statement of Income and Expenses" form from Revenue Canada outlines some of the expenses that you may wish to consider. This form is contained in the *Business and Professional Income Tax Guide* available from Revenue Canada. Your accountant may suggest other expenses that you could be eligible for.

You may only claim expenses for the business use of a workspace in your home if either of the following applies:

√ The work space is your principal place of business for the part-time or full-time self-employed aspect of your career (you could have a salaried job elsewhere; it is not required that you meet people at your home).

√ You use the workspace only to earn income from your business, and it is used on a regular basis for meeting clients, customers, or patients. In this case you could also deduct expenses from an office outside the home.

Also, the expenses you may deduct for the business use of your home cannot exceed the income from the business for which you use the workspace. This means that you must not use these expenses to create or increase your business loss. You may carry forward any expenses that are not deductible in the year and deduct them, subject to the same limitation, in the following year.

To deduct expenses, you take that portion relating to the space used for a home office. For example, you can divide the total number of rooms in the house by the number of rooms used for business to find the percentage of square feet used for business. So if you were using 20% of your home for business purposes, including the basement for storage of inventory, then you would deduct 20% of all your related expenses from your business income.

There are direct and indirect expenses relating to your home business that are deductible in part or in full. Here is a description of the most common expenses. (Refer to Checklist 4 in the Appendix, which is an outline of the home business tax-deductible expenses that you should be familiar with, and discuss expenses with your accountant.) Remember that tax law changes can and do occur from time to time, which could affect any of the following deductions.

Maximizing Expense Deductions

Direct Business Expenses

These are expenses that would benefit only the business part of the home. Some of these costs are depreciated (applying CCA) and others are deducted:

√ *Room Furnishings*

Office furniture and equipment would have to be depreciated (use the CCA schedule from Canada Revenue Agency (CRA). Other items such as office supplies and materials can be deducted.

√ *Remodelling or Decorating Costs*

This would include repairs or renovations done to a room to turn it into an office (e.g., painting, carpentry, floor covering, plumbing, electrical). If you added an extension to your house, that would be covered as well. This should be listed as an improvement and should be depreciated as discussed under "Room Furnishings" above.

Combined Business/Personal Expenses

These are expenses that benefit both the personal and the business parts of the home business, but only the business part is deductible as a business expense. Expenses should be apportioned on a reasonable basis between business and non-business use (e.g., a percentage of the floor space used).

Rent

If you rent a house or apartment and use part of it for business purposes, you may deduct the portion of your rent attributable to business use. For example, you may decide to claim 20% of your apartment or 20% of your home costs as "rent." Common ranges for an apartment would be from 10% to 25%, and for a house between 5% and 25%. It could be more, of course, depending on use.

Mortgage Interest

You can deduct the percentage of interest expense related to use of your home for business. For example, if your monthly mortgage payments are $2,000, generally about 99% of that payment is interest and 1% goes toward the principal. This would be the case, especially in the first three years of the mortgage (assuming it is a 20-year amortization period). Therefore, for practical purposes, let's assume the interest portion is $2,000. If you were claiming 20% of your house as business-use related, you would claim $400 per month × 12 months, which would equal $4,800 a year, as a business expense.

Insurance Premiums

You can deduct that portion of insurance expense that relates to your business (e.g., fire, theft, liability coverage). If you were claiming 20% usage of your house or apartment, you would claim that portion of the premium as a business expense.

Depreciation of Your Home

You can claim depreciation on the building portion (not land portion) of your home. This is a CCA category, as explained earlier. There are different percentage rates depending on the item being depreciated. You can get these rates from Revenue Canada. A house would normally be 4%, which means that you take 4% of the depreciated balance each year as a starting point. If the house was worth $100,000, that would be $4,000 depreciation in the first year. The second year would be $100,000 less $4,000, which would equal a $96,000 base. Four percent of that amount would therefore be a $3,840 starting point in the second year. If you were claiming 10% of the house was related to business use, you would claim $400 in year one and $384 in year two, for example.

In practical terms, most home business owners do not claim CCA. The reason is that if you later dispose of the property, a taxable capital gain could arise on the portion of the property that you used for business purposes. You could also be subject to recapture (having to claim on the following year's tax return as income) of the CCA previously claimed. If you are interested in claiming depreciation, speak to your accountant and have these concepts explained in further detail.

Utilities

You can deduct the portion of your expenses related to business (e.g., 20%) for oil, gas, electrical, and water costs.

Home Maintenance

You can deduct a portion of your expenses for labour and material for house maintenance and repairs for business use (e.g., furnace or roof repair). You cannot claim, though, for your own labour. You can pay other family members for labour.

Services

You can deduct a portion of municipal or private services such as snow and trash removal, yard maintenance, etc., for business use.

Automobile

If your auto is used for personal and business travel, you need to take a portion of the expenses and depreciation relating to business use. Incidentally, Revenue Canada has put a ceiling of $30,000 plus GST plus PST on the value of your car, regardless of its market value. Check with your accountant as tax legislation can change at any time. In addition to depreciation, you can claim a portion of all other car-related expenses, such as oil, gas, repairs, insurance, maintenance, and interest, relating to financing costs.

Telephone

If you have a separate telephone and business line, the full amount of costs is deductible (e.g., monthly service charge). If you were using your residence phone for business use, you would deduct the portion of costs that is business related. All long-distance charges that are business related are, of course, totally deductible. Other phone-related costs that you could deduct (in full or in part) would be installation costs, telephone equipment, answering machine, or answering service.

Entertainment and Meals

Generally you may deduct costs incurred for business meals and for entertaining business associates if you incur these expenses in the ordinary course of business. However, Revenue Canada will accept a claim for only 50% of entertainment and meal expenses.

Travel

If you travel to go to conferences, conventions, or trade shows, or conduct other business activities relating to being a landlord or your real estate investments, you can write off the costs of travel, e.g., airfare and accommodation. If the trip combined personal and business activities, you would take a percentage that was the business portion, e.g., 75%.

Child Care Expenses

If you are self-employed and need to pay someone to care for your child so you can work, it may be possible to claim an expense deduction for a portion or all of the cost.

The expenses discussed are just some of the many tax deductions that may be available to you. As recommended earlier, refer to Checklist 4 for a detailed list of possible expense deductions. Remember, you may be able to claim 100% of the cost of the expense or a depreciated amount over time, depending on the item.

To clarify what you can deduct and how to do it, as well as other home business tax issues, speak to your accountant. It is also very important that you speak with your lawyer about the various types of legal issues when starting a business. (Chapter 6: Understanding the Legal Aspects gives an overview of the three main types of legal structures.)

Keeping Records

If you are renting out part of your principal residence to a tenant, or intend to have a home-based business, make sure that you keep detailed records of all money collected and paid out. Purchases and operating expenses must be supported by invoices, receipts, contracts, or other documents.

You do not need to submit these records when you file your return. If you do not keep receipts or other vouchers to support your expenses, all or part of the expenses claimed may be disallowed. (More information on recordkeeping is covered Chapter 10: Managing Your Property.)

Real Estate Investment Property

It is important to understand the concepts and options outlined in this section. It will save you time when discussing the issues with your accountant and enhance your decision making. The following is only an overview to highlight some of the key areas. By the time you finish reading this section, you will appreciate the need and benefit of using professional advisers to maximize your tax savings and net after-tax profit.

Capital Gains or Income

Many investors assume that when property is sold for a profit, the profit will be treated as a capital gain for income-tax purposes. This would result in a lower tax rate than other types of income. You have to be very careful, though, as Revenue Canada could consider the profit as regular income at regular tax rates.

Capital gains are usually taxed at 50% of the capital gain. In other words, if you bought a property for $100,000 and sold it for $225,000, but after all expenses were taken into account you net $200,000, the net profit (gain) would be approximately $100,000. You would normally have to pay tax on 50% of the net gain, e.g., $50,000. If the profit were deemed to be income instead of a capital gain, you would have to pay tax on 100% of the amount; that is, on the full $100,000.

Revenue Canada applies various types of criteria to determine whether the profit is deemed to be a capital gain from a real estate investment, or income from a business of speculating in real estate without any investment intent. Each situation depends on the individual circumstances, so make sure you get tax advice from a professional accountant in advance.

For example, if you purchased a property with the intention of selling it as soon as possible in a "hot" real estate market, the profit from that could be deemed to be income. In other words, you "flipped" the property or sold your rights under an agreement of purchase and sale. Another example would be a situation in which a person bought vacant land with the intention of selling it quickly. The key tests are what your original intent was when you purchased the property, the facts and the circumstances, and how quickly you sold it. There are many credible and logical reasons to refute the income theory and argue that it should be considered a capital gain. It would be very frustrating to plan on specific after-tax money from a sale, and then find that you owe more money to Revenue Canada than you had planned. That is why you need good tax planning and advice from a professional accountant, a point that is reinforced throughout this chapter.

Business Income or Property Income?

Depending on the circumstances, rental income may be income from either a business or property. There are certain factors to be considered in determining if a rental operation is a source of business income or a source of property income. Revenue Canada recognizes as businesses very few rental operations carried on by individuals. One notable exception is when renting real property is incidental to, or part of, your business. In such cases, the rental activity is regarded as forming part of your business income or loss.

If your rental operation is not part of, or incidental to, an existing business, the number and kinds of services that you provide for your tenants will determine if you are earning income from a business or from property. Generally you are considered to be earning income from property if you merely rent space and provide basic services such as:

√ heat

√ light

√ water

√ elevators

√ parking

√ laundry facilities

√ general maintenance of the property.

However, if you provide services to tenants in addition to those basic services that have come to be considered part of property rental, you may be carrying on a business rather than merely renting property. For example, as the landlord of a building, your rental operation would be considered a rental business in the following situation:

√ You rent apartments and, in addition to providing your tenants with the basic services listed above, you supply meals and drinks, operate a restaurant or lounge on the premises, or provide maid or linen services.

The more services you provide, the greater the likelihood that your rental operation is a business. However, the following factors are *not* to be taken into account when determining whether a rental operation is a business:

√ the size or number of properties you are renting

√ the amount of time you spend on managing or supervising the properties

√ whether the accommodation is rented furnished or unfurnished.

If two or more individuals participate in a rental operation, the same factors must be considered in determining whether the rental operation is a source of business income or property income. In the case of a legal partnership, if all factors indicate that your rental operation is not a business, your income from the operation is treated as property income, even though partnership income usually relates to a business operation.

Capital Expenses

These expenses are usually outlays that provide a lasting benefit beyond the current year. This would include such expenses as purchasing or improving your property. Generally, capital expenditures are not fully deductible in the year they are incurred. Instead, you may deduct a portion of their cost each year as capital cost allowance (CCA). This percentage may vary between 4% and 100% each year. In effect, you are depreciating the value of the item according to the CCA classification table, and writing off the depreciated amount against your rental income.

You cannot claim CCA on the cost of land, as it is not a depreciable property. On the contrary, as an investor, it is your hope and intention that the property will appreciate!

Revenue Canada considers the following types of expenses as capital in nature:

√ the purchase of rental property

√ legal fees and other costs in connection with the purchase of property

√ the cost of furniture and equipment rented with the property

√ major repairs and expenditures that extend the useful life of your property, or improve it beyond its original condition.

Here are some of the guidelines that Revenue Canada uses in determining whether an expense is capital or current in nature. A discussion of current expenses follows shortly.

Maintenance or Betterment

An expense that merely restores a property to its original condition is usually a current expense. However, an expenditure that materially improves a property beyond its original condition is likely a capital outlay. For example, the cost of reinforcing wooden steps would be a current expense. If you replaced the wooden steps with concrete steps instead, the expenditure would be capital in nature.

Integral Part or Separate Asset

The cost of repairing an integral part of a property is a current expense. However, the cost of replacing the whole property or even a considerable part of it is a capital outlay. For instance, since electrical wiring is an integral part of a building, an amount spent to rewire would normally be considered a current expense, if it were not a betterment. The purchase and installation of air conditioning window units in a building that was not previously air conditioned, however, is a capital expenditure because the units are separate assets and not integral parts of the building.

Enduring Benefit

A capital expenditure generally provides a lasting benefit or advantage. On the other hand, a current expense is one that usually recurs after a relatively short period. The installation of an air conditioning system in a building is an example of a capital expenditure.

Relative Value

An additional factor that you may have to consider is the cost of the expenditure in relation to the value of the property. For example, while a filter for a furnace could be considered a separate asset, it is logical to treat its cost as a current expense. If you replace the furnace itself, you acquire a separate asset of substantial value in relation to the building where the furnace is installed. The cost of the furnace is therefore a capital expenditure. On the other hand, you might spend a substantial amount for normal maintenance and repair work to your property all at one time. If this expenditure was for normal maintenance that for some reason was not done on an ongoing basis, it is nevertheless a maintenance expense and, as such, would be deductible as a current expense.

Obtain professional tax advice on the issue of capital expenses before making decisions.

Current Expenses

These types of outlays are usually ones that benefit the current year only, e.g., repairs made to maintain the rental property in the same condition it was in when you originally bought it. You may deduct current expenses from your gross rental income in the year you incur them. Current expenses are also referred to as operating expenses.

The following is a list of typical costs associated with renting a property. These are general guidelines only. You may deduct these expenses from your gross rental income in the year they are incurred unless otherwise stated. As mentioned many times, tax rules can change, so obtain current tax advice. In addition, there may be various tax-planning options on which your accountant can advise you.

Accounting Fees

Accounting fees include amounts paid for bookkeeping services, auditing books and records, and preparing financial statements.

Advertising

Amounts paid for advertising that you have space available to rent.

Capital Expenditures

Capital expenditures are not fully deductible in the year they are incurred. This was discussed in the previous section on page 225.

Commissions

Amounts paid or payable to agents for collecting rents or finding new tenants.

Computer-Related Expenses

As you are probably using a computer to manage your properties, doing research on the Internet, or doing letters or e-mailing, all related directly or indirectly to your business, investment, or landlord activities, you should be entitled to deduct all the related costs, for example, copy paper and toner, high-speed Internet connection, computer repairs, printer, and fax machine.

Condominium Expenses

If you earn rental income from a condominium unit, you are entitled to deduct any expenses that are normally deductible from rental income. These may include condominium fees representing your share of the upkeep and maintenance of the common property, and other rental expenses you incur for the upkeep and maintenance of the unit.

Education

If you are spending money to keep current with your landlord, investment, or business activities, you would be able to write off that legitimate expense to keep informed on issues of interest and to protect your investment and risk, for example, taking seminars or courses; attending conferences, conventions, and trade shows in town or out of town; subscribing to newspapers, magazines, newsletters; buying books and CDs, related directly or indirectly to your business or investment activities, cable costs for your TV, which you are using as a medium for education and so on.

Finder's Fee

A finder's fee is an expense incurred for arranging a mortgage or loan for the purpose of purchasing or improving the rental property. The expense is deductible in equal portions over five years. However, if you repay the mortgage or loan before the end of the five-year period, you can deduct any undeducted balance in the year of repayment.

Insurance

Premiums for current insurance coverage on your rental property are deductible in the year. If your policy provides coverage for more than one year, you may deduct only the current-year premiums.

Interest

Interest on money borrowed to purchase or improve your rental property is deductible. You may also deduct interest paid to tenants on rental deposits. However, if you refinance your rental property to obtain funds for purposes other than the acquisition or improvement of your rental property, you may not deduct the interest against your rental income.

Landscaping

The cost of landscaping the grounds around your rental property is deductible in the year of payment.

Lease Cancellation Payments

These are amounts paid or payable to tenants to obtain cancellation of their leases. You must amortize the payments over the remaining life of the lease, including renewals, to a maximum of 40 years. If you dispose of the property, the tax treatment will vary, depending on the particular circumstances.

Legal Expenses

Fees incurred for legal services such as lease preparation or collection of overdue rents are deductible. However, legal fees incurred for the purchase or sale of your rental property are not deductible against your gross rental income. Instead, legal fees you incurred to acquire your rental property are treated as part of your cost of the property. When you sell the rental property, any legal fees you incurred in connection with the sale may be deducted from the proceeds of disposition when calculating your gain or loss.

Maintenance and Repairs

If you do the repairs yourself, you can deduct the cost of the materials. The value of your own labour is not generally deductible unless you structure your services with the advice of a professional accountant. There are various creative and legitimate ways of getting paid for your services.

Mortgage Payments

Repayments of the principal portion of your mortgage or loan to purchase or improve your rental property are not deductible. See "Interest" regarding the interest portion of your mortgage.

Motor Vehicle Expenses

Travel expenses you incur to collect rents are considered personal expenses and are usually not deductible. However, reasonable travelling expenses may be deductible if incurred in certain circumstances. For example, if you receive income from only one rental property that is located in the general area where you live, you may deduct motor vehicle expenses to the extent you personally do part or all of the necessary repairs and maintenance on the property, and incur the expenses transporting tools and materials to the rental property.

If you own two or more rental properties, you may deduct reasonable motor vehicle expenses incurred for the purpose of collecting rents, supervising repairs, or generally providing management of the properties. This is the case whether your rental properties are located in or outside the general area where you live. However, technically the properties must be located in at least two different sites away from your residence for your motor vehicle expenses to be deductible.

Office Expenses

Expenses for items of stationery such as journals, receipt books, and photocopying, pens, printer paper and toner and stamps, are deductible.

Penalties

Amounts paid for early retirement of your mortgage (even on its renewal) are not deductible. Penalties for the late filing of your income tax return are also not deductible.

Property Taxes

They are deductible if assessed by a province, territory, or municipality and relate to your rental property.

Salaries and Wages

Amounts paid or payable to superintendents, maintenance personnel, and others employed by you for the operation or supervision of your rental property are deductible. Your professional accountant should be able to suggest creative and legitimate ways of structuring your contribution, so that your services would be legitimately deductible as an expense—if you incorporate a management company, for example, and your company bills for your services that you are providing to it.

Tax Return Preparation

Fees and expenses for advice and assistance in preparing and filing tax returns are deductible when the nature of your rental operation is such that it is a normal part of operations to obtain legal and accounting services.

Travelling Expenses

Costs of travel related to your landlord and investment activities are deductible, for example, if you are checking out other potential properties or land to buy, and need to fly to the location. Possibly you want to attend a trade show, conference, or convention out of town, which is related directly or indirectly to your real estate investment and management activities.

Utilities

Utilities are deductible if your rental arrangement specifies that you will pay for the lights, heat, water, or cable used by your tenants.

Tax Implications of the Purchase Structure When Buying an Apartment Building

There are several important tax implications to the way you structure the purchase of a revenue property, such as an apartment building. Here are some examples to illustrate the point and to discuss with your accountant.

Allocating Purchase Price Value

There are tax implications to the way you structure the purchase price. In other words, the purchase price could consist of several components such as land, building chattels (e.g., appliances), inventory (e.g., supplies), and possibly goodwill. Goodwill is an intangible concept; essentially it is the value of the positive image or reputation that the investment property (e.g., an apartment building) enjoys. This has implications for keeping vacancy low and tenancy high. Negotiations relating to the purchase should include how you are going to apportion the purchase price, considering the above points. That is why you want to make sure you receive tax advice before you submit your offer. Once you have negotiated the terms of the offer, it is more difficult to revise them to your benefit.

If you are purchasing an apartment building for $800,000, for example, you may want to allocate as high a value for the land as realistically possible in the circumstances, say, $600,000. That would mean you have less of a capital gain on your eventual sale than if you valued the land on purchase at $300,000. If you did not agree in writing at the time of the original purchase and eventual sale as to the value of the land portion, you could have problems in convincing Revenue Canada as to the capital gain portion if you were ever audited.

Another example is the value allocated for the building and for chattels. These two main categories can be depreciated over time, the amount of depreciation depending on the CCA classification of the building or land. The higher the value allocated for the building or chattels, the greater the amount of depreciation you could claim after you have purchased the property. These three examples—land, building, and chattels—are only a few of the issues you need to discuss with your tax accountant before making an offer. Basically you want to agree to a purchase allocation price package that benefits your interests. Conversely, if you are selling the revenue property, you want to negotiate quite a different allocation-of-value package. It all comes down to the tax implications, in terms of taxes saved or deferred.

Purchasing the Shares or Assets of a Corporate Vendor

If you are buying an apartment building, for example, the vendor could be an individual or a limited liability company (corporation). There are tax implications if you are buying the shares or assets of that corporation. If you are buying the shares of the company, here are the implications relative to buying the assets:

√ You would be assuming any liability that the company has, e.g., debts owing or pending lawsuits. If you bought the assets (e.g., land, building, and chattels), you would not have this liability.

√ If the company has losses from previous years that have not yet been used up to set off against future revenue property income, you could have a bonus in that regard, depending on the nature and amount of unclaimed losses. If you bought the assets as described earlier, you would not have this loss available to you.

√ You would probably be able to avoid paying the property purchase tax applicable in several provinces. The tax is normally triggered and payable upon transfer of title of the property. If you buy the shares of the corporation, that does not change the title on the property. The same corporation shows up as owner. If you bought the assets, as described earlier, you would have to pay the tax.

√ You could end up losing money in terms of depreciation available. The corporation could have depreciated most of its depreciable assets such as building and chattels. Therefore, you would not have that depreciation benefit. If you bought the assets, as described earlier, you could negotiate the value of the building and chattels when allocating the purchase price. You could then start depreciating them at that higher value, thereby having more tax deductions.

√ You could end up losing money in terms of the value of the land. The land in terms of the corporation's valuation of it could be artificially low. You could therefore have a higher capital gain tax to pay if a future purchaser wanted to buy the apartment building assets from you and wanted to have a current market value on the land at that time.

Purchasing in a Personal or Corporate Name

Whether you purchase the apartment building in your own name or with others, or through a limited company (corporation), has considerable tax implications. You could purchase the shares or assets of the apartment owner personally or with your own corporation. (Refer to Chapter 6: Understanding the Legal Aspects for an explanation of the available options.)

Soft Costs

Certain outlays made in connection with the construction, renovation, or alteration of a building to make it rentable are referred to as "soft costs," which include interest, legal fees, accounting fees, and property taxes.

Soft costs may be incurred during construction, renovation, or alteration of a building or outside that period, as long as the outlays are attributable to that period. You must treat soft costs as capital expenditures until the work is completed, or until all or substantially all of the building is rented, whichever comes first.

If you are going to renovate a building, you should discuss with your tax accountant which costs during the period of renovation you can claim as an expense, and which have to be capitalized, e.g., would be deemed capital expenditures. Current and capital expenses were discussed earlier (page 225).

Vacant Land

If you are holding vacant land for investment purposes, there are various tax rules that may restrict the deduction of interest on borrowed money used to buy the land, and property taxes paid on the land. If you are not earning rental income from the vacant land, Revenue Canada will probably consider your costs as capital expenditures and therefore they would be added on to the original cost of the property on sale. Because of this approach, when the property is sold, the cost for tax purposes is higher than it otherwise would be and therefore the capital gain is lower.

On the other hand, you may decide to rent or lease out the vacant property, e.g., to a farmer, in order to generate revenue. If you earn rental income from the vacant land, there are limitations to the amount you may deduct for interest on money borrowed to acquire the land, as well as property taxes and related land assessments. Your deduction is restricted to the amount of rental income remaining after you have deducted all other expenses from your rental income. You cannot create or increase a rental loss, nor can you reduce other sources of income by claiming a deduction for the above expenses. However, if you are unable to deduct a portion of the expenses because of the limitation, you may add the undeducted portion to the cost of the land.

The above are general guidelines. Check with your tax accountant for specific and current advice.

Investing in Real Estate in the United States

Tax issues can be very confusing to many Canadians. If you own property or other investments in the U.S., it can become quite complex. That is because the tax laws of both countries could affect you. In the United States, for example, you could be liable under certain circumstances for income tax, capital gains tax, estate tax, and gift tax.

Rental Income from U.S. Real Estate

You may be renting out your U.S. property part-time or full-time. As a non-resident "alien," you are subject to U.S. income tax on the rental income.

Tax on Gross Rental Income

The rents you receive are subject to a 30% non-resident withholding tax, which your tenant or property management agent is required to deduct and remit to the IRS. It doesn't matter if the tenants are Canadians or other non-residents of the United States, or if the rent was paid to you while you were in Canada. The Canada–U.S. Tax Treaty allows the United States to tax income from real estate with no reduction in the general withholding rate. Rental income is subject to a flat 30% tax on gross income, with no expenses or deductions allowed. The 30% withholding tax therefore equals the flat tax rate.

Tax on Net Rental Income

Since a tax rate of 30% of gross income is a high rate, you may prefer to pay tax on net income after taking all deductible expenses. This step results in reduced tax and possibly no tax. The Internal Revenue Service (IRS) permits this option if you choose to permanently treat rental income as income that is effectively connected with the conduct of a U.S. trade or business. You are then able to claim expenses related to owning and operating a rental property during the rental period, for example, mortgage interest, property tax, utilities, insurance, and maintenance. You can also deduct an amount for depreciation of the building. However, the IRS permits only individuals (rather than corporations) to deduct the mortgage or loan interest relating to the rental property if the debt is secured by the rental property or other business property. If you borrow the funds in Canada, secured by your Canadian assets, you would not technically be able to deduct that interest on your U.S. tax return. Obtain strategic tax-planning advice on this issue.

Selling U.S. Real Estate

If you are a non-resident alien, any gain or loss that results from a sale or disposition of your U.S. real estate has tax-reporting implications. The purchaser or agent of the purchaser is generally required to withhold 10% of the gross sale price at the time the sale transaction is completed and the balance of payment is made. The 10% holdback is to be forwarded to the IRS as a non-resident withholding tax credit.

Waiver of Withholding Tax

If you anticipate that the U.S. tax payable would be less than the 10% withheld, you can apply to the IRS in advance to have the withholding tax reduced or eliminated by completing a withholding certificate. If the 10% had already been paid, you would still be entitled to a refund after you filed your U.S. tax return if the 10% was greater than the amount due.

You may be exempt from withholding tax if the purchase price of your property is less than U.S. $300,000 and the buyer intends to use the property as a residence at least half of the time it is used over the subsequent two-year period. The buyer does not have to be a U.S. citizen or resident or use the property as a principal residence. To obtain this type of exemption, the buyer must sign an affidavit setting out the facts related above. If the purchase price is over U.S. $300,000 or the buyer is unwilling or unable to sign the affidavit, you can request the waiver from withholding discussed in the previous paragraph.

Reporting to Revenue Canada

Under the *Income Tax Act,* you are required to report all your income and capital gains from your worldwide activities to Revenue Canada. You pay tax on all your financial activities, no matter where the activities occurred. However, Canada has tax treaties with many countries throughout the world, for example the U.S. The implication for a Canadian taxpayer is that there would be a foreign tax credit, so that you are not paying tax twice, i.e., in both countries. For example, if you paid $10,000 tax in the U.S. on the sale of a property there, you would receive that as a credit for whatever tax you owed in Canada for the taxable capital gains on the sale of the property.

U.S. Internal Revenue Service (IRS) Shares Information with Revenue Canada

The IRS and Revenue Canada's ability to exchange data on Canadian and U.S. taxpayers by computer has increased dramatically now that certain Canadians are required to have a U.S. taxpayer identification number (ITIN).

When you apply for your ITIN, you must provide some brief but very personal information to the IRS. Of course you must provide your name, and your name at birth, if different. In addition, you must provide your address in Canada. Post office boxes and care-of addresses are not allowed. Your date and place of birth are also required, along with your sex, your father's complete name, and your mother's maiden name. In addition, you are asked for your passport number and U.S. visa number, if any.

You are also asked for your Canadian social insurance number. You can imagine the potential co-operation between the IRS and Revenue Canada this will facilitate. The IRS has a fast, sophisticated computerized cross-referencing capability between your U.S and Canadian taxpayer numbers. For example, information on certain U.S. tax-related activities in which you are involved, such as the sale or rental of U.S. real estate, or your claim for a U.S. tax refund on U.S. investment or pension income can be transmitted to Revenue Canada by computer, giving Revenue Canada your name, your Canadian address, and your Canadian social insurance number.

Need to Obtain Expert Tax Advice

Obtain professional tax advice on IRS filing requirements from an accountant who specializes in U.S. and cross-border tax and financial planning issues and strategies. Dealing with Canadian and U.S. tax matters is complex, and laws and regulations are always changing. There is an excellent cross-border financial planning and tax newsletter for Canadians written by Richard Brunton, CPA. His firm provides tax and financial planning consultations to Canada. You can get more information from his site at www.taxintl.com.

Tax Effects on Different Legal Structures

√ If you are the sole proprietor of your business, your salary is included as an expense. The profits that you earn in your business constitute your personal income and are taxable as such in that taxation year. When you file your personal income tax return, you have to complete the "Statement of Income and Expenses," available on request from Revenue Canada. It outlines the basic sources of income and type of expenses and allowances.

√ If your business is a partnership, all partners are taxed on their salaries and their share of the profits, whether withdrawn or not. The same "Statement of Income and Expenses" form is used for a partnership, although you must also provide the percentage share of profit or loss that is being declared.

√ A corporation files a corporate tax return, which is separate and distinct from the individuals involved in the company. It is therefore not filed with the personal income tax return, as with a proprietorship or partnership.

√ A corporation in Canada is entitled to a small business tax deduction, assuming various conditions are met, such as generating an active business income. This deduction, which is approximately one-half the regular tax rate, is designed to help Canadian-controlled private companies accumulate capital for business expansion. Many provinces also allow a provincial tax rate reduction as well as other incentives. An active business, as the name implies, is one in which people are actively generating income, rather than passively receiving income.

For more detail on the above three business structure options, refer to Chapter 6: Understanding the Legal Aspects.

What Constitutes an Expense?

√ An expense is tax-deductible if its purpose is to earn income; it is not of a capital nature; and it is reasonable in the circumstances. A capital expense means an asset that is depreciated over a period of time according to the capital cost allowance (CCA) class interest deduction. The allowance must not exceed the maximum rate allowable in any year. The percentages range from 4% to 100% depreciation in a year. Obtain a copy of these CCA categories from CRA.

√ Your accountant will advise you as to which categories of expenses are deductible in your particular business and which are not. Also, if some of the expenses are related to personal use, you are supposed to deduct that portion from the business expense. Reasonable remuneration paid to spouses or partners for service rendered to the business is also deductible. The "Statement of Income and Expenses" from Revenue Canada outlines some of the expenses to consider. Your accountant can suggest other expenses you could be eligible to claim.

Keeping Records

If you are investing in real estate or are generating revenue from your investment, keeping detailed records is essential. Make sure that you have all the documents necessary to verify money collected and paid out. This includes all receipts, invoices, and contracts. If you don't have the proper documents, your claim could be disallowed by Revenue Canada. You do not need to submit these records when you file your return. Revenue Canada requires you to report rental income using the accrual method. This means that:

√ Rents are included in income for the year in which they are due, whether or not you received them in that year, and

√ Allowable expenses are deducted in the year they are incurred, regardless of when you actually made the payments.

Refer to Chapter 10: Managing Your Property for more information.

Summary

This chapter discussed the wide range of taxes that you need to be aware of. Topics covered also include practical ways of saving on taxes, maximizing your deductions, pitfalls to avoid, tax planning strategies, and money-saving tips. The need to select the right professional accountant and obtain expert tax advice is critical to reaching your short- and long-term financial goals and minimizing the risk.

Insurance is another key aspect to owning property and is discussed next.

CHAPTER 8

Understanding the Insurance Aspects

Although it is possible to buy too much insurance, many people don't purchase enough or the right type of insurance. Considering the time, energy, commitment, and resources that you are putting into your business venture as a real estate investor, you want to minimize the inherent risk by making sure you have adequate insurance protection. There will be references to business-related insurance. If you are investing in, and possibly managing, residential real estate, you are operating a business.

This chapter will cover a wide range of types of insurance to enhance your awareness and the quality of your decision making. The discussion will include organizing your insurance program for all your needs, including property and general insurance. Then the different types of property insurance coverage will be explained, followed by the different types of general insurance that are important to consider for your total protection, as well as life and disability insurance. You need to look at your complete insurance picture. Tips to follow and pitfalls to avoid will also be discussed. There is a list of Web sites of interest for your further research.

Organizing Your Insurance Program

It is important to consider all criteria to determine the best type of insurance for you and your business. Your goal should be adequate coverage. That can be achieved by periodic review of the risk you are insuring for and by keeping your insurance representative informed of any changes in your business that could affect the adequacy or enforceability of your coverage. Such changes could include additional equipment purchases, extensions to your property, the business use of your personal car, or starting a home-based business.

The following advice will help you plan an insurance program.

Assess your business and identify the likely risk exposure:

√ cover your largest risk(s) first

√ determine the magnitude of loss that the business can bear without financial difficulty, and use your premium dollar where the protection need is greatest

√ insure the correct risk.

Decide which of these three kinds of protection will work best for each risk:

√ absorbing the risk (e.g., budgeting to cover loss or expense without getting insurance)

√ minimizing the risk (e.g., reducing the factor that could contribute to the risks, rather than getting insurance)

√ insuring against the risk with commercial insurance.

Reducing Cost of Insurance

Use every means possible to reduce the cost of insurance:

√ Negotiate for lower premiums if your loss experience is low or if you have had no claims.

√ Increase deductibles as much as you can if you need the protection, but can't afford a low deductible premium.

√ Shop around for comparable rates and analyze insurance terms and provisions offered by different insurance companies. Try to get a minimum of three comparative quotes.

√ Avoid duplication of insurance; have one agent handle all your business insurance if possible and practical. However, as there are different categories of insurance, e.g., property, general, life and health, you would most likely have two different brokers.

√ Ask about the types of discounts available, e.g., for age, monitored fire alarm system, security alarm system.

√ Check out group insurance coverage at lower rates from various membership organizations such as the Chamber of Commerce or Board of Trade.

√ If you have a financial planner, ask him or her about different types of life, health, and disability insurance coverage. Generally, financial planners do not deal with property insurance, but could recommend some brokers they know.

√ Incorporate if necessary to further reduce personal liability.

Selecting an Insurance Broker

√ Refer to the section on "Selecting an Insurance Broker" in Chapter 4: Selecting Your Advisory Team.

√ For property and business-related insurance, refer to the Web site of the Insurance Brokers Association of Canada (www.ibac.ca) for a list of members to obtain comparative quotes.

√ For life and health-related insurance, refer to the Web site of the Canadian Life and Health Insurance Association (www.clhia.ca) for a list of members and helpful consumer information.

Regular reviews of risk exposure can help avoid overlaps and gaps in coverage, and thereby keep your risk and premiums lower. This is especially important if your real estate investment and management business is growing. Reviews can also help you keep current with inflation.

Types of Property Coverage

When you are buying real estate for personal use, investment, or rental purposes, it is important to understand the jargon of the property insurance trade, and how premiums are determined and risk assessed. This will enhance the quality of your decision making, improve your negotiating skills, and save you money. It will also protect you from having inadequate insurance coverage or running the risk that a claim could be denied. Here is an overview of the key concepts.

Inflation Allowance

This coverage protects you against inflation by automatically increasing the amount of your insurance during the term of your policy without increasing your premium. On renewal, the insurance company will automatically adjust the amount of your insurance to reflect the annual inflation rate. The premium you pay for your renewal will be based on those adjusted amounts of insurance.

Inflation allowance coverage will not fully protect you if you make an addition to your building or if you acquire additional personal property. This is why you need to review the amount of your insurance every year to make sure it is adequate.

Special Limits of Insurance

The contents of your dwelling are referred to as "Personal Property." Some types of personal property insurance such as jewellery, furs, and money have "Special Limits of Insurance." This is the maximum the insurer will pay for those types of property. If these limits are not sufficient for your needs, you can purchase additional insurance.

Your policy automatically includes some additional coverage to provide you with more complete protection. The individual types of coverage that are included are listed in the section "Additional Coverage."

Insured Perils

A peril is something negative that can happen, such as a fire or theft. Some policies protect you against only those perils that are listed in your policy. Other policies protect you against "all risks" ("risk" is another word for peril). This means you are protected against most perils.

All insurance policies have exclusions. Even if you have selected "all risks" coverage, this does not mean that "everything" is covered. It is important that you read the exclusions carefully in order to understand the types of losses that are not covered by your policy. For example, floods and earthquakes may not be covered if you reside in a high-risk location for these types of perils.

Loss or Damage Not Insured

This is the "fine print," the section that tells you what is not covered. They are also known as "exclusions." Exclusions are necessary to make sure that the insurance company does not pay for the types of losses that are inevitable (e.g., wear and tear), uninsurable (e.g., war), or for which other specific policy forms are available to provide coverage (e.g., automobiles).

Basis of Claim Settlement

This section describes how the insurer will settle your loss. It's the real test of the value of your policy and the reason why you purchased insurance.

Replacement Cost

You should purchase replacement-cost coverage for your property. This is particularly important for your personal property (e.g., the contents of your dwelling and personal effects). Otherwise the basis of settlement will be "actual cash value," which means that depreciation is applied to the damaged property when establishing the values. You therefore would get less money, possibly considerably less.

"New for old" coverage is available. All you have to do is ask for "replacement-cost coverage" and then make sure that your amounts of insurance are sufficient to replace your property at today's prices.

Guaranteed Replacement Cost

This is one of the most important types of coverage available to a homeowner. You can qualify for this coverage by insuring your home to 100% of its full replacement value. If you do, then the insurance company will pay the full claim, even if it is more than the amount of insurance on the building. Make sure this is shown on your policy.

The guaranteed replacement cost coverage applies only to your building, not your personal property.

There is usually an important exclusion. Many insurance companies won't pay more than the amount of insurance if the reason the claim exceeds that amount is the result of any law regulating the construction of buildings. Check this out.

Bylaws

Some municipalities have laws that govern the height of a house, what materials you have to use, or even where you can build it. These are known as bylaws. If the insurance company has to rebuild your house to different standards, this can increase the amount of your claim significantly.

Your policy doesn't cover this increased cost because the insurance company has no way of knowing which laws may apply in your municipality, but you can find out. Then make sure that your amounts of insurance are high enough to cover the increased cost, or increase them if necessary, and ask for a bylaws coverage endorsement. It'll cost a bit more now, but it can save you a lot later.

Deductible

There is a deductible and the amount is shown on the coverage summary page of your policy. It means that you pay that amount for most claims, for example, $250 or $500. The insurance company pays the rest.

As you can imagine, the cost to investigate and settle a claim can be considerable, often out of proportion when the size of the claim is relatively small. These expenses are reflected in the premiums you pay. By using deductibles to eliminate small claims, the insurance company can save on expenses and therefore offer insurance at lower premiums.

Conditions

This is a very important part of your policy. It sets out the mutual rights and obligations of the insurer and the insured. This section governs how and when a policy may be cancelled, as well as your obligations after a loss has occurred.

Purchasing Adequate Amounts of Insurance

Purchasing adequate amounts of insurance that reflect the full replacement value of everything you own is without a doubt the single most important thing you can do to protect yourself. The penalty is that insurance companies will not pay more than the amounts of insurance you have purchased, so it is up to you to make sure the coverage is adequate and realistic. Review it annually.

Establish how much it would cost to rebuild the home from scratch. This is the amount for which you should insure the house, in order to make sure that you are fully protected.

If you put an addition onto the house or carry out major renovations, you should recalculate the replacement value, as your current amount of insurance doesn't take this into consideration. Notify your insurance company representative. The inflation allowance feature of your policy does protect you against normal inflation, but is not sufficient to cover major changes.

You may also want to check with municipal authorities to see whether there are any bylaws that govern the construction of houses in your area, as you may need a higher amount of insurance so that the reconstruction of your home will be fully covered.

Contents Coverage

If you are using the home personally, the following discussion relates to personal use. Your policy provides coverage for your contents. You should make sure that this amount is enough to replace all your possessions at today's prices. If the home is rented to a tenant, they are responsible for obtaining tenant's insurance. You should make that a condition of any rental agreement.

If you have a claim, the insurance company will ask you to compile a complete list of everything that you have lost. Ideally, you should maintain an inventory of everything, furniture, appliances, clothes, and other possessions. Estimating what it would cost you to replace them is a good way to check if the amount of insurance you carry is enough.

At the very least you should keep the receipts for all major purchases in a safe place. Another good idea is to take pictures of your contents or make a video of everything by walking from room to room. In addition, most insurance companies will provide you with a checklist, so you can compile a list of your contents. This may seem like a chore right now, but it can really save time and aggravation if you do have a claim.

As you could lose your inventory or photographic evidence in a major loss, you should store your records away from your house. The best place is a safety deposit box. Whatever method you use, remember that you should update it periodically (ideally annually) to make sure that it remains accurate.

How Insurance Companies Calculate the Premium

The pricing of insurance is governed by a principle known as the "spread of risk." This means that the premiums paid by many people pay for the losses of the few.

When more dollars in claims are paid out than taken in as premiums, then the premium paid by everyone goes up.

The premium you pay therefore represents the amount of money needed by the insurance company to pay for all losses, plus their expenses in providing the service, plus a profit factor divided by the number of policyholders.

The potential for loss assessment is based upon a number of risk factors. Most of these risk factors are based upon where you live. Here are the three most important ones:

Fire

Although theft losses occur more often, fire still accounts for most of the dollars insurance companies pay out in claims. The potential damage due to fire is therefore based upon a municipality's ability to respond to, and put out, a fire.

If you own property in an area with fire hydrants, your premium will be lower because the fire department will have access to a large water supply. Fires in hydrant-protected areas can be extinguished at an earlier stage than those in less well-protected areas.

If you own property in an area without hydrants or even a fire department close by, the premium will be even higher.

Theft

Statistics show that theft is narrowing the gap with fire for dollars paid out. Generally, there is a much higher number of break-ins in cities than in rural areas. Insurance companies track the loss experience caused by theft by area, which is reflected in the premium you pay.

Weather

If your geographic area has a history of severe weather storms, such as windstorms, snowstorms, hail, or flooding, insurance companies obviously look at these risks as well.

Ways to Reduce Your Premiums

Higher Deductible

Many people don't realize there are ways to reduce the premium payment significantly. What exactly do you want protection for? What you are really concerned with is the possibility of a catastrophe or a total loss. If so, you can save money by increasing your deductible. By doing so, you save the insurance company the expense of investigating and settling small claims. That saving is passed back to you in the form of a reduced premium.

Discounts

You can reduce your premium if you qualify for any of the discounts insurance companies offer. Generally, discounts recognize a lower risk of category, for example, buying a newer home, installing an approved burglar alarm system, non-smoking policyholders, or seniors. Always ask what discounts are available and see if you are eligible.

Claims-Free Discount

This is a discount you don't have to ask for. Most insurance companies will reduce your premium automatically if you have been claim free for three or more years.

You should never reduce your amount of insurance so that you pay a lower premium. If you ever do have a claim, it could cost you a lot more than any amount you might save.

Personal Liability Protection

This is the part of the policy that protects you if you are sued. If someone injures himself or herself on your property, i.e., falls on your stairs, slips on your driveway, etc., and a court determines that you are responsible, your insurance company should defend you in court and pay all legal expenses and the amount up to the limit of the policy. The normal minimum limit is $1 million. However, you can increase this amount if you want.

There are specific exclusions that apply to this section of the policy. They are listed under the heading "Loss or Damage Not Insured." Make sure you read this carefully.

How to Avoid Being Sued

Every year, many people are injured while visiting the premises of others. The last thing you want is to be sued. The process is stressful, time-consuming, negative, protracted, and uncertain. Here are some suggestions to avoid problems. If you are renting to a tenant, your contract should cover hazard reduction and require the tenants to have tenant insurance coverage as a condition of your tenancy agreement. You should receive a copy of the policy.

Maintain Your Premises

Most injuries are caused by "slip and fall." They are usually the result of a lack of maintenance. In winter, you should clear ice and snow from all walkways on your premises and the stretch of sidewalk in front of your house. Exterior steps should be kept in good repair and a handrail provided.

Inside your house, carpets should be secured to stairs and floors and kept free of toys or objects that could trip a visitor.

Alcohol

If you serve alcohol to guests, you could be found responsible, to some extent, for their subsequent actions. Some courts have gone to extraordinary lengths to assign responsibility to a host. Good judgement is required. In particular, never allow an intoxicated guest to drive a car.

Other Hazards

You are potentially responsible for everything that happens on your premises. If you have a swimming pool, you are responsible for the safe use of the pool. If you have a dog, you are responsible for the actions of the dog. The list is almost endless. If you are renting to a tenant, you want to pass on the responsibility and liability as much as possible on to your tenant. As mentioned earlier, you should make it a condition of tenancy that the tenant obtain tenant insurance prior to moving in and provide you with a copy of it.

The good news is that most injuries can be avoided by using nothing more than common sense. All you have to do is be alert to the potential hazards on your own premises.

Types of General Insurance

The following brief overview is intended to alert you to the main types of coverage you may wish to consider, depending on the nature of your business needs. After you review them, you will see the wide range of coverage that you might require for your peace of mind. It includes a discussion of life, health, and disability insurance.

General Liability

This type of policy covers losses that you would be liable to pay for causing bodily injury to someone (e.g., in an accident) or damage to the property of others. Make sure that your policy covers all legal fees for your defence and related costs. This policy generally covers negligence on your part that accidentally causes injury to clients, employees, or the public.

Business Property

If you are operating a business out of your home, your current basic home-owners' or apartment owners' policy may void any coverage of business-related assets. Request that coverage be added to include the business assets, or purchase a separate policy. If you own a computer, you may wish to get a special "floater" policy covering risks unique to computer owners, including power-surge and fire damage and theft of hardware and software.

Fire

This coverage enables you to replace or rebuild your office or home as well as replace inventory and equipment. Make sure your policy is a replacement policy. (This was covered in the previous section on property insurance.)

Automobile

Automobile coverage insures physical damage to the car and bodily injury to the passengers as well as damage to other people's property, car, or passengers. It also includes theft of your car. Make sure that your car is insured for business use. Otherwise, if the facts came out on a claim that it was being used for that purpose, your policy would be void and your claim disallowed.

Mortgage

If you owe money on your mortgage and die, the bank insurance offered by your lender will pay off the outstanding mortgage. However, there are drawbacks and other options available to this type of insurance. The good news is that almost everyone is considered insurable. The drawbacks are that the premiums are high and the insurance is not portable. In other words, it is only for the purpose of paying off your mortgage. A better alternative is to get your own private term life insurance coverage. The premiums will be lower, and you can keep the insurance coverage long after the mortgage has been paid off. It gives you that flexibility. Also, if you become uninsurable in the future due to health reasons, at least you will have your own portable life insurance protection.

Life

Term life insurance insures a person for a specific period of time or term, and then stops. Term life does not have a cash-surrender value or loan value as with a whole-life plan. Term premiums are less expensive than whole-life premiums. If you have a bank loan or personal or business obligations, consider term life coverage. Whole-life insurance costs more as it includes a "term" component plus an investment savings component—you obtain interest on the investment part of your premium.

Home Office

It is important to recognize the potential risks of working from home and the policies available for protection against them. If you don't have insurance protection, you could be personally liable for all financial losses. Always advise your insurance agent that you are operating a business from your home. You will need extra coverage for any risk areas involved directly or indirectly with your business operation. The home office coverage is normally an extension endorsement of your regular homeowner insurance policy coverage.

Almost all homeowner policies exclude home businesses. However, the increased premium on your current home insurance policies will still be a saving compared to the higher insurance premium you would pay if your business were located in commercial premises. Use the same insurance broker for all your policies if possible, as you should be able to negotiate better rates. Ask for copies of the extra policy coverage for your file.

Disability

Good health is by far our greatest asset. With it, we can improve our financial net worth; without it, we have only liabilities.

Statistics show that the chance of becoming disabled between 45 and 65 years of age for a minimum of three months is almost 40%. Almost one-half of those still disabled after six months will still be disabled at the end of five years.

Depending on the disability, you might be covered by Workers' Compensation benefits, CPP benefits, or Employment Insurance disability benefits. You may have group or personal disability insurance benefits. Group and individual plans will cover only a portion of your gross earnings before you were disabled by injury or illness.

Definitions of disability vary. Whether or not you receive benefits may well depend on how the company defines disability. Carefully read the wording of your contract, as some are so restrictive that it might be almost impossible to be eligible for a claim. Most contracts define disability according to one of four types, from the least to the most restrictive.

Own Occupation

Disability is defined as the inability to work in your own occupation only. If you can prove that you are disabled from doing your own job and are under the care of a doctor, you will qualify for benefits. Even if you went to work in another occupation, you may still qualify for benefits. Individual insurance contracts may offer an "own occupation" clause to age 65.

Regular Occupation

This type would provide coverage in the event that you are disabled and unable to work in your own occupation, provided that you choose not to work in an alternative occupation.

Any Occupation

This would cover disability from any suitable occupation, based on your education, training, and/or experience. Most, but not all, group insurance contracts specify an "any occupation" disability after the first two years of disability.

Total and Permanent

Some insurance contracts require that you not only be totally disabled from working, but also that your disability must be permanent. Naturally, this insurance is high risk for you due to the severe nature of disability required before coverage commences. The insurance premium is lower as the risk is lower to the insurance company.

Web Sites of Interest

Here are some Web sites to obtain consumer information and contact names of members in your area:

Canadian Life and Health Insurance Association: www.clhia.ca
For a list of members in the area of life, health,
and disability insurance.

Financial Advisors Association of Canada: www.advocis.ca
The organization formed from the merger
of the Canadian Association of Financial Planners
and the Canadian Association of Insurance and
Financial Advisors.

Financial Planners Standards Council of Canada: www.cfp-ca.org
The organization licenses financial planners with
the certified financial planner (CFP) designation.

Insurance Brokers Association of Canada: www.ibac.ca
Contact them for a list of members to obtain
comparative quotes in the area of property
and business insurance.

Summary

With insurance, it is important to be realistic. Weigh the risks and potential business and personal financial exposure if you have no insurance or inadequate coverage. You need to look at your total insurance picture to make sure that you have adequate and integrated coverage. Always comparison shop, and make sure you understand the jargon of the trade. Speak to accredited insurance brokers and financial planners.

With the fine points out of the way, we're going to enter the world of negotiations

CHAPTER 9

Negotiating Strategies

Understanding the art and science of negotiating will be important for you if you want to make money buying or selling real estate. Whether you are a first-time homebuyer or an experienced or novice real estate investor, you will benefit from the practical tips and street-smart strategies and insights explained in this chapter.

Most interactions with people—personnel, professionals, business associates, suppliers—involve some dynamics of the negotiation process. If you are attempting to sell, persuade, convince, or influence another person's thinking or feeling to accord with your own wants and needs, you are using negotiating skills. If, at the same time, you have defined and satisfied the other person's needs, you have attained an optimal or "win-win" type of negotiation. However, in practical terms in real estate negotiations, you may not satisfy the seller's or buyer's needs, as his or her needs and expectations may be unrealistic in the circumstances.

Different players in the real estate market frequently use psychological negotiating games and techniques. You will learn the concepts and step-by-step process in this chapter. This will help you save more money and therefore make more money on any type of real estate purchase or sale. You will learn how to obtain the best price and terms, how to buy low and sell high.

This chapter will cover the necessary steps to follow to prepare for real estate negotiation, understanding the reasons why the property might be for sale, and what to put in the offer.

Preparing for Real Estate Negotiation

There are various preliminary steps you should go through to maximize your success before any offer is made:

√ Determine the amount of mortgage that you are entitled to, the maximum price that you are prepared to pay, and the terms that you would prefer.

√ Have alternative properties so that you have fallbacks.

√ Have your realtor thoroughly check out the property. (The services a realtor can offer in this regard were covered in an earlier chapter.) Find out such factors as how long it has been for sale, why it is for sale, how the vendor determined the asking price, recent market comparables in the area, and any vendor deadline pressure. The following section in this chapter discusses in more detail why a property might be for sale.

√ Be thoroughly prepared.

√ Stick to your investment plan.

√ Ideally, use a realtor as a negotiating buffer between you and the vendor.

√ Obtain legal and tax advice on the implications of your purchase.

√ Don't get emotionally involved with the property. Be totally objective and realistic, otherwise it could taint your judgement.

√ Train yourself to appear patient and unemotional to the vendor or vendor's agent.

√ To increase your bargaining leverage, look for negative features of the property in advance. All properties can be found to have something negative. For example, it could be a large lot with a high property tax. Some people would like a large lot. However, others would look at it from a negative perspective in terms of maintenance, e.g., cutting grass. Write down a list of the positive and negative features.

√ Establish a relationship with a building inspector and contractor in advance; you might need their services on short notice.

Reasons Why a Property Is for Sale

Why Principal Residence Properties Might Be for Sale

It is important to determine the owner's real motivation for selling the property. This will assist you in knowing how to negotiate in terms of your offer price and terms and general strategies. The motivation for sale could be a positive or negative one. If the vendor is selling in a buyer's market, be particularly thorough in finding out why the vendor is selling in a market that is clearly disadvantageous in terms of the negotiating climate and eventual sale price.

Some of the most common reasons for sale of a principal residence include the following:

√ Separation or divorce.

√ Death of owner or co-owner.

√ Loss of job of principal wage earner or of one of two wage earners when two wage earners are necessary to pay for the home expenses.

√ Job relocation.

√ Ill health of one or both homeowners.

√ Retirement and therefore relocation or downsizing house size needs, or desire to take some of the equity out of the house for retirement purposes.

√ Owner lost money in a business or other investment venture and needs to sell the house to pay off the debt.

√ Owner has not made payments on the mortgage due to personal or financial problems, so the lender has started court proceedings. This could be in the form of an order for sale or foreclosure proceedings. The length of time before the house could be sold in the above circumstances varies depending on the provincial jurisdiction. In Canada, though, all distress sales of real estate, especially principal residences, are sold by the lender with or without court approval of the price, depending on the nature of the litigation and province. In practical terms, the lender obtains a current real estate appraisal and makes legitimate and sincere attempts to sell the property at fair market value. Otherwise, the owner could complain to the court or sue the lender, claiming that the sale price was not fair market value.

√ Municipal property tax sales in Canada are also a rarity. In normal circumstances, depending on the province, a municipality waits for three years' arrears of taxes before a tax sale by sealed bid or auction can take place. The purchaser of the tax sale property cannot obtain title to the property until one year after the sale, so that the owner can pay the arrears and be current again. For all these reasons, in practical terms, an owner of a principal residence is not going to let the property go and lose all the equity built up for the relatively small amount of property tax arrears. One way or the other, the owner will raise the money, or alternatively put the house on the market and sell it at fair market value.

√ Owner wants to sell in a seller's market.

√ Owner is concerned that the market is changing and could become a buyer's market.

√ Owner is testing the market to see what the market will pay without making any serious attempt to sell.

√ Children are leaving the home and therefore the owner is downsizing house size needs.

√ Owner wants to buy a larger home due to increasing family size or needs. This could also be due to having an extended family, e.g., in-law suite or extra space for parents or relatives, or blended family due to a second marriage or common-law relationship.

√ Owner wants to trade up to a nicer home or better neighbourhood.

√ Owner wants to buy a house with a rental suite in basement for revenue purposes.

Why Investment Properties Might Be for Sale

There are many reasons why an investment property could be listed for sale. It does not necessarily mean the property has serious problems or is a bad investment. Possibly the property is poorly managed, poorly maintained, or has excessive vacancies. In many cases, an astute investor could turn the property into an attractive investment by identifying the exact problems and opportunities, devising a plan for turnaround, and buying at below market value. Explore to find out the real reasons why the property is for sale.

Here are a few of the common reasons for sale:

√ *Inexperienced Owner:* Possibly the owner was a first-time investor who bought beyond his skills, resources, and comfort zone, and feels intimidated by the responsibilities, time, and risk involved. He may now have changed his mind and wish to sell due to the associated personal stress.

√ *Partnership Disputes:* About 80% of business partnerships at some point break up or have conflict. (This topic was discussed in Chapter 1: Understanding Real Estate Investment.) Maybe the property is for sale due to unresolved disputes. Another possibility is that some investors need to get out for financial reasons or changed investment goals; therefore, the partnership splits up and that triggers the sale.

√ *Tax Benefits:* Maybe the owner has depreciated the building as much as possible and wants to sell because the land value has increased. The owner wants to minimize the capital gain aspects by selling in the current market.

√ *Settling of an Estate:* If the owner of the property has died, the executor of the estate wants to settle the estate reasonably quickly, and the property could therefore be priced at fair market value or below in order to effect a sale.

√ *Run-down Properties:* Due to management or financial difficulties, the property could visibly deteriorate, causing the owner to want to sell. Some of the reasons are discussed in further detail below.

√ *Poor Management:* This could be because the owner is attempting to manage it himself, but lacks the skills, knowledge, or personality to do it profitably. Maybe the owner has hired the cheapest management firm and they do the least amount possible. If an owner lives outside the city, province, or country, possibly the management company is indifferent and allows the property to deteriorate, causing problems to occur. Another reason for poor management is that the owner is draining the revenue property by taking out too much money personally. This could result in a shortfall of the revenue required to meet necessary expenses.

√ *Excessive Vacancies:* If an apartment building suffers from ongoing vacancies, it could be because the building is run-down or has poor management; there are unstable employment opportunities in the community; there is the wrong mix of tenants in the building; there are more attractive competing apartments; or the rents are too high. Whatever the cause, the vacancy situation is probably causing serious cash flow problems for the owner.

√ *Financing Problems:* For various reasons the owner could have, or anticipate having, difficulty refinancing the property. For example, possibly the value has decreased resulting in 15% owner's equity, and the lender requires a minimum of 25% owner's equity. This could be the motivation to sell the property because any legal action by the mortgage company could result in a distress sale, thereby causing the property to diminish further in value.

√ *Distress Sale:* This means that the owner is forced to sell, generally due to legal action by the mortgage company in the form of a court order for sale or foreclosure litigation. The reason for legal action would be due to breach of the payment terms or other conditions of the mortgage by the owner. The practical effect is that the lender is requiring that the property be sold. Due to the circumstances of sale, a buyer might be able to pick up the property for less than fair market value. It really depends on the circumstances, market demand, nature of the price and terms, and other factors.

In practical terms in Canada, most properties that are forced sales by lenders either have to be court-approved sales or otherwise have to pass the scrutiny of fairness if the lender sells it. The owner could later take the lender to court, alleging that the sale price was not a fair market value. In other words, the court or lender wants to make sure that they have received top price for the property in the circumstances and in the market at that time. It is very rare that property tax sales occur. (This was covered above in "Why Principal Residence Properties Might Be for Sale.")

√ *Personal Problems of Owner:* The owner could be having personal, marital, health, employment, or financial problems. This could result in the owner wanting to sell the investment.

√ *Change in Investment Strategies of Owner:* The owner could have revised his or her personal investment strategies and goals, and decided to change the nature of the real estate investment or get out of real estate altogether.

√ *More Attractive Investment:* The owner may be interested in purchasing a different real estate investment property that is a more attractive investment package in every respect.

√ *Seller's Market:* Possibly the market is an attractive one for selling revenue property and there is more demand than supply, hence sale prices have gone up. The owner could decide to take advantage of the increased market activity.

√ *Concern That a Downturn Might Be Coming:* The owner could foresee that the real estate cycle could soon be taking a downturn, and that property values could drop. This concern could result in the property being listed for sale.

Negotiating Tips and Techniques

After you have gone through the preparation steps, the next negotiating stage is the presentation of your offer to the vendor. Here are some guidelines when presenting an offer.

√ *Name of Purchaser:* Depending on the nature of your purchase, you may want to put your name and the words "or assignee" if it is your intent to sign over the agreement to someone else. However, you need to get legal advice on this issue as there could be legal implications as to who actually is the purchaser. Alternatively, if you are purchasing an investment or speculative property with a degree of risk, you may want to incorporate a company and put the offer in the corporate name. If you back out of the deal before closing, your company could be sued for breach of contract and damages (losses) by the vendor, but not you personally. Presumably your new company does not have any assets at that stage. You would need experienced legal advice on these matters in advance.

√ *Deposit:* Try to put down the smallest deposit. You don't want to tie up any more money than you have to. Also, if you back out prior to closing, your deposit funds could be at risk of being kept by the vendor. Whatever deposit money you put down, never pay it directly to the vendor. Always have it paid to a realtor's or lawyer's trust account. Make sure you write in the offer that your deposit funds are to accrue interest to your credit pending the closing date.

√ *Price:* Attempt to offer the lowest possible price the market and circumstances allow. Always start with your ideal price and terms. You never know what the vendor will find to be acceptable or not, so don't anticipate disfavour. Think positive. If the vendor counter-offers, you may want to extract concessions from the vendor due to the variation of your original offer.

√ *Closing Date:* Depending on your objectives, you may want to have a long closing date such as three or four months. Maybe you will be receiving funds by then. Maybe the market will have gone up in an escalating market, and you would be entitled to a higher mortgage on closing.

√ *Financing Terms:* You may want to ask the vendor for vendor-take-back financing for a first or second mortgage. Depending on your objectives, you may want to ask for a long-term open mortgage (say, five years) with an attractive interest rate, and assumable without qualifications. This latter provision would make it easier for resale. The vendor may be willing to provide such favourable terms because the market is slow and he is anxious to sell.

√ *Conditions:* Conditions are sometimes referred to as "subject" clauses. You should include as many conditional clauses as you feel are appropriate for your needs, such as subject to "financing" or "satisfactory building inspection." Also include any warranty confirmations from vendor. Examples may include the vendor's assertion that "the furnace is functioning properly and still covered under a manufacturer's warranty" or "the house was built under the New Home Warranty Program" if such a program exists in your province. (Refer to the section on "Understanding the Purchase and Sale Agreement" in Chapter 6: Understanding the Legal Aspects for more "subject clause" examples.)

Summary

This chapter covered the steps necessary to successfully prepare for real estate negotiation, and understand the dynamics at play. Advance research knowledge is critical to ensure a profitable purchase.

Once you have purchased a property, you will need to ensure it is managed well in all respects. The next chapter discusses property management.

10 Managing Your Property

Effective property management is a vital part of making the maximum amount of profit on a revenue property with a minimum amount of stress and risk. Property management has many objectives, the primary ones being to attain the highest possible cash flow, net income, and property value by using successful management techniques. These in turn will give you the best return on your investment. Other objectives, which are fundamental to achieving the primary objectives, include making the right type of management decisions to result in ideal tenants, few vacancies, maximum revenues, and minimal expenses. In addition, the maintenance of the property at its optimal condition is part of those general objectives.

Many novice landlords eventually put their properties up for sale, frequently at a loss, when it otherwise would not have been necessary. This is likely due to the lack of property-management knowledge and skills. Difficulties often arise because the investor gets tired of the chronic frustration, stress, and time involved in dealing with the problems created by poor management, for example, problems such as late-paying tenants, disruptive tenants, vacancies, high turn-over, vandalism, negative cash flow or sporadic cash flow, creditor or lender demands, tenant disputes, complaints, and high repair and maintenance costs.

This chapter will assist you in attaining your personal objectives of stress-free property management and avoidance of the common pitfalls. The following sections will cover types of management, keeping records, finding the right tenant, and understanding the tenant documentation. It will also cover how to save on expenses and increase the income from your revenue property. Common home-maintenance problems and avoiding common fire hazards will also be discussed.

Types of Management

The initial decision that you make regarding the form of management will be largely determined by the size of the property, the type and number of investments, the number of tenants, your interest and experience in management, and the time you have available. If you are purchasing a condominium, the same considerations are taken into account by the condominium corporation on behalf of and under instructions from the condominium owners.

There are essentially three forms of property management: self-management, resident management, and professional management. A combination of these alternatives may also be used.

Self-Management

In the case of small revenue properties, it is often more practical for the owner to be responsible for managing the investment directly. For example, in a duplex or single-family house situation, this self-management alternative could be attractive. It is not necessary in a self-management situation that the owners themselves clean the grounds, cut the grass, do the gardening, and sweep the driveways. In does mean, though, that the owners, or a representative of the owners, would have to be directly involved in supervising the performance of these types of services. Frequently the jobs are done by firms under contract or by the tenants themselves.

Clearly, there are cost savings to managing the property yourself, but not everyone is suited for it. Ask yourself how much free time you have and are prepared to spend. For example, if you are retired or semi-retired, you could comfortably manage several single-family properties or a combination of different types of properties. Even if you work full-time, if you manage your time well and are an efficient and effective landlord, you may be capable of managing several properties successfully.

You also have to look realistically at your skills and interest in doing minor repairs and maintenance. In addition, consider whether you really enjoy dealing with tenants and their problems, and have the patience, temperament, and personality to do so. If not, maybe one of your family members does.

Another reason for self-management or resident management is that the property may be outside the metropolitan area, so there may be difficulty in obtaining the services of a professional management company.

Remember, in terms of real estate management, you can involve yourself as little or as much as you want. It comes down to personal choice and circumstances and desire for profit. Although it is easier to have someone else assume the management responsibilities, there will be a cost factor. You may wish to work at it on a part-time basis and have the right tenant assist on matters such as minor cleanup, cutting the lawn, and watering the plants.

You could negotiate some minor monetary or non-monetary benefit for the tenant. Many tenants would probably be willing to do such tasks without a benefit if the duties were minor and seasonal in nature. Everyone is unique in his or her motivations, needs, and wishes. Tips covered later in this chapter, as well as those discussed in Chapter 1: Understanding Real Estate Investment under "Establishing Your Investment Strategies" will provide you with a better basis for making your decision. If you decide to maintain the properties yourself, you may wish to take a residential property manager course offered through a local college or apartment owners' association.

Resident Management

In this situation, the owner employs one or more people directly to perform the daily management requirements. These people would normally operate out of an office on the property and would be paid a full-time or part-time salary, or have a partial rent or rent-free apartment in exchange for services. It is important to be very careful in selecting the resident manager and to thoroughly check out their references beforehand. Generally only apartment buildings with more than eight suites can financially justify employing a full-time resident manager, but this can vary.

The prospective resident manager could already be a tenant living in the building, rather than someone new. It is not uncommon to have a husband-and-wife team share the responsibilities. Frequently this is an excellent arrangement. The chief qualities and qualifications to look for in a resident manager would include:

√ honesty and integrity

√ conscientiousness and willingness to do the job

√ capable of assuming the responsibilities required

√ personable and pleasant to get along with

√ has the time available to monitor the property and perform the duties

√ enjoys being a handyman and doing minor repairs and upkeep

√ takes pride in the services performed

√ ideally has past experience dealing with tenants or is familiar with the service industry in some form, although this is not essential if the other attributes are present.

The responsibilities of the resident manager can vary, but generally include: collecting rent, making deposits, keeping the grounds neat and clean, making minor repairs and maintenance, showing vacant suites, signing up new tenants, keeping records, promptly advising you of any problems, and generally following your instructions and procedures.

If your local college or apartment owners' association has a course or seminar on residential property management, you may wish to offer that as a paid incentive to your property manager, in order to increase his or her knowledge and skills. The cost-benefit of this approach has to be assessed.

Professional Management

Many owners of apartment buildings over 12 units, owners of several single-family dwellings, absentee owners, or inactive owners use a professional management company. These companies tend to be very experienced at residential property management and have many systems and procedures for efficient operation of their support function. The types of services and benefits provided could include:

√ experienced staff

√ computerized accounting, bookkeeping procedures, and management systems

√ access to suppliers who can provide bulk-buying discounts and good service

√ careful selection of, and contracting out for, competent tradespeople for repair or general maintenance service, subject to a limit beyond which any expenditure would require your written authorization

√ finding and selecting tenants, showing apartments, and negotiating tenancy agreements or leases, and using forms supplied or approved by you and your lawyer

√ monitoring tenant problems and evicting, if necessary

√ collecting rents

√ paying all bills and mortgage payments on your behalf

√ maintaining all necessary records

√ sending you a monthly statement on the operation of the building

√ ensuring that the grounds and buildings are maintained properly

√ selecting and supervising the resident manager.

One of the key benefits of using a professional management company is that such a company will provide the continuity of management to ensure a consistent level of quality. Professional management fees can range from 2% to

5% or more of the gross monthly revenue from the property. Like any business activity, fees are negotiable. It is important to give the management company guidelines in writing, as well as to incorporate them in the overall management contract. Make sure you have your lawyer review the contract before you sign it. Check out the company thoroughly and ask for references from owners of other properties being managed. Look in the Yellow Pages under "Property Management." In Canada, one of the highest levels of professional certification is called Certified Property Manager or CPM. This credential is awarded by the Real Estate Institute of Canada. Check out their Web site for information and members in your area (www.reic.ca).

Remember, before making your final decision, attempt to shortlist at least three desirable candidates for resident manager or professional management company.

Keeping Records

Why Keeping Records Is Necessary

Records must be kept regardless of how small your real estate investment is. If you are renting out property, records such as bank deposit books, invoices, receipts, sales slips, contracts, and numerous other documents are continually generated. It is critically important to develop systems for recording and filing the various types of records, so they can be retrieved and examined quickly and efficiently.

Accurate records should be kept for both external and internal reasons.

External Reasons for Keeping Records

√ Government regulations—federal government departments have set rules and regulations related to record keeping. For example, Statistics Canada requires that information be supplied upon request, and Canada Revenue Agency (CRA) requires you to pay income tax on net revenue income and to remit deductions at source from any employee taxes and contributions to Unemployment Insurance and the Canada Pension Plan. If Revenue Canada requires an audit, you will need to produce your records for review.

√ Raising bank financing and lender requirements.

√ Attracting potential investors.

√ Selling the property.

√ Meeting insurance company requirements for a loss claim.

Internal Reasons for Keeping Records

√ Keeps you better informed about the financial position of your investment.

√ Makes it easier to complete accurate income tax returns with supporting receipts for expenses.

√ Provides the basis for evaluating the condition, efficiency, and operation of the revenue property.

√ Reminds you when creditor obligations are due.

√ Provides an opportunity for comparing budget goals with historical records and future projections.

√ Provides the basis for preparing cash flow, income and expense projections, and break-even analyses to enable you to improve your cash management and revenue operational position.

√ Prepares for sale of the property.

The *Income Tax Act* requires that you keep your records and books in an orderly manner at your place of business or your residence, as Revenue Canada may request this material at any time for review or audit purposes.

You are required to maintain business records and supporting documents for at least six years from the end of the last taxation year to which they relate. If you filed your return late for any year, records and supporting documents must be kept for six years from the date you filed that return. Revenue Canada permits computer storage of records, as long as those records provide adequate information to verify taxable income.

Typical Financial Records

Some examples of typical financial records to be maintained manually or on a computerized program are as follows (not all will be applicable):

√ sales journal

√ cash receipts journal

√ accounts receivable ledger

√ accounts payable journal

√ cash disbursements journal

√ credit purchases journal

√ credit sales journal

√ payroll journal

√ general synoptic ledger.

Some of the non-financial records include documents relating to personnel, equipment, inventory, and tenants.

Record-Keeping Systems and Equipment

The equipment and systems that a real estate investor uses for record keeping can range from simple, inexpensive manual procedures to more complex computer systems. You should ask your accountant to recommend the most efficient record-keeping system for your type of operation. There are some excellent software programs available, and some that are geared for real estate investors.

If you are just investing in a single-family house, you may require only a one-write system for cheque writing, a general ledger, and a ledger system for receivables and payables. As your real estate investment expands in terms of numbers and types of properties, you will likely want and need to use one of the excellent computer software programs available.

Finding the Right Tenant

To leave a property vacant costs you money on a daily basis. Therefore, to minimize your losses, you should prepare yourself for the process of finding tenants. There are a variety of effective techniques for finding tenants. As with the real estate cycle, factors such as the economy, the vacancy rate, the time of year, and what is happening in and around the community itself will make some of these methods more effective at one time over others. No single method is best, nor should one method be used exclusively. Using a combination of techniques will help you to build your own experience and to know which method works best for your area.

√ community newspaper classified advertisements

√ referrals from realtors

√ referrals from property-management companies

√ referrals from tenant rental agencies

√ signs on lawn or in house window

√ sign on bulletin board in local supermarket, college, or university

√ Internet advertising on sites that could attract your target market.

If it is an apartment building you are trying to find tenants for, here are some additional suggestions:

√ referrals from other tenants in the building

√ notice inside building on bulletin board

√ daily newspaper classified or display advertisements

√ direct mailing

√ advertising on the selected Web sites.

Once you have shortlisted potential prospects, the next section covers the steps to take to narrow down the list of applicants, finalize your decision, select the right tenant, and confirm the arrangement in writing.

Understanding the Tenant Documentation

Experienced landlords and property managers are unanimous in their opinion that it is better to leave a suite vacant than to rent it to a "bad" tenant. Therefore, do not underestimate the importance of the application, screening, and interviewing process before making a selection. Most provinces have legislation relating to landlord/tenant relationships. Before proceeding with your tenant selection, you should obtain a copy of your provincial *Landlord/Tenant Act* and become familiar with it. At the same time, pick up any brochures and forms available relating to your rights and responsibilities as a landlord. You may wish to consider joining your local apartment owners' association or take an adult education course on landlord responsibilities, offered through community colleges and school boards.

The process leading to actual tenancy will include having each of your prospective tenants complete a detailed tenant application form. Following careful review and reference checking, a second meeting should be held to draft a tenancy agreement and complete a suite-inspection report. Each of these is described below. Copies of standard forms may be obtained from your provincial or local apartment owners' association, or a stationery store.

Tenant Application Form

The application form provides you with some critical background information on the prospective tenant. It requires details on the employer's name, length of employment at that firm, current residence address, length of time at that address, reason for moving, name and phone number of present landlord, current bank, and personal, credit, and previous landlord references. In addition to these details, the form should have a line in which the applicant provides his or her written consent to permit you to do credit checks. Always contact the previous landlord and the personal and credit references. Taking that extra effort could save you unnecessary grief later. Allow yourself three to five days to process the application.

Tenancy Agreement

The legislation covered in the *Landlord/Tenant Act* and the standard forms available for tenancy agreements are not all-encompassing, so you want to reflect in writing your specific policies for the suite or house rental. Some types of issues you may wish to cover in the agreement include:

√ no-smoking policy

√ pet policy

√ number of occupants

√ when the rental payment is due

√ penalty for late payment

√ penalty for cheques that do not clear the tenant's account

√ term of the tenancy (month to month or fixed period)

√ proportionate share payment of utilities

√ amount of security deposit and deposit interest

√ tenant's obligations, such as care and maintenance of premises

√ landlord's access to premises

√ tenant's notice to landlord of extended absence

√ no assignment or subletting of rental suite by tenant without the landlord's prior written permission and consent.

For your peace of mind, and to ensure that all aspects have been considered, you should have your lawyer review the additions you have made to the standard lease agreement. To get more information on the landlord/tenant legislation in your province, go to www.google.ca and type in the key words "landlord tenant law" and the name of your province.

Landlord/Tenant Suite-Inspection Checklist

Before the tenant assumes occupancy of a suite, it is important for both of you to walk around the suite for an initial inspection. (For an example of a landlord/tenant suite-inspection checklist, refer to Checklist 5 in the Appendix.) By reviewing the suite together, you will be able to agree on and document its current condition. Don't forget to make sure the form is signed by both parties. It will provide a reference point to review any damages that have occurred during the tenancy. Any such damages or items that need repair, other than normal wear and tear, will be a rationale for withholding part or all of the deposit monies as compensation for repair costs.

Saving on Expenses

Part of making money from your rental property is ensuring that you save money wherever possible. Here are some of the common methods:

- √ appealing a high property tax increase to the property assessment authority
- √ hiring tenants who will handle maintenance, such as snow removal, gardening, minor painting
- √ utilizing government subsidy program for insulation, gas conversion, etc.
- √ buying supplies in bulk
- √ getting at least three competitive bids for any major expense, such as landscaping, painting, and renovating
- √ reviewing present property-insurance coverage and premiums
- √ reviewing property-management contract and commission
- √ employing your children to do cleanup and odd jobs, if appropriate, thereby keeping the money in the family
- √ enforcing warranties and contracts to ensure quality service or operation.

Increasing Revenue Property Income

Like other income properties, the expenses of a multi-unit apartment building are relatively fixed. Therefore, if you can increase revenues through innovative management techniques, you can have a measurable impact on cash flow. Here are some additional ways to generate income, assuming there is no provincial residential tenant legislation restricting such methods.

Tenant Application Fee

It takes time to process an application, including the expense of a credit bureau search. You may want to charge a non-refundable processing fee of $15 to $25 or more.

Late Payment Charge

If these penalties are included in the written tenancy agreement signed by the tenant, it will result in a benefit due to prompt rent payments or the late charges themselves.

Parking Fees

Space not specifically allocated for tenants could be rented out monthly as additional space to tenants of your building, or an adjacent apartment or commercial building.

Pets

Assuming that pets are allowed, you could put a clause in the written tenancy agreement outlining the restrictions on the kind, size, and number of pets that are permitted, and the amount of a monthly pet rent (e.g., $5 to $10).

Additional Tenants

You may wish to have a limit on the number of tenants at the base rent price. Any tenants over and above the limit would result in a set monthly extra rent for each extra tenant.

Coin-Operated Machines

This can be one of the best extra revenue sources. You have a choice of buying or leasing the equipment and paying for a service contract, or contracting with a company who will supply and service the equipment and give you a commission of a percentage of gross revenue collected. This is negotiable, but can be up to 75%. Clearly there could be advantages to this latter option over the purchase option. Make sure the equipment used is energy-efficient or utility costs could consume most of the extra revenue.

Vending Machines

A vending machine is another related revenue generator that can be installed on a commission basis. It is important to have trash receptacles in the vending machine and to site the machine where they are accessible. A common location is the laundry room and/or recreation or community room. You may also want to consider offering coin-operated video games.

Recreation Facilities

Some of the more modern buildings have recreational amenities such as recreation area, community room, swimming pool, and tennis courts. You should consider charging tenants for use of these facilities. If that is already being done, review the rates in terms of increasing them. If the tenants had the amenities originally included for free, consider revising future tenancy agreements or leases to charge a fee for usage. Your lawyer can best advise you on the appropriate content and approach. You may also wish to allow outsiders to use the amenities on a selective basis and charge a higher fee than for tenants.

Daycare Facilities

If the apartment building that you own or co-own has a large number of young children, you may wish to consider the benefits of operating a daycare facility. Of course, you would have to comply with any government zoning, licensing, and health regulations, and have an appropriate location. You may prefer to hire people to operate the facility. For obvious reasons, you will have to be very selective. Another alternative is to contract with an existing qualified, experienced, and credible daycare operator to operate the daycare facility. You would charge them a fee for the business opportunity or split the net proceeds on an agreed formula. A daycare facility could also be a positive and attractive feature to bring in new tenants as well as provide additional revenue.

Furniture Rental

If your apartment building has younger tenants who stay for short periods (e.g., college or university students), you may want to consider renting furniture. Rather than buying your own furniture and having that capital cost and inventory, you may want to rent the furniture directly from a furniture rental company for a discount, of course, or refer your tenants to a specific furniture-rental company, with the inducement of a "special discount for tenants." You would then arrange for the furniture-rental company to pay you a referral fee or percentage of the monthly rental. Make sure you have any such agreement in writing in advance so there is no misunderstanding.

Storage Facility

In addition to whatever storage lockers come with the apartment rental, you may wish to rent out extra storage areas. Conversely, you may want to charge extra for storage lockers over and above the base rent, and not include free storage space. Not everyone wants or uses storage space, so the latter example could be a good source of additional revenue, rather than giving it away for free. In addition, you may want to make an arrangement with a nearby mini-warehouse company to give a "special discount" to your tenants. In return, you would arrange to receive a referral fee or monthly commission from the mini-warehouse company along the same lines as with furniture rental discussed earlier.

Newsletter Advertising

If the number of units in your apartment building warrants, you may wish to consider publishing a monthly newsletter. It is an excellent way to improve tenant relations as well as to provide a source of income by selling advertising to local businesses. The newsletter could be two to eight pages in length and easily desktop published on your own computer. Get competitive quotes if you are going to hire someone to do the desktop publishing or printing for you. You may wish to clone your newsletter idea by selling the newsletter to other non-competing apartment building owners. You get the advertising revenue and they get the public relations benefit. It could be a generic content and name, or you could customize the name for each apartment building. The whole concept, of course, would have to be economically feasible to begin with.

Avoiding Common Homeowner Maintenance Problems

Most people do not look on their home or investment property as a mechanical device, like a car, which should have regular maintenance checkups, yet a house needs to be maintained regularly to preserve the home value on resale. Simple, inexpensive maintenance can enhance the value of the house considerably.

The elements, such as water, snow, ice or wind, and the sun, are the main culprits when it comes to deterioration of the property.

A recent Canadian study has shown that the 10 conditions most neglected by homeowners are as follows:

Furnace Filters

Accumulated dust and debris on the furnace and filter require the motor and fan to work harder to pull air through the filter. The harder the furnace has to work, the shorter its life expectancy. If you don't use a quality filter and replace it regularly, you might have to pay hundreds of dollars to replace the fan and motor, or several thousands of dollars to replace the entire furnace. In 80% of homes, the furnace filters needed replacing.

Water behind Walls

In three out of four houses, the caulking between the tub and surrounding wall (or shower pan and shower walls) is either deteriorating or missing altogether. If not corrected, this condition will allow water to leak behind the walls, promoting dry rot and mildew. Eventually, the wall will deteriorate. The removal of tile walls can be expensive.

Doors and Windows

Sixty percent of houses that are 20 or more years old have inoperable, improperly fitted, or non-weather-stripped windows and doors.

Windows and doors that don't open and close properly can be life threatening if they are needed as an escape route. If they are loose and improperly sealed, they allow warm or conditioned air to escape, creating climate-control problems. This not only drives up your monthly heating and cooling bills, it forces your furnace and air conditioner to run overtime to attain the desired temperature, shortening their life span significantly.

Leaky Plumbing

Leaking water-supply valves under sinks and faucets, found in one of every two houses, cause the floor (or wall if the faucet is also leaking) to deteriorate. If neglected, it could cost anywhere from $200 to $1,000 to repair the damage, depending on how long the leak has been ignored. Even when some owners are aware of this problem, the typical solution is duct tape and a bucket.

Overgrowth

Ivy growing up the side of your house may be beautiful but it is terribly damaging, as are tree branches that hang over your roof, yet both conditions were found in two out of every five houses examined.

Retained water in vegetation contributes to accelerated deterioration and rot. An ivy's root system is so strong that it can move mortar and get behind siding and pop it out, and leaves deposited on a roof are a breeding ground for degeneration. Depending on the extent of growth, you may need a new roof or new siding on your house at a cost of several thousand dollars. At best, your roof's life expectancy will be reduced by 20%.

Poor Grading

About a third of all houses have grading problems. Even if the lot was graded properly when the house was built—it should slope away from the structure—the grade can shift over time.

The cause is usually heavy rain and erosion from overwatering shrubs placed too close to the house. But sometimes the ground simply settles. If the ground within 10 feet (3 metres) of the house slopes toward the house, water will collect adjacent to the building. This can be eliminated by a few wheelbarrows of dirt and some digging. If water is allowed to remain over a period of time, it will flow under the structure and weaken the foundation.

Clogged Gutters

A third of all houses also have gutters and downspouts clogged by vegetation. This will allow water to back up on the roof, not only causing the roof to deteriorate more quickly but also leading to erosion, which causes a negative grade at the foundation.

Broken Exhaust Fans

The exhaust fan in bathrooms without windows is either disconnected or inoperable in one out of every three houses inspected. This will allow condensation to accumulate, causing moisture damage. Eventually the walls and flooring can rot out completely.

Worn-out Caulking

Fifteen percent of the houses examined have either worn-out caulking or none at all. Deteriorating or missing caulking on exterior walls where dissimilar materials meet can allow water to leak into wall cavities, where it will cause the framing to rot.

Caulking wears out. It shrinks, cracks, blisters, and hardens, so it needs to be evaluated annually. If it's not checked and, when necessary, replaced, you may end up replacing sill plates, interior studs, and framing at a cost of several thousand dollars.

Blocked Attic Vents

Many homeowners add new or additional insulation in the attic, and in many cases block the necessary attic ventilation passages. Blocked vents can create moisture buildup, mildew, and rot in the attic.

Avoiding Common Fire Hazards

Fire, whether minor or major, is a traumatizing experience. Even if no one is injured, there can be the loss of treasured family photos, memorabilia, and memories. However, with some advance planning, you can go a long way in avoiding accidental fires. Here are some tips.

Overloaded Fuses

Fuses are the safety valves in your electrical circuits. They prevent wires from overheating, which can cause a fire. If a fuse keeps on blowing, then the circuit is overloaded. Never try to circumvent blown fuses by the use of pennies or foil. Call a qualified electrician.

Permanent Wiring

All additions or alterations to permanent wiring should be done by a qualified electrician and must be inspected and approved by your local City Hall electrical inspector.

Careless Smoking

This is possibly the only cause of fire that is 100% preventable. If you have a no-smoking policy with your tenants, that should include any guests as well, so that your policy is 100% non-smoking. Make this provision in writing in your tenancy agreement. This will also have the added advantage of making your home more saleable when the time comes to resell. Many people are allergic to smoke and can detect the odour of smoke in a dwelling, no matter how hard one tries to conceal or mask it.

Wood Stoves

All types of auxiliary heating appliances, such as wood stoves or portable heaters, require extra precaution. To avoid problems, you should note the following guidelines:

√ Always look for a Underwriters' Laboratories of Canada (ULC) or Canadian Standards Association (CSA) label on the unit, which means the unit meets the minimum safety standards and has been approved for use in Canada.

√ If you install the unit yourself, follow the installation instructions precisely. In particular, pay close attention to the clearances required between the unit and any combustible material. It is better to have it installed by a professional.

√ Use the unit strictly in accordance with the instructions.

√ You can call your local fire department or fire-prevention bureau for information and advice on any fire safety-related topic, including wood stoves.

Fireplaces and Chimneys

Always use a fireplace screen and dispose of the ashes in a closed metal container. Chimneys (for wood stoves as well as fireplaces) require cleaning by a chimney sweep service at least every two years to remove and prevent the buildup of creosote deposits. Creosote is flammable and can be ignited by the hot gases from your fireplace. This can spread to any combustible material, such as your roof.

Fire Extinguishers

Buy at least one portable fire extinguisher and keep it in an easily accessible place in the kitchen. Ideally, you should have one extinguisher for every level of your house. Try to select an extinguisher with chemical contents to deal with A (paper and wood), B (flammable liquids, e.g., oil), and C (electrical) types of fire.

Smoke, Fire, and Gas Alarms

These are absolute necessities. They are inexpensive and effective. Smoke alarms should be placed outside bedroom doors, kitchen, workshop area, and other key areas. When you are researching which units to buy, refer to the recommended home sites on the box. Some alarms are heat sensitive, rather than detecting the by-products of a fire (e.g., smoke). If you are using natural gas in the dwelling, make sure you get detectors for that risk as well (e.g., carbon monoxide). Don't forget to replace the batteries twice a year on a memorable date (e.g., when you change your clocks forward for daylight saving time or back for standard time).

Other Safety Measures You Can Take

√ Be sure you have proper locks and that all doors and windows can be secured.

√ Be sure you have well-lit entrances and trim all shrubbery so that it does not obscure entries.

√ Be sure you have all ladders locked away, so that they cannot be used by an intruder.

√ Be sure you review your property periodically to check for potential access points for burglars.

Summary

The property-management tips discussed in this chapter cover a range of issues to consider. Topics include the different types of property-management options, keeping good records, locating the right tenant, and understanding the tenant documentation required. Practical suggestions were given for saving on expenses and increasing income from your revenue property. Finally, tips were offered on avoiding common home-maintenance problems and fire hazards.

We now turn to how to prepare a property for sale as eventually owners and investors will want to dispose of their property.

11 Selling Your Property

Selling is an integral part of the real estate process, whether it is your own home or an investment property. Most of the emphasis in real estate, though, is on buying and managing real estate. Many people take the selling process casually without a full appreciation of the skills and techniques that should be used. They rely on luck or their realtor to get the top price. If you don't know how to maximize the selling price, you will probably make the wrong decisions and lose your potential profit. One of the main motivations for purchasing your principal residence or investment property is, of course, to make as much money on resale as possible. With that in mind, this chapter will give you the foundation to take full advantage of your new insight and knowledge.

There are many questions you have to ask yourself before deciding to sell, including the reasons you should sell, the timing, the price, the terms, and the benefits. You also have to consider how you will sell, including selecting and negotiating with a realtor, a lawyer, and the buyer.

The key topics that will be covered in this chapter include determining when to sell, preparing to sell your property, selecting a real estate agent, and the potential disadvantages of selling the property yourself. Practical home-selling tips will also be discussed.

Determining When to Sell

One of the critical decisions of any real estate investor is deciding when to sell. There are many factors that would suggest a sale is appropriate. Of course, you want to make sure the sale is not perceived as a distress sale. (See also discussions in Chapter 9's section on why a property might be for sale.) The following factors could justify a decision to sell:

√ market is reaching its peak in terms of upward momentum of sales

√ appreciation of the property is plateauing or starting to decline

√ income is plateauing

√ return on investment is decreasing

√ capital expenditures will increase

√ tax shelter or tax benefits are declining

√ financial needs have been met

√ you are interested in other priorities or opportunities

√ area is not economically healthy; it is either stagnating or declining

√ reached appropriate stage in original strategic holding period

√ reduction in net operating income

√ you are getting frustrated with property-management problems.

In short, monitor the market and your investment regularly. Anticipate problems and act accordingly.

Preparing to Sell Your Property

Once you have made the decision to sell, there are other issues you have to deal with. These would include the following:

Timing

The optimal rule here is to sell when everyone else is buying, although this is not always possible. The best times for selling homes, for example, would generally be in the spring, summer, or early fall, rather than the winter months.

Pricing

The property has to be priced right for the market—without emotion and based on objective assessment or value. How to evaluate property value was covered earlier. It is normal to determine the ideal price and then add another 5% or more for negotiating margin.

Documentation Preparation

Prepare all necessary documents for the realtor or purchaser. For example, if a mortgage is assumable without qualification and has an attractive interest rate, get a copy of the mortgage. If you have a revenue property or small apartment building, get all the financial and other records for a purchaser to review.

Financing

If you have an assumable mortgage or you are prepared to take a first or second mortgage back in terms of vendor financing, clarify the terms.

Professional Advice

Depending on the nature of your property, obtain advice from your tax accountant and lawyer with regard to pricing, apportioning value, and timing.

Select a Realtor

Most experienced real estate investors utilize realtors extensively. (The benefits of selecting and using a realtor were discussed in Chapter 4: Selecting Your Advisory Team.) The different types of listing agreements with a realtor were discussed in Chapter 6: Understanding the Legal Aspects. Make certain your realtor is experienced in selling the type of real estate you have.

Competition

Check out similar properties for sale and the positive or negative features about your own property relative to others you have reviewed.

Promotion

Have your realtor advertise and promote the property as extensively as possible. This would usually be done through a Multiple Listing Service (MLS), an open house for public viewing, an open house for realtor viewing, newspaper advertising, and lawn signage.

Make the Property Attractive

First impressions are lasting, so give your property special "curb appeal." This issue is covered in more detail in the last section of this chapter.

Set Terms

Determine what your best deal and bottom-line position will be and why. The purchaser will attempt to negotiate the best deal, so be prepared. (Review Chapter 9: Negotiating Strategies.) Although the points on making the offer are designed from the purchaser's perspective, it will give you a good idea on which matters to counter-offer. (In addition, review Chapter 6: Understanding the Legal Aspects relating to subject clauses in the agreement.)

Calculate Closing Costs

Determine what you will net after all costs and before taxes. For example, you might have a three- or six-month penalty clause in your fixed-term mortgage for prepayment. There would be an exception, of course, if the purchaser assumes the mortgage.

Disadvantages of Selling the Property Yourself

You may be tempted to sell the property yourself. There is primarily only one reason for doing so, and that is saving on a real estate commission. You may indeed save money. On the other hand, the saving could be an illusion. The only other motivation could be a personal challenge or learning experience, but basically the desire to save money is the main motivator. Depending on the nature of the property, the market at the time, the specific realtor you are considering, and the real estate company involved, you can negotiate a reduced real estate commission. The problem with a reduced commission structure, though, is that if you want it listed on the Multiple Listing Service (MLS), other realtors will see the reduced commission involved, and may not be too inspired to spend time attempting to sell it when they can make a higher commission on other properties.

Here are some general disadvantages of selling a property yourself as opposed to using a carefully selected and experienced realtor. The comments apply whether you are selling your principal residence or investment property. The following remarks are not intended to dissuade you from attempting to sell your own property, but to place the process in a realistic perspective. In the end, you will have to balance the benefits and pitfalls and make up your own mind.

Inexperience

If you don't know all the steps involved, from the presale operation to completing the deal, you could and probably would make mistakes that could be costly to you. If you use a realtor who knows the market well in your community, you can capitalize on making the correct decisions.

Emotional Roller-Coaster

Many people, especially with a principal residence, tend to get emotionally involved in the sale process because of the direct interaction with the prospective purchasers. For example, vendors can experience frustration if prospective buyers reject the house, if there are negative comments or fault-finding, if they don't like the personalities of prospective buyers or or people who negotiate aggressively on the price. These one-on-one direct dynamics or comments can sometimes be taken personally and therefore be a cause of stress.

If you use a realtor to act as an agent, you rarely (if ever) meet the prospective purchaser directly, either before the agreement of purchase and sale is signed, or before or after closing. This degree of anonymity reduces stress.

Time Commitment

You have to have open houses and show your property at times that may not necessarily be convenient for you. In addition, you will have to spend time preparing the ad copy and staying at home to respond to telephone calls or people knocking on the door.

If you use a realtor, you will be able to save time by not having to be around when the property is shown or to answer phone calls. The realtor does all that for you as enquiries go directly to the realtor.

Expense, Nature, and Content of Advertising

Costs include any daily or weekly newspaper classified and/or box ads, as well as a lawn sign. You would pay for these yourself. In addition, you may not know what specific types of advertising would be appropriate for your type of property, how to write ad copy that would grab the attention of a reader and prospective purchaser, nor how to identify and emphasize the key selling features of your property.

If you use a realtor, he or she would pay for all the advertising costs. The nature and amount of advertising is negotiated at the time the listing agreement is signed. Not only could you get listed in the MLS book, which normally comes out weekly and is circulated to all member realtors, you could also be on the MLS computer database, which is accessible to all realtors on the Internet through the MLS Web site or through the real estate company Web site if they have one. Your property could also be advertised in daily and/or community newspapers, plus in special weekly real estate newspaper publications, which are available in most major cities. In addition, your realtor can show your property at a special realtor open house once the property is listed. All interested realtors therefore have an opportunity to personally view it. All the techniques described are various forms of advertising. An experienced realtor should also know how to write good ad copy and accentuate the key selling features of your property.

Limited Market Exposure

The previous point covered the comparative differences in market exposure in terms of advertising that you do yourself and the types of advertising a realtor could do for you. There is obviously a direct correlation between the nature and degree of market exposure and the end price. Clearly, self-advertising has limited exposure.

Potential Legal Problems

The prospective purchaser may supply you with his own agreement of purchase and sale. This contract may have clauses and other terms in it that could be legally risky, unenforceable, unfair, or otherwise not beneficial to you. You may not recognize these potential problems or risks. In addition, you could end up agreeing to take back a mortgage (vendor-take-back mortgage) when it would not be necessary or wise, or to accept a long-term option or other legal arrangement that could be risky.

If you use a realtor, the realtor should recognize those aspects of the agreement that are unfair, unenforceable, or unclear, and advise you accordingly. The importance of having a real estate lawyer protect your interests before signing an agreement of purchase and sale is mentioned several times throughout this book. It is an inexpensive investment for peace of mind.

Lack of Familiarity with the Market

You may not have a clear idea of exactly what a similar property in your market is selling for, or the state of the real estate market at that point. This can place you at a distinct disadvantage. For example, if you are unrealistic in your pricing and have limited advertising exposure, you could literally price yourself out of the market. Prospective purchasers may not even look, let alone make an offer. You may eventually sell your property, but only after several price reductions and after a long period. Naturally, of course, this depends on the market and the nature of your property.

If you use a realtor, he or she should be familiar with the market in your area, especially if you carefully select a realtor who is experienced with your type of residential property and knows your geographic area well. The pricing and overall marketing strategies recommended would therefore be customized for market conditions and general saleability.

No Prescreening of Prospective Purchasers

You would not generally know the art of prescreening prospects in terms of which questions to ask them over the phone. The end result is that you could waste your time talking to people over the phone or showing people through the house who are not and never will be serious prospects. You could also end up accepting an offer from someone who does not realistically have a chance of financing the house, or who asks for unrealistic time periods for removing purchaser conditions, which effectively would tie up your property during that time.

A realtor can prescreen the potential prospects over the phone or in person to limit a potential waste of time for you. When the offers are finally presented, you will have more serious prospects involved.

Offer Price Not Necessarily the Best

You may think the offer is the best offer from that prospective purchaser, or any purchaser, and therefore may accept it. That price may not be the best price at all. You may have started too low or too high for your initial asking price based on emotion or needs (not reality); you may have received a "low-ball" offer from the purchaser that was never intended to be accepted but was designed to reduce your expectations; you may be inexperienced in applying real estate negotiating skills; or you may be subjected to effective closing skills on the part of the prospective purchaser.

If you use a realtor, the realtor should be able to eliminate all the above problems. The realtor would normally provide the following services: do the initial research and set the original asking price realistically and objectively, depending on the market conditions, nature and condition of the property, etc.; recognize a "low-ball" offer as a tactical ploy, and attempt to find out the reasons for the offer and whether the prospect was a serious one; suggest to you how to deal with offers in terms of counter-offers; know what negotiating skills to use in a given situation, and use them on your behalf; and know how to use effective closing skills.

Lack of Negotiating Skills

This problem was referred to in the previous point. You may lack any negotiating or sales skills, and as a consequence the price and terms you eventually settle for may not be as attractive as they otherwise could be.

If you use a realtor who is experienced and competent in selling your type of property in your area and who has a successful track record, you will benefit from that realtor's astute use of professional negotiating and sales skills. Another advantage is that the prospective purchaser will be dealing with your realtor, and you will probably never personally meet the purchaser before or after you accept the offer and the deal closes. Removing yourself from direct interaction with the prospective purchaser and using an agent instead enhances your negotiating position and the effective use of strategies.

Purchaser Wants Discount in Price Equal to Commission Saved

It is not uncommon for the prospective purchaser to determine what the fair market value is, and then ask to have an additional discount equal to the real estate commission you are saving. The primary reason why prospective purchasers are attracted to a "For Sale by Owner" is the prospect of getting a better deal than a property listed with a realtor due to the commission otherwise built into the sale price. The primary reason why you are selling the property yourself is to save the full amount of any commission otherwise payable, hence the problem. A compromise may be possible whereby the price is further reduced by 50% or 75% of the commission saved. Again, in practical terms, it is normally an illusion to think that you will save the full amount of the commission. The other related issue is that if you save on a commission (say, $5,000), after the purchaser saves an additional $5,000 on the purchase price (e.g., splitting the commission saving), would you not have a lingering doubt that you could have netted more if it was listed through a realtor and with MLS?

If you use a realtor, the above problem, of course, will not occur. Also, there is a good chance a realtor's efforts will result in a higher selling price for your property. Statistically, if you had listed it and had greater market exposure, better pricing, and a realtor who had applied more experienced real estate negotiating and selling skills than you possess, a higher sale price would be achieved.

Tough to Sell in a Buyer's Market

Buyers in this type of market are very price sensitive, negotiate aggressively because they want the best deal, and have the time to be selective after comparing what is available in the market. You are at a disadvantage if you don't get all the exposure possible and use all the negotiating and selling skills available. You could wait a long time before finally selling, and the market could go down further by that time in a declining sale market (e.g., substantial supply of property but limited demand).

If you use a realtor, whether the market is a buyer's or seller's market, for the reasons outlined in this section, the statistical odds are that you would benefit, in general terms, in your net sale proceeds.

The above summary of the key points shows that there are distinct benefits to consider selling through a realtor who is experienced and carefully selected. Of course, there are exceptions in certain situations where you may choose to sell yourself, but you have to be very aware of the disadvantages and pitfalls. Most real estate investors realize the benefits of using a realtor and do so as a business decision, whether for buying or selling.

Home-Selling Tips

It is essential to make your property as attractive in appearance as possible, whether you are selling it yourself or through a real estate agent. Realtors will give sellers a package that includes tips on improvements to assist in selling a property. Both the inside and outside of the home must evoke a positive feeling with the prospective buyer in order to obtain a quick sale and the highest price. Ask yourself objectively what you perceive a prospective buyer's first impression would be of your home, exterior and interior. If you feel you cannot be objective or want a second opinion, have a relative or friend look at your home with a critical eye and ask him or her to tell you all the negative aspects.

Part of preparing your home for sale means getting rid of unnecessary possessions that detract from a sale. Give yourself plenty of time to remove items before putting your home up for sale, in order to make the process more acceptable and less stressful. You may have to allocate three or four months of weekends before you have cleaned out the excess. Many people are packrats and have difficulty in letting go of possessions accumulated over time. They feel more comfortable about being surrounded by familiar items, no matter how unattractive, junky, or impractical. Ask yourself about each item if you are having difficulty about whether to keep it or not. For example, ask yourself if you have used the item over the past year. If so, consider keeping it as long as it is still usable. If not, then ask yourself if it has any real value to you, or considerable sentimental value. If not, then get rid of it by selling it at a garage sale or donating it to charity.

Another important step, once you have completed all the home-improvement procedures, is to prepare a list of things about your house that you like, e.g., special or unique features such as a workshop or solarium, or a beautiful garden. Make a list of the key selling points about the house, in your view. For example, if you have repainted the house, inside or out, replaced the carpets or had new landscaping done, those are key points to make your home attractive. Finally, make a list of the main points that you like about the neighbourhood, such as convenient shopping, transportation, schools, parks, or playgrounds. In addition, such factors as a quiet neighbourhood, friendly and helpful neighbours, lots of babysitters nearby, and a community spirit are important points to note. If you are using a realtor, give this list to your agent.

The following points discuss the main internal and external factors that you should deal with in the process of getting your home ready for the market.

Home Interior

Keep Things Clean

Keep windows sparkling and clean, inside and outside. Clean all mirrors. Have drapes, carpets, and rugs cleaned and vacuumed. If the carpet is especially worn, consider replacing it. Your home will likely sell faster, although you may not recover your full cost. Keep front and back entrances clear, clean, and inviting. Clean up any corridors, halls, or walkways.

Make the Interior Decorating Attractive

Major decorating before selling may be neither necessary nor desirable because many buyers will probably prefer to select their own paints and colours. On the other hand, if the paint is old, dirty, or dull, you may wish to paint the key areas or all of the inside of the house in a light, bright, natural colour, such as white or beige. Make sure it is washable latex paint. Lighter colours make the room appear larger and brighter. Neutral colours make the room more flexible for any type of furniture. A dingy closet or a badly marked wall can be made much more attractive with a good scrub, a touch of fresh paint, or a bright strip of wallpaper. Try to have a natural flow from room to room, rather than having rooms that are not uniform or complementary.

Get Rid of Clutter

Keep things tidy. Rooms can look comfortable and lived in without being untidy. Vacuum and dust thoroughly. Keep kitchen and bathroom counters uncluttered and gleaming, tables uncluttered and dirty dishes out of sight. Clean up books, magazines, newspapers, and clothes that might be lying around. Store or sell excess furniture if it makes the room look cluttered and small with little floor space. As you want to make the home look more spacious, remove kids' toy bins from the living room, wall-to-wall sports trophies from the family room, and general clutter.

Clean Up All Closets

Make the best use of space. Show your closet and storage areas off to their best advantage. Stack linen neatly, hang clothes carefully, and use garment bags and shoe racks. Crammed closets look small, but well-organized ones appear larger than they really are. Closet organizers would show how efficiently space could be utilized. Remove all "junk" from storage space and discard it, give it away, or sell it at a garage sale.

Make Kitchens and Bathrooms Inviting

The two most important rooms to many buyers are the kitchen and the bathroom. It is particularly important to make those areas appealing. Keep both rooms immaculately tidy and spotlessly clean. You want to create the impression that the home is easy to maintain.

Tidy the Garage

Keep your garage or carport neat and organized to emphasize all the extra storage space. A garage can be a selling point, particularly if viewers are accustomed to the parking or storage problems associated with apartment living.

Make Necessary Repairs

You may be accustomed to a broken window catch, dripping tap, sticking or squeaky door, broken switch covers, and loose doorknobs, but potential buyers will notice and develop a negative impression. Therefore, fix everything that could be irritating from the buyer's viewpoint as described, and anything else, such as wobbly towel racks, loose mouldings, holes in window screens, and stuck windows. Walk around your home, inside and out, and make a list.

Make the Environment as Peaceful as Possible

Keep noise to a minimum to let prospective buyers and the real estate agent examine your home without distraction. Quiet music in the background might have a pleasant effect, but noisy children or TV or stereo sounds can annoy prospective buyers. Try to be out of the house, along with the children and pets, while the realtor shows your home.

Provide a Comfortable Environment

Make sure the building is at a comfortable temperature—fresh and airy on hot summer days and warm during cold days. The right number of lights should be turned on after dark, and a crackling fire lends a homey feeling on a fall or winter evening, or even during the day. Consider replacing your light bulbs with a higher wattage, in order to create a brighter impression. Freshly cut flowers in various rooms such as the kitchen, living room, dining room, bathroom, and master bedroom would be inviting. Potted plants are attractive. The delicious smell of baking in the kitchen can be appealing and make one feel at home. Be cautious about cooking odours, though.

Keep Pets Out of the Way

Buyers may not enjoy being welcomed by a cat or dog. Some people are allergic to animals and others don't like them. Many people could be turned off by knowing that various animals have resided in the home. Ideally, remove the pets from the home during the showing. Also remove cat litter boxes and use a deodorant spray to minimize any odour.

Remove Ashtrays and Odour of Smoke

Many people do not smoke and are allergic or otherwise negatively affected by the odour of cigarettes. Most people do not smoke. Therefore, if you or anyone else who occupies the house or condominium for sale smokes, make sure you remove all ashtrays, dry clean the drapes, and shampoo the carpets. Also consider washing or painting the walls to remove any odour of smoke, which might discourage a prospective purchaser.

Home Exterior

Maintain Your Landscaping

Keep your lawn, shrubs, hedges, and garden tidy and trimmed. Sweep the sidewalks and driveway. Have colourful flowers and/or hanging baskets to project a positive and warm feeling.

Consider Buying a Doormat

If you don't have a doormat or if it is old, consider buying a new one.

Remove Junk

Store or remove any outdoor items that may create a "junkyard" image, such as old tires, cars, or broken fixtures or appliances.

Organize Outdoor Items

Arrange and organize items neatly, such as firewood, outdoor furniture, and play equipment.

Repair Exterior of Home

Paint or stain areas that require it and repair any broken fencing. Repair any broken windows or screens, and then wash them for a brighter appearance.

Consider Painting the House

It may not be necessary to paint the house, but do a touch-up and paint the trim. On the other hand, if the exterior is peeling badly or looks dull and dirty, it will negatively affect the sale of your home, both in price and speed of sale. Therefore, consider repainting.

Check the Front Door

One of the first items a buyer will see will be your front door. Make sure it looks attractive, otherwise consider replacing it. Get new brass house numbers or repaint the old numbers.

The preceding hints are simply basic guidelines to remind you how important it is to set the correct mood and enhance the environment so a person will want to buy your property. As mentioned earlier, the best approach is to try to see your property through the eyes of a prospective buyer.

Summary

The topics in this chapter are critical to obtaining an optimal sale price. The key strategies and tips discussed include determining when to sell, preparing to sell your property, and selecting the real estate agent. Also explained are the potential disadvantages of selling the property yourself, and practical tips on making your home more attractive to a buyer.

The final chapter in the book is about your future—and that of your family. We now turn to financial and estate planning.

CHAPTER 12

Understanding Financial and Estate Planning

If you are investing or thinking of investing in real estate, it is particularly important to make sure that you have a financial and estate plan in place.

This chapter provides an overview of the financial and estate planning issues that you need to consider, and update regularly as your needs change. At the end of the chapter is a section of Web sites of interest.

An Introduction to Financial Planning

As part of your personal life plan, you need to have a detailed written plan of your financial-planning needs and goals. This would include your short- and long-term investment plan. The cliché of "How do you know if you have arrived unless you know where you are going?" is a truism. A realistic and objective plan, prepared with the support of your professional advisers, will provide you with peace of mind and a sense of control and financial security.

You will need to obtain the right advisers to assist you in attaining your goals. You want to maximize your profit potential and minimize your financial risk. (Chapter 4: Selecting Your Advisory Team gives guidelines and tips on how to carefully select the right advisers to assist you in your financial plan.) This would include an integrated professional approach to all your personal and investment needs, utilizing a financial planner, insurance broker, accountant, and lawyer to protect your interests and accomplish your objectives.

There are five basic steps involved in financial planning. These include selecting the right financial planner and other professionals, assessing your current and future financial situation, establishing your goals and priorities, developing a realistic and attainable plan, and monitoring and evaluating the results on an ongoing basis. The plan should cover all the aspects of your financial life, including insurance, investments, loans, tax, retirement planning, and estate planning.

An Introduction to Estate Planning

Your will is the most important document you will ever draw up. With very few exceptions, everybody should have a will. A will is the only legal document that can ensure that your assets will be distributed to your beneficiaries according to your wishes, instead of by a government formula, in a timely manner and with effective estate planning. Your will takes effect only after your death and is kept strictly confidential until that time.

There are no estate taxes or succession duties in Canada, but estate planning can minimize the amount that is taxed in other ways. Part of estate planning also includes having a power of attorney and possibly a living will. For a more detailed discussion of estate and tax planning, refer to the book, *The Canadian Guide to Will and Estate Planning* by Douglas Gray and John Budd. Check out the website: www.estateplanning.ca.

Why You Need a Will

About one out of four people dies suddenly, leaving no opportunity for tax or estate planning if such a plan was not already in place. It is estimated that only one out of three adults has a will, which means that when the other two-thirds die, the government has to become involved. Some people just procrastinate by nature or have busy lives and simply do not put a priority on preparing a will. Others do not appreciate the full implications of dying without a will or even think about it. And some people simply resist the reality that they are mortal. Preparing a will and dealing with estate-planning issues certainly faces the issue of mortality in a direct way.

Of those who do have a will, many do not modify it based on changing circumstances. People first think of preparing a will when they marry, have children, fly for the first time without their children, or when they hear news of a sudden death of a friend or relative. Once they complete a will, they forget about it. Not updating your will can be as bad as not having one and could cause your beneficiaries much grief, stress, time, and expense. Your marital status may have changed, assets increased or decreased, or you may have started or ended a business, moved to a new province, or a new government tax or other legislation could be introduced that should prompt you to revisit your estate plan. For those who consider writing their own will, there is a risk of serious mistakes and oversight.

What Is Estate Planning?

Estate planning refers to the process of preserving and transferring your wealth in an effective manner. From a tax perspective, your estate objectives, including a properly drafted will, include:

√ minimizing and deferring taxes

√ moving any tax burden to your heirs to be paid only upon future sale of the assets.

There are techniques to attain the above objectives, including:

√ arranging for assets to be transferred to family members in a lower tax bracket

√ establishing trusts for your children and/or spouse

√ setting up estate freezes, generally for your children, which reduce the future tax they pay on assets of increased value

√ making optimal use of the benefits of charitable donations, tax shelters, holding companies, or dividend tax credits

√ taking advantage of gifting during your lifetime

√ minimizing the risk of business creditors encroaching on personal estate assets

√ having sufficient insurance to cover anticipated tax on death

√ avoiding probate fees by having assets in joint names or with a designated beneficiary.

What's in a Will?

Depending on the complexity of your estate, your will could be either simple or complex. A basic will contains:

√ name and address of the person who is making the will (the testator)

√ a declaration that the document is your last will and testament and it revokes all former wills and codicils (a supplementary document that may change, add, or subtract from the original will)

√ appointment of an executor (person or an organization who will administer your estate) and possibly a trustee (required where you have included trust provisions in your will)

√ authorization to pay outstanding debts, including funeral expenses, taxes, fees, and other administrative expenses before any gift of property can be made

√ disposition of property and cash legacies to beneficiaries, or a gift of part or the entire residue of your estate (what is left after all debts, funeral and administrative expenses, taxes, and fees have been paid and specific property gifts and cash legacies distributed)

√ attestation clause that states that the will was properly signed in the presence of at least two witnesses who were both present at the same time, and who both signed in your presence and the presence of each other

√ appointment of a guardian for infant children.

Special Provisions

Consult a lawyer who specializes in wills and estates to assist you in identifying and preparing special provisions for your situation. A few of the many special provisions include:

√ *Alternative beneficiaries and 30-day survivorship clause:* When spouses die together or within a very short time of each other, if they have wills leaving everything to each other without naming alternate beneficiaries, the situation is similar to not having a will at all. Although uncommon, you still should provide for the possibility that your spouse may not be able to benefit from the estate. A 30-day clause provides that in order for your beneficiaries to benefit from the estate, they have to survive you by 30 days. If it is impossible to determine which of a married couple died first, it is presumed that the younger spouse survived the older spouse.

√ *Trusts:* If you want to give someone a gift but do not want him or her to have direct control of the property, you can set up a trust provision in your will to manage the gift. Trusts are discussed in more detail later.

Funeral Instructions

Some people detail in their will their instructions regarding funeral arrangements and the disposition of the body. These instructions are not legally binding on the executor for various legal reasons. Inform your executor and immediate family of your funeral arrangement wishes. Your will is generally not located and read until after the funeral has already occurred. Your comments in the will should simply reinforce what you have stated verbally.

What Happens If You Don't Have a Will?

If you don't have a will, or don't have a valid will, the outcome could be a legal and financial nightmare and an emotionally devastating ordeal for your loved ones. This is compounded greatly if you have a business. Not having a will at the time of death is called being intestate. Under provincial legislation, the court will appoint an administrator. If no family member applies to act as administrator, the public trustee or official administrator is appointed. Your estate will be distributed in accordance with the legal formulas of your province, which are inflexible and many may not reflect either your personal wishes or the needs of your family or loved ones.

While the law attempts to be fair, it does not provide for special needs. A home or other assets could be sold under unfavourable market conditions in order to distribute the assets. Your heirs may pay taxes that might easily have been deferred or reduced. There may not be sufficient worth in the estate to pay the taxes. Your family could be left without money for an extended period, and your assets may be lost or destroyed. There may be a delay in the administration of your estate and added costs such as an administrator bond. This is similar to an insurance policy if the administrator makes a mistake.

If you die without a will appointing a guardian for your young children, and there is no surviving parent who has legal custody, provincial laws come into effect. The public trustee becomes the guardian and manager of the assets that your children are entitled to. The provincial child welfare services assume responsibility for their care, upbringing, education, and health. A relative or other person can apply to the court for guardianship, but it is up to the court's discretion.

Is Your Will Valid in the U.S. for U.S. Assets?

In general terms, if you have a valid will that is legally enforceable in your province, it would probably also be valid in the U.S. state in which you have assets. Possibly you own recreational property or are thinking of buying property in the U.S. for business purposes.

There could be a serious problem if you have two wills, one Canadian, one American. Because they are different legal jurisdictions, a beneficiary (or someone who would like to be one) might challenge the contents of the will in one jurisdiction but not in the other one. Standard boilerplate clauses often state that the most recent will automatically revokes any and all previous wills. If you inadvertently included that clause in a U.S. will, it could automatically nullify your Canadian will!

You could instruct your Canadian lawyer to include specific terms in your Canadian will relating to your U.S. assets and have affidavit attestation of the witnesses of your will at the same time. All this must be done in conjunction with feedback from a U.S. lawyer who has expertise in will matters in the state in which you own assets. Another option is to have a U.S. lawyer transfer your U.S. assets into joint names, with right of survivorship, so that those assets would automatically go to your surviving spouse. Consider having your U.S. property in a living trust or revocable trust. This bypasses your estate, and therefore probate procedures, as the trust is not in the deceased's name, but a trustee's name. Your lawyer will help you assess the options in your situation.

Preparing a Will

There are basically three ways to prepare a will: writing it yourself, having a lawyer do it for you, or having a trust company arrange a lawyer to do it for you. The advantages and disadvantages of each are outlined in the following:

Self-Written Wills

This is the poorest choice because the inadequacies of a self-written will could result in a legal, financial, and administrative nightmare for your family, relatives, and beneficiaries. How you expressed your wishes may be legally interpreted differently than what you intended. Worse still, a clause or the whole will could be deemed void for technical reasons. Some people draft a will from scratch or use a "standard form" of will format purchased in bookstores or stationery stores. The risk is very high and it is false economy as, depending on your situation, you could have a lot to lose.

Lawyer-Prepared Wills

In almost all cases, wills should be prepared by a lawyer who is familiar with wills because he or she is qualified to provide legal advice and is knowledgeable on how to complete the legal work. For more information, refer to the book *The Canadian Guide to Will and Estate Planning* by Douglas Gray and John Budd, and the website: www.estateplanning.ca.

Depending on the complexity of the estate, however, you may also need to enlist the expertise of the other specialists, including a professionally qualified tax accountant or a financial planner. (Refer to Chapter 4: Selecting Your Advisory Team to assist you in finding professional assistance.)

The fee for preparing a basic will is modest, ranging from $200 to $300 or more per person. If your affairs are complex, the fee could be higher due to the additional time and expertise required. A "back-to-back" will is a duplicate reverse will for each partner, and is generally done at a reduced price.

Key Reasons for Consulting a Lawyer

To reinforce the necessity of obtaining a legal consultation before completing or redoing a will, just look at some of the many reasons when legal advice is specifically required because of the complex legal issues and options involved:

√ You own or plan to own investment real estate.

√ You currently jointly own investment real estate with others or plan to do so.

√ You own or plan to own foreign real estate on your own or jointly with others.

√ You own or plan to own your own business.

√ You own or plan to own a business with partners.

√ You are separated from your spouse but not divorced.

√ You are planning to separate from your spouse or partner.

√ You are divorced and paying support.

√ You are living in, entering, or leaving a common-law relationship.

√ You are in a blended family relationship.

√ Your estate is large and you need assistance with estate planning to reduce or eliminate taxes on your death.

√ You anticipate being a beneficiary of a substantial inheritance.

√ You have a history of emotional or mental problems such that someone could attack the validity of your will on the basis that you did not understand the implications of your actions.

√ You want to have unbiased, professional advice rather than being influenced by or under duress from relatives.

√ You want to live outside of Canada for extended periods of time, for example, retire and travel south in the winter. Your permanent residence at the time of your death has legal and tax implications. For more information, refer to the book *The Canadian Snowbird Guide (Everything You Need to Know about Living Part-Time in the USA and Mexico)* by Douglas Gray.

√ You have a will that was signed outside Canada or plan to have one.

√ You want to forgive certain debts, or make arrangements for the repayment of debts to your estate should you die before the debt is paid.

√ You want events to occur that have to carefully worded, such as having a spouse have income or use of a home until he or she remarries or dies, at which time the balance goes elsewhere.

√ You want to set up a trust for your family, business, or investment real estate.

√ You want to donate money to a charitable organization.

√ You want to make special arrangements to care for someone who is incapable of looking after himself or herself or unable to apply sound financial judgement, for example, a child, an immature adolescent, a gambler, an alcoholic, a spendthrift, or someone with emotional, physical, or mental disabilities or who is ill.

√ You wish to disinherit a spouse, relative, or child because of a serious estrangement or the fact that all your children are now independently wealthy and don't need your money.

√ You have several children and you want to provide one specific child with the opportunity to buy, have an option to buy, or receive in the will a specific possession of your estate.

As you can see, there are many reasons to consult with a legal expert for a will that is customized for your needs. The general factors to look for when selecting a lawyer are discussed in Chapter 4: Selecting Your Advisory Team.

Other Key Factors to Consider

Selecting a Trust Company

A trust company can offer extensive services in terms of will and estate planning, generally in conjunction with a lawyer of your choice, or they could recommend one. Always obtain independent legal advice. A trust company is invaluable when a trust is set up as part of your estate planning, as well as to act as your executor, for example, if you don't have anyone who has the time, ability, skill, temperament, or desire to be the executor or trustee of your estate. Needs vary and, after obtaining advice, you may not require a trust company.

Selecting an Executor

Your executor acts as your personal representative and deals with all the financial, tax, administrative, and other aspects of your estate. You grant your executor the power to convert any part of your estate into money as he or she thinks best in order to wind up the estate. It is difficult to find a layperson or family member who could adequately fulfill all the qualifications that might be required. Not only can the process be time consuming and complicated, it can also expose the executor to personal legal liability if errors are made. The executor is accountable to all beneficiaries.

There are two kinds of executors. The professional executor is a lawyer, accountant, or trust company staff. The other type is an inexperienced layperson, generally a relative or family friend. Many people consider being asked to be an executor an honour, a reflection of the trust in the relationship. However, conflicts can and do occur between executors and beneficiaries. The executor may be perceived as overzealous or indifferent, authoritarian or showing favouritism, lacking necessary knowledge or making decisions too hastily. An executor can retain a lawyer or a trust company as an agent. You can also name more than one person to administer the estate, referred to as co-executors. For example, you could consider having a spouse and a trust company as co-executors. If you are naming an individual, make sure you have an alternate executor in case the first one is unwilling or unable to act.

Selecting a Trustee

Trusts that operate during your lifetime are generally called inter-vivos trusts. A trust that is operable upon your death as outlined in your will is a testamentary trust. You would need to have a trustee manage either type; both are discussed later in this chapter.

You may wish to appoint a trustee to manage a portion of your assets for an extended period. If you are selecting a layperson to be the executor, you may not want the same person to be the trustee to prevent a potential conflict of interest. Trustees are normally responsible for taking in and investing money, selling assets, and distributing the estate proceeds in accordance with the trust terms. The trustee must maintain a balance between the interests of income beneficiaries and beneficiaries subsequently entitled to the capital. In addition, a trustee should maintain accounts and regularly issue accounting statements and income tax receipts to beneficiaries, make income payments, and exercise discretion or early withdrawal of capital to meet special needs.

Finally, the trustee makes the final distribution of the trust fund in accordance with the will. You can see why trust companies perform a vital role. An individual may not have the long-term continuity required due to death or lack of interest or ability. Selecting the right executor and trustee will enhance the smooth disposition of your assets and reduce your family's stress. Use professionals to act as an executor or trustee, or appoint a family member to be a co-executor or co-trustee if the circumstances warrant. Remember to shortlist three prospects and/or trust companies before you decide whom to select as your executor and/or trustee.

Selecting a Guardian

If you have children, it is in your children's best interests to thoroughly plan for their upbringing and care in the event of your death. When you appoint a guardian, you are really just making a request, as your wishes are not legally binding as children are not property and therefore cannot be willed. If the guardian is willing and able to perform the responsibilities, the courts will generally uphold your wishes. Make sure you name an alternate guardian in case the first one is unwilling or unable to assume the responsibility or predeceases you.

Talk with, and obtain the consent of, the main and alternate guardians before naming them in your will. Leave with your will, in your safety deposit box, a letter detailing your wishes with regard to raising your children. This would include fundamental issues such as religion, education, values, and general upbringing. Discuss these issues with the guardian.

Appointing different people to be the trustee and guardian of the children should eliminate any potential conflict of interest. The trustee is responsible for protecting the child's inheritance. A guardian frequently attempts to obtain more funds for the upbringing, health, and education of the child. One way of making sure there is sufficient money for the trust is to purchase life insurance.

Understanding Trusts

Trusts are a very common way of dealing with a range of personal choice, family, or business options. Basically, a trust is a legal structure whereby a trustee deals with property or assets, e.g., cash, stocks, bonds, over which the trustee has control for the benefit of beneficiaries. The trustee could also be one of the beneficiaries. Although the trustee has legal title to the trust property, beneficial ownership rests with the beneficiaries.

A trustee derives only certain limited powers by provincial statute. Therefore, your will should specify exactly what powers you want to give your trustee in carrying out the provisions of the trust. For example, if you do not want your trustee restricted in the type of investments of trust funds, you must provide your trustee with expanded investment powers in your will.

Living Trusts

There are a number of creative ways that you can use a living trust, including the following examples.

Family Trust

This trust would involve having some of the shares in a company owned by a spouse held in the name of a family trust. These shares could be non-voting shares. This family trust could be comprised of your spouse and children. The monies that would go to the trust by means of dividends could then be distributed through dividends to each of the trust members. If the members of the trust were not receiving any other income, they could each take out $30,000 (indexed for inflation) of dividend income each year tax-free. As the tax legislation can change at any time, check with your accountant. If the family members were minors and if the trust were formed properly, the normal CRA policy of attributing income to a minor to the parents for tax purposes (the attribution rule) would not be applicable.

Unfortunately, several years ago, the government clamped down on income-splitting arrangements by introducing a special income-splitting tax. This tax will apply at the marginal income tax rate to individuals under 18 years of age who directly or indirectly receive taxable dividends on shares of Canadian private corporations and foreign corporations. This special tax will also apply to some business income allocated to a minor from a partnership or a trust. Seek advice from your tax accountant.

Estate Freeze

If your company or other assets have shown a consistent pattern of growth over time, which you anticipate will continue, an estate freeze using a corporation set up for the purpose, along with a living trust agreement, could be an effective strategy. This technique freezes the value of your assets as of the effective date of the agreement. All future capital gains will accrue to the benefit of your beneficiaries, e.g., children.

Providing for Family Members with Special Needs

If you have family members who are not able to handle their own affairs due to mental or physical incapacity or other reasons, a living trust could be established to provide for their financial needs for their lifetime. On the recipient's death, the remainder of the funds could be left for some other purpose, e.g., charity.

Giving to Charity

You may wish to set up what is referred to as a "charitable remainder trust." In this situation, you could assist your charity of choice by donating a residual interest in a trust to the charity. The common format is for the capital in the trust to go to the charity on your death, and in the meantime, you receive the income earned from the assets in the trust. It is possible that the trust could be structured so that you receive a non-refundable tax credit when the trust is established, representing the projected fair market value of the residual interest (the "remainder"), e.g., the capital available on your death. If the capital is not going to be eroded during your lifetime, it is easy to project the remainder.

Managing Retirement Needs

With the advances in medical science and people being more aware of healthy living and eating, the average life span has increased greatly over the years. It is not uncommon for people to live into their eighties and nineties.

However, many people do not feel comfortable managing their own affairs. Possibly their children do not have money-management skills, are very busy, or live out of town. For these reasons, many people consider the benefits of a living trust, managed by a trust company and a responsible family member as co-trustees. Assets are set aside and put into the trust. Normally it is structured so that the parents receive income for life, with the capital distributed to the children and/or grandchildren on the death of the surviving parent.

The trust could also have a provision stating that the capital of the trust could be used under certain conditions, such as greater financial needs dictated by health such as, for example, paying for a long-term care facility in a retirement home.

Testamentary Trusts

Testamentary trusts, created in your will, include the spousal trust, trusts set up for minor children or grandchildren, providing for family members with special needs, discretionary trusts for children who are spendthrifts, and gifts for charities. Here are some examples:

Spousal Trust

In this situation, you set up a trust to provide income for the life of your spouse, with the capital remaining at death to go to the children or grandchildren. This type of trust is common when a spouse is ill or incapacitated or lacks financial expertise. A variation of this format, if there are no children or grandchildren, is to leave the capital to charity on the death of the surviving spouse.

Trusts for Minors

This is probably an obvious one for most people. You may probably already have it stated in your will that in the event that both parents die at the same time, or when the surviving parent dies, that a portion of your estate shall be held in trust for minor children or grandchildren until they reach a certain age. In the meantime, the trustee can encroach on the capital for specific needs of the children. Many people then arrange to have the money disbursed over various time periods as the children mature. For example, one-third at age 19, one-third at age 25, and one-third at age 30.

Trust for Charities

You may wish to set up a trust that provides family members with income for life, but on their death the remaining capital in the trust is distributed to a charity of your choice.

Spendthrift Trust

Perhaps you have a child who has a history of financial irresponsibility. One solution is to set up a trust to control the funds or assets that the child would otherwise receive.

Living Will

A living will is designed for those who are concerned about their quality of life when they are near death. It is a written statement of your intentions to the people who are most likely to have control over your care, such as your family and your doctor. Have a copy of the living will where it can be readily obtained, such as in your wallet. Give a copy to your spouse and family doctor. You should also review your living will from time to time.

The purpose of a living will is to convey your wishes if there is no reasonable expectation of recovery from physical or mental disability. Such a will requests that you be allowed to die naturally, with dignity, and not be kept alive by "heroic medical measures." In some provinces, a living will is merely an expression of your wishes and is not legally binding on your doctor or the hospital. Other provinces have officially endorsed the concept through legislation if your written instructions are correctly done. For further information, contact the Joint Centre for Bioethics, University of Toronto, through their Web site: www.utoronto.ca/jcb.

Power of Attorney (PA)

Many lawyers recommend a power of attorney (PA), sometimes referred to as an "enduring" PA, at the same time that they prepare a will. The purpose of a PA is to designate a person or a trust company to take over your affairs if you can no longer handle them due to illness or incapacitation, for example. Another reason is that you may be away for extended periods on personal or business matters. A power of attorney is important if you have substantial assets that require active management. You can grant a general PA over all your affairs, or a limited one specific to a certain task or time period. You can revoke the power of attorney at any time in writing. A PA is valid only in your province. You would need to have a separate PA if you own assets in the U.S. or elsewhere.

If you do not have a power of attorney and become incapacitated, an application has to be made to the court by the party who wishes permission to manage your affairs. This person would be called a committee. If another family member does not wish to perform this responsibility, a trust company can be appointed, with court approval. Committee duties include filing with the court a summary of assets, liabilities, and income sources, with a description of the person's needs and an outline of how the committee proposes to manage the accounts and/or structure the estate to serve those needs.

Personal Information Record

If you died suddenly, or had a serious head injury or stroke, would anyone have an accurate and current knowledge of your personal, business, and investment matters? For most people, the answer to that question would be no. That is why you need to prepare one, and keep it updated annually and when any financial matters change. Your family, executor, and trustee will think of you fondly for having the foresight to make the administration of your estate so much easier. This personal information record is normally kept with your will, for example, in your safety deposit box, with a copy at your home.

To obtain a copy of a personal information record template, go to the Web site: www.estateplanning.ca. The types of matters covered in a typical personal information record would include:

- √ personal information such as partners, children, dependants
- √ key documents and location of documents
- √ names of professionals or advisers you deal with
- √ details of banking information
- √ details of investment information
- √ details of personal property
- √ details of personal or investment real estate
- √ details of ownership in a business
- √ details of mortgages and other debts
- √ details of insurance
- √ funeral information.

Web Sites of Interest

Here are some Web sites that will assist your information search on financial and estate-planning matters. The federal government has some excellent Web sites, as noted. In addition, check out the Web sites of banks, trust companies, credit unions, mutual fund companies, brokerages, and insurance companies.

Canada Revenue Agency: www.cra-arc.gc.ca
Also known as Revenue Canada; contains
information on tax, child and family
benefits, and more.

Canadian Estate Planning Institute:
Contains articles on financial and estate
planning, personal finance, and excellent
checklists, charts, personal information
record, financial calculators, and more.

www.estateplanning.ca

Canadian Consumer Information Gateway:
A federal government initiative designed
to enhance consumer awareness of
the marketplace.

www.consumerinformation.ca

Canadian MoneySaver:
A personal finance site that has articles
from past and current issues of the
magazine of the same name.

www.canadianmoneysaver.ca

Financial Consumer Agency of Canada:
A federal government agency with a
mandate to educate and protect consumers
in the financial services area; ensures that
financial institutions comply with federal
consumer-protection requirements.

www.fcac-acfc.gc.ca

Financial Planners Standards Council:
Learning Centre: Provides consumer
information on financial-planning
articles and links.

www.cfp-ca.org

Government of Canada:
General information on a wide
variety of topics.

www.canada.bc.ca

Human Resources Development Canada:
HRDC is a federal government agency
that administers the Canada Pension
Plan and the Old Age Security Program.

www.hrdc-drhc.gc.ca

Joint Centre for Bioethics:
University of Toronto: This organization
has an excellent Web site with information
on the concept of living wills and provides
free copies for different types of purposes
that can be downloaded from the site.

www.utoronto.ca/jcb

Money Savvy 101:
An on-line course program designed to
address common financial questions
during various life stages; the program
is designed by Industry Canada, a federal
government agency.

http://strategis.ic.bc.ca

MoneySense:
A personal finance site that has articles
from past and current issues of the
Canadian magazine of the same name;
has excellent financial calculators for a
wide range of decision-making issues,
including mortgages

www.moneysense.ca

Summary

Proper and professional financial planning is an integral part of your short-
and long-term personal and investment strategy. It encompasses an integral
range of matters, such as personal, business, insurance, tax, retirement, and
estate planning.

A will is part of your estate planning, and should be customized for your
specific needs and updated on a regular basis. As a will is a legal document, the
wording and necessary clauses to reflect your wishes should be approved by
your lawyer. Most people would not choose to inflict the consequences of not
having a will on their family. There is no logical reason not to have a will, an
enduring power of attorney, and a living will—all necessary components of a
prudent estate plan.

Appendix

FORM 1: Personal Cost-of-Living Budget (Monthly)
(See Chapter 1)

I. Income (Average monthly income, actual or estimated)

Salary, bonuses, and commissions	$_____
Dividends	$_____
Interest income	$_____
Pension income	$_____
Other:	$_____
	$_____
TOTAL MONTHLY INCOME	$_____(A)

II. Expenses

Regular Monthly Payments:

Rent or mortgage payments	$_____
Automobile(s)	$_____
Appliances/TV/Cable	$_____
Internet charges	$_____
Home improvement loan	$_____
Credit card payments (not covered elsewhere)	$_____
Personal loan	$_____
Medical plan	$_____
Instalment and other loans	$_____
Life insurance premiums	$_____
House insurance	$_____
Other insurance premiums (auto, extended medical, etc.)	$_____
RRSP deductions	$_____
Pension fund (employer)	$_____
Investment plan(s)	$_____
Miscellaneous	$_____
Other:	$_____
	$_____
TOTAL REGULAR MONTHLY PAYMENTS	$_____

Household Operating Expenses:

Telephone $_____

Gas and electricity $_____

Heat $_____

Water and garbage $_____

Other household expenses (repairs, maintenance, etc.) $_____

Other: $_____

$_____

TOTAL HOUSEHOLD OPERATING EXPENSES $_____

Food Expenses:

At home $_____

Away from home $_____

TOTAL FOOD EXPENSES $_____

Personal Expenses:

Clothing, cleaning, laundry $_____

Drugs $_____

Transportation (other than auto) $_____

Medical/dental $_____

Daycare $_____

Education (self) $_____

Education (children) $_____

Dues $_____

Gifts, donations, and dues $_____

Travel $_____

Recreation $_____

Newspapers, magazines, books $_____

Automobile maintenance, gas, and parking $_____

Spending money, allowances $_____

Other: $_____

$_____

TOTAL PERSONAL EXPENSES $_____

(Continued)

Tax Expenses:

    Federal and provincial income taxes $_____

    Home property taxes $_____

    Other: $_____

         $_____

    TOTAL TAX EXPENSES $_____

III. Summary of Expenses

Regular monthly payments $_____

Household operating expenses $_____

Food expenses $_____

Personal expenses $_____

Tax expenses $_____

TOTAL MONTHLY EXPENSES $_____ **(B)**

TOTAL MONTHLY DISPOSABLE INCOME AVAILABLE $_____ **(A – B)**

(subtract total monthly expenses from total monthly income)

FORM 2: Personal Net Worth Statement (Format Commonly Requested by Lenders)
(See Chapter 1)

Name:_____

Date of birth: MM_____/DD_____/YR_____   Social Insurance No.: _____

Street Address: _____

City: _____   Province: _____   Postal code: _____

Home phone: _____   Residence: ☐Own ☐Rent ☐Other

How long at address?   _____Years   _____Months

☐Married   ☐Unmarried   ☐Separated   Number of dependants: _____

Occupation: _____   Employer's Phone _____

Currently employed with How long with employer? _____Years _____Months

Your principal financial institution and address: _____

_____

Personal Data on Your Spouse

Under the laws of Canada and of some provinces, your spouse may have a legal interest or obligation arising from your business dealings and may also have an interest in your personal assets.

Spouse's name: _____

Spouse's occupation: _____

Spouse currently employed by:_____

Spouse's work phone: _____

How long with employer? _____Years   _____Months

(Continued)

Financial Information

As of _____ day of _____ month, 20_____

Assets	Value
(List and describe all assets)	
Total of chequing accounts	$_____
Total of savings accounts	$_____
Life insurance cash surrender value	$_____
Automobile: Make _____ Year _____	$_____
Stocks and bonds (see Schedule A attached)	$ _____
Accounts/notes receivable (please itemize):	
_____	$_____
_____	$_____
_____	$_____
Term deposits (cashable)	$_____
Real estate (see Schedule B attached)	$_____
Retirement plans:	
RRSP	$_____
Employment pension plan	$_____
Other	$_____
Other assets (household goods, etc.)	$_____
Art	$_____
Jewellery	$_____
Antiques	$_____
Other	$_____
TOTAL ASSETS (A)	$_____ (A)

Liabilities

(List credit cards, open lines of credit, and other liabilities including alimony and child support.)

	Balance Owing	Monthly Payment
Bank loans	$ _____	$_____
Mortgages on real estate owned		
(see Schedule B attached)	$ _____	$_____
Monthly rent payment	$ _____	$_____

Credit cards (Please itemize):

_____	$ _____	$ _____
_____	$ _____	$ _____
_____	$ _____	$ _____
_____	$ _____	$ _____

Money borrowed from life
insurance policy $ _____ $ _____

Margin accounts $ _____ $ _____

Current income tax owing $ _____ $ _____

Other obligations (Please itemize):

_____	$ _____	$ _____
_____	$ _____	$ _____
_____	$ _____	$ _____

TOTAL MONTHLY PAYMENTS $ _____

TOTAL LIABILITIES (B) $ _____ **(B)**

NET WORTH (A − B) $ _____ **(A − B)**

Income Sources

Income from alimony, child support, or separate maintenance does not have to be stated unless you want it considered.

Your gross monthly salary $ _____

Your spouse's gross monthly salary $ _____

Net monthly rental (from Schedule B attached) $ _____

Other income (Please itemize.):

_____	$ _____
_____	$ _____
_____	$ _____

TOTAL $ _____

Sundry Personal Obligations

Please provide details below if you answer yes to the following question:

Are you providing your personal support for obligations not listed above

(i.e., co-signer, endorser, guarantor)? ___ Yes ___ No

Details of any of the above: _____

Schedule A: Stocks, Bonds, and Other Investments

Quantity	Description	Where Quoted	Market Value	Pledged as collateral?	
				Yes	No

TOTAL _____

Schedule B: Real Estate Owned

Please provide information on your share only of real estate owned.

Property address (primary residence):_____

Legal description: _____

Street _____

City _____ Province _____

Type of property _____

Present market value : $ _____

Amount of mortgage liens: 1st $ _____ 2nd $ _____

Gross monthly income rental _____

Monthly mortgage payments 1st $ _____ 2nd $ _____

Monthly taxes, insurance, maintenance, and miscellaneous: _____

Net monthly rental income $ _____ $ _____

Name of mortgage holder(s)

First mortgage _____

Second mortgage _____

Percentage ownership: _____ % Month/year acquired: _____

Purchase price $ _____

General Information

Please provide details if you answer yes to any of the following questions:

Have you ever had an asset repossessed?	Yes ____ No ____
Are you party to any claims or lawsuits?	Yes ____ No ____
Have you ever declared bankruptcy?	Yes ____ No ____
Do you owe any taxes prior to the current year?	Yes ____ No ____

Details:

_____

_____

_____

_____

_____

_____

_____

_____

_____

_____

_____

The undersigned declare(s) that the statements made herein are for the purpose of obtaining business financing and are to the best of my/our knowledge true and correct. The applicant(s) consent(s) to the Bank making any enquiries it deems necessary to reach a decision on this application, and consent(s) to the disclosure at any time of any credit information about me/us to any credit reporting agency or to anyone with whom I/we have financial relations.

Date:_____   Signature of applicant(s) above:_____

FORM 3: Calculating Your
Gross Debt-Service (GDS) Ratio
(See Chapter 5)

Your GDS ratio is calculated by adding the total of your monthly mortgage principal, interest, and taxes (PIT) together and dividing that figure by your monthly income. Guidelines have been set that generally allow a maximum of 27% to 30% or more, depending on the financial institution, of your gross income to be used for the mortgage PIT

$$\text{GDS ratio} = \frac{\text{Monthly Principal} + \text{Interest} + \text{Taxes (PIT)}}{\text{Monthly income}}$$

Gross (pre-tax) *monthly* income of purchaser(s) $_____

Other forms of income (e.g., annual)
averaged to monthly $_____

TOTAL MONTHLY INCOME $_____

Estimate monthly property tax on home

(net after any provincial homeowners' grant is
taken into consideration, if applicable) $_____

1. To estimate the *maximum* monthly mortgage payment plus property taxes you could carry (monthly PIT), calculate 30% of the total monthly income:

30% of $ _____ $_____

2. To estimate the *maximum* monthly mortgage payment, not including taxes (PI), that you could carry, subtract the monthly tax amount from the monthly PIT:

Monthly PIT $_____

Less: Monthly property tax $_____

MAXIMUM MONTHLY MORTGAGE PAYMENT $_____

(not including taxes) = Monthly PI

Use Chart 7 to determine the maximum mortgage (not including taxes) for which you qualify under your GDS ratio guidelines. Simply look up your maximum monthly mortgage payment under the current interest rate. Maximum mortgage available under GDS

Ratio guidelines $_____

FORM 4: Calculating Your Total
Debt-Service (TDS) Ratio
(See Chapter 5)

Most lenders require that an applicant meet a TDS ratio, in addition to looking at the GDS ratio. The TDS ratio is generally a maximum of 35% to 40% or more of gross income—actual rules may vary between financial institutions. The TDS ratio is calculated in much the same way as the GDS ratio, but takes into consideration all other debts and loans you may have.

$$\text{TDS ratio} = \frac{\text{Monthly Principal} + \text{Interest} + \text{Taxes (PIT)} + \text{Other monthly payments}}{\text{Monthly income}}$$

Gross (pre-tax) monthly income of purchaser(s)	$_____
Other forms of income (e.g., annual) averaged to monthly	$_____
TOTAL MONTHLY INCOME	$_____

Other monthly payments:

Credit cards	$_____
Other mortgages	$_____
Car loan	$_____
Other loans	$_____
Alimony/child support	$_____
Charge accounts	$_____
Other debts (list):	$_____
_____	$_____
_____	$_____
_____	$_____
TOTAL OTHER MONTHLY PAYMENTS	$_____

(Continued)

To calculate your TDS ratio, take 40% of $ _____ (total monthly income)
= $ _____ available for monthly principal + interest + taxes + other payments
(PIT + Other).

To estimate the *maximum monthly mortgage payment* you could carry within your allowable TDS ratio:

Monthly PIT + Other	$_____
Less: Other monthly payments	$_____
SUBTOTAL	$_____
Less: Estimated property taxes	$_____
MAXIMUM MONTHLY MORTGAGE PAYMENT	$_____

Use Chart 7 to determine the maximum mortgage for which you qualify under the TDS Ratio guidelines. Simply look up your maximum monthly mortgage payment under the current interest rate.

Maximum mortgage available under
TDS Ratio guidelines $_____

FORM 5: Projected Cash Flow (Three Months)
(See Chapter 3)

	Month 1		Month 2		Month 3		Quarterly Summary	
	Projected	Actual	Projected	Actual	Projected	Actual	Projected	Actual
INCOME:								
Contributed capital Loans Miscellaneous Rent received Other_____								
TOTAL INCOME (A)								
EXPENSES								

Accounting fees
Advertising
Bank interest and
  charges
Equipment purchase
  (appliances)
Insurance
Interests on rent
  deposits
Legal fees
Loan repayments
Maintenance services
Major repairs
Management fees
Minor repairs and
  maintenace
Miscellaneous expenses
Mortgage payments
Property taxes
Renovations
Utilities
Other_____								

TOTAL EXPENSES (B)								
OPENING CASH BALANCE								
PLUS TOTAL INCOME (A)								
LESS TOTAL EXPENSES (B)								
CLOSING CASH BALANCE								

FORM 6: Projected Income and Expense Statement
(as of _____)
(See Chapter 3)

INCOME:

Rental income	$_____	
Other sources of income	$_____	
TOTAL INCOME	$_____	(A)

OPERATING EXPENSES:

Accounting fees	$_____	
Advertising	$_____	
Bank interest and charges	$_____	
Equipment purchase (appliances)	$_____	
Insurance	$_____	
Interest on rent deposits	$_____	
Legal fees	$_____	
Loan repayments	$_____	
Maintenance services	$_____	
Major repairs	$_____	
Management fees	$_____	
Minor repairs and maintenance	$_____	
Miscellaneous expenses	$_____	
Mortgage payments	$_____	
Property taxes	$_____	
Renovations	$_____	
Utilities	$_____	
Other	$_____	
TOTAL OPERATING EXPENSES	$_____	(B)
NET INCOME	$_____	(A − B)

FORM 7: Projected Balance Sheet (as of _____)
(See Chapter 3)

ASSETS

CURRENT ASSETS:

Cash	$ _____	(a)
Rent receivables	$ _____	(b)
Prepaid expenses	$ _____	(c)
TOTAL CURRENT ASSETS	$ _____	= (A) [a + b + c]

FIXED ASSETS:

Land	$ _____	(d)
Buildings	$ _____	(e)
Less accumulated depreciation	$ _____	(f)
Chattels	$ _____	(g)
Less accumulated depreciation	$ _____	(h)
TOTAL FIXED ASSETS	$ _____	= (B) [d + e + g − f − h]
TOTAL ASSETS	$ _____	(C) [A + B]

LIABILITIES

CURRENT LIABILITIES:

Accounts receivable	$ _____	(i)
Accrued expenses	$ _____	(j)
Rent deposits	$ _____	(k)
Interest on rent deposits	$ _____	(l)
Interest on mortgage	$ _____	(m)
Due in next 12 months	$ _____	(n)
TOTAL CURRENT LIABILITIES	$ _____	= (D) [i + j + k + l + m + n]

LONG-TERM LIABILITIES:

Mortgage principal payable	$ _____	(o)
TOTAL LONG-TERM LIABILITIES	$ _____	= (E) [o]
TOTAL LIABILITIES	$ _____	= (F) [D + E]

NET WORTH	$ _____	(C − F)

FORM 8: Income Approach Worksheet
(See Chapter 3)

Date:_____

Name of apartment building: _____

Address: _____

City: _____

Type of property: _____

Number of suites: _____

Asking price: _____

Cost per suite: _____

Cost per building sq. ft. _____

Zoning: _____

Age of building:_____

		%	Amount	Comments
1	MAXIMUM POTENTIAL RENTAL INCOME (assuming no vacancies)			
2	Less: Vacancy/bad debt losses			
3	EFFECTIVE RENTAL INCOME (A)			
4	Plus: Other income (B)			
5	GROSS OPERATING INCOME (C) [A + B]			
6	Less: OPERATING EXPENSES			
7	Advertising, licences			
8	Accounting and legal fees			
9	Resident manager			
10	Property management company			

11	Government payments (EI, CPP, Workers' Compensation)			
12	Property insurance			
13	Other			
14	Property taxes			
15	Repairs and maintenance			
16	Services: Elevator			
17	Janitorial			
18	Lawn			
19	Pool			
20	Rubbish			
21	Other			
22	Supplies			
23	Utilities: Electricity			
24	Gas and oil			
25	Sewer and water			
26	Telephone			
27	Other			
28	Miscellaneous			
29	GROSS OPERATING EXPENSES (D)			
30	NET OPERATING INCOME (E) [C − D]			
31	Less: Annual debt service (F) (mortgage and loan payments)			
32	CASH FLOW BEFORE TAX (E − F) (positive or negative)			

CAP RATE _____ GIM_____ NIM _____

RATING OF PROPERTY (circle)   1   2   3   4   5   6   7   8   9   10
                              Low   High

FORM 9: Investment Property Analysis Checklist
(See Chapter 3)

Date of analysis _____

Property _____
Present use _____
Year built _____
Type of construction _____
Architectural style _____
Summary of physical condition _____
Square footage of building _____
Square footage of land _____

Assessed Value for Property Tax Calculation Purposes
Date of assessment _____
Land $_____
Building $_____
Total $_____
Total annual tax bill $_____
Tax rate per $1,000 assessed value $_____
Cost per square foot (building) $_____

Restrictions on Property Use
Most feasible use(s) _____
Building code restrictions _____
Zoning restrictions_____
Other restrictions _____

Calculations of Value

MARKET COMPARISON
Estimate value range to   _____ to _____
Estimate of value $_____
Terms: Down payment $_____
First mortgage rate $_____ %
Total amount of first mortgage $_____
Annual total payment of first mortgage $_____

COST METHOD

New building cost $ _____

Minus:

   Physical depreciation $_____

   Functional depreciation $_____

   Economic depreciation $_____

   Depreciated cost of building $_____ (A)

Add:

   Land value $_____ (B)

Total cost value $_____ (A + B)

INCOME CAPITALIZATION METHOD

Gross income $_____

Total expenses $_____

Net income (before taxes) $_____

Expenses represent what % of gross income?   _____ %

Gross operating income × multiplier $_____

Net operating income × multiplier $_____

Estimate of value using NOI and CAP rate $_____

Summary of Value Calculations

Using market comparisons $_____

Using cost (minus depreciation) $_____

Using income capitalization $_____

Most probable value (average of above) $_____

Property Feasibility Summary

Feasible use(s) recommended _____

Feasible use(s) considered _____

Major benefits_____

Minor benefits_____

Major costs _____

Minor costs _____

Major disadvantages _____

Minor disadvantages _____

CHART 1: Criteria for Determining Real Estate Cycles
(See Chapter 1)

	A	B	C	D	A
Values	Depressed	Increasing	Increasing	Declining	Depressed
Rents	Low	Increasing	Increasing	Declining	Low
Vacancy level	High	Beginning to decrease	Low	Increasing	High
Occupancy level	Low	Increasing	High	Decreasing	Low
New construction	Very little	Increasing	Booming	Slowing	Very little
Profit margins	Low	Improving	Widest	Decline	Low
Investor confidence	Low	Negative to neutral	Positive	Slightly negative	Low
Media coverage	Negative and pessimistic	Positive and encouraging	Positive and optimistic	Negative and pessimistic	Negative and pessimistic
Action	Buy	Second best time to buy	Sell	Be cautious	Buy

CHART 2: Recovery on Renovation Costs
(See Chapter 2)

Renovation project	Recovery on resale
Adding a full bath	96%
Adding a fireplace	94%
Remodelling kitchen (minor)	79%
Remodelling kitchen (major)	70%
Remodelling bathroom	69%
Adding a skylight	68%
Adding new siding	67%

Renovation project	Recovery on resale
Adding insulation	65%
Adding a room	62%
Re-roofing	61%
Adding a wood deck	60%
Adding a greenhouse	56%
Replacing windows, doors	55%
Adding a swimming pool	39%

CHART 3: Amortization Period in Year
(See Chapter 5)

The following examples assume a $50,000 mortgage loan and an interest rate* of 6% for the amortization period selected.

Amortization period in years

Payment	10	15	20	25
Monthly payment of principal and interest	$553.26	$419.95	$356.10	$319.91
Total of mortgage payments over the amortization period	$66,390.31	$75,558.58	$85,461.45	$95,968.63

*Interest being compounded semi-annually.

CHART 4: Interest Payments
(See Chapter 5)

Interest* on each $1,000 of mortgage is based on payment period

Interest rate %	Weekly $	Every two weeks $	Twice a month $	Monthly $
3.50	$0.67	$1.33	$1.44	$2.90
4.00	$0.76	$1.52	$1.65	$3.31
4.50	$0.85	$1.71	$1.86	$3.72
5.00	$0.95	$1.90	$2.06	$4.12
5.50	$1.04	$2.08	$2.26	$4.53
6.00	$1.13	$2.27	$2.47	$4.94
6.50	$1.23	$2.46	$2.67	$5.34
7.00	$1.32	$2.64	$2.87	$5.75
7.50	$1.41	$2.83	$3.07	$6.15
8.00	$1.51	$3.01	$3.27	$6.56

*Interest being compounded semi-annually.

CHART 5: Prepayment or Increased Payment Savings
(See Chapter 5)

Based on a $50,000 mortgage at a 6% interest rate.*

	Standard mortgage 25-year amortization	10% annual increase in mortgage payment	10% annual prepayment of principal
Mortgage repaid in months	300	164	97
Total interest charged	$45,968.63	$29,504.54	$14,060.22
Interest savings vs. standard 25-year mortgage	N/A	$16,464.09	$31,908.41

*Interest being compounded semi-annually.

CHART 6: Mortgage Amortization Chart
(See Chapter 5)

Follow the chart *down*, under the current interest rate, to the amount of your maximum monthly mortgage payment (not including taxes).

Follow that line *to the left* to determine the maximum mortgage, after down payment, for which you may qualify.

Maximum Mortgage*	4%	5%	6%	7%	8%
30,000	$157.81	$174.49	$191.95	$210.13	$228.97
40,000	$210.41	$232.65	$255.93	$280.17	$305.29
50,000	$263.02	$290.81	$319.91	$350.21	$381.61
60,000	$315.62	$348.97	$383.89	$420.25	$457.93
70,000	$368.22	$407.13	$447.87	$490.30	$534.25
80,000	$420.82	$465.29	$511.85	$560.34	$610.58
90,000	$473.42	$523.45	$575.83	$630.38	$686.90
100,000	$526.03	$581.61	$639.81	$700.42	$763.22

Maximum Mortgage* (Continued)	4%	5%	6%	7%	8%
110,000	$578.63	$639.77	$703.79	$770.46	$839.54
120,000	$631.23	$697.93	$767.77	$840.50	$915.86
130,000	$683.83	$756.09	$831.75	$910.55	$992.18
140,000	$736.43	$814.25	$895.73	$980.59	$1,068.50
150,000	$789.04	$872.41	$959.71	$1,050.63	$1,144.83
160,000	$841.64	$930.57	$1,023.70	$1,120.67	$1,221.15
170,000	$894.24	$988.73	$1,087.68	$1,190.71	$1,297.47
180,000	$946.84	$1,046.89	$1,151.66	$1,260.75	$1,373.79
190,000	$999.44	$1,105.05	$1,215.64	$1,330.79	$1,450.11
200,000	$1,052.05	$1,163.21	$1,279.62	$1,400.84	$1,526.43

*Based on 25-year amortization period. Amounts are approximate. Interest compounded semi-annually.

CHART 7: Monthly Mortgage Payments for Principal Plus Interest
(See Chapter 5)

The table gives the monthly payments for principal and interest* (not including taxes) for each $1,000 of the amount of the mortgage.

Interest rate %	5 years $	10 years $	15 years $	20 years $	25 years $
3.50	$18.19	$9.88	$7.14	$5.79	$5.00
4.00	$18.41	$10.11	$7.39	$6.05	$5.27
4.50	$18.63	$10.35	$7.63	$6.31	$5.54
5.00	$18.85	$10.59	$7.89	$6.58	$5.82
5.50	$19.08	$10.83	$8.14	$6.85	$6.11
6.00	$19.30	$11.07	$8.40	$7.13	$6.40
6.50	$19.53	$11.32	$8.67	$7.41	$6.70
7.00	$19.76	$11.56	$8.94	$7.70	$7.01
7.50	$19.99	$11.82	$9.21	$7.79	$7.32
8.00	$20.22	$12.07	$9.49	$8.29	$7.64

*Interest being compounded semi-annually.

CHECKLIST 1: Real Estate Assessment Checklist
(See Chapter 2)

1. This assessment checklist has most of the essential features to look for in a house, condominium, or apartment building.
2. Not all the categories are necessarily applicable in your individual case. Terminology in some instances can vary from province to province.
3. On the line provided, indicate your rating of the listed factor as: excellent, good, poor, available, not available, not applicable, further information required, etc.

A. General Information

Location of property   _____

Condition of neighbourhood   _____

Zoning of surrounding areas   _____

Prospect for future increase in value   _____

Prospect for future change of zoning   _____

Proximity of

- Schools   _____
- Churches   _____
- Shopping   _____
- Recreation   _____
- Entertainment   _____
- Parks   _____
- Children's playgrounds   _____
- Public transportation   _____
- Highways   _____
- Hospital   _____
- Police department   _____
- Fire department   _____
- Ambulance   _____

Traffic density   _____

Garbage removal   _____

Sewage system   _____

Quality of water   _____

Taxes:

- Provincial   _____
- Municipal   _____

Maintenance fees/assessments (if condominium)   _____

Maintenance fees/management fees (if apartment building)   _____

Easements _____

Quietness of

- Neighbourhood _____
- Condo or apartment complex _____
- Individual condominium unit _____
- Individual apartment unit _____
- House _____

Percentage of units that are owner-occupied (if condominium) _____

If next to commercial centre, is access to residential
section well controlled? _____

Is adjacent commercial development being planned? _____

Size of development related to your needs
(small, medium, large) _____

Does project seem to be compatible with your lifestyle? _____

Style of development (adult-oriented, children, retirees, etc.) _____

Age of development (new, moderate, old) _____

B. Exterior Factors

Privacy _____

Roadway (public street, private street, safety for children) _____

Sidewalks (adequacy of drainage) _____

Driveway (public, private, semi-private) _____

Garage

- Reserved space (one or two cars) _____
- Automatic garage doors _____
- Security _____
- Adequate visitor parking _____

Construction material (brick, wood, stone) _____

Siding (aluminum, other) _____

Condition of paint _____

Roof:

- Type of material _____
- Age _____
- Condition _____

Balcony or patios:

- Location (view, etc.) _____
- Privacy _____
- Size _____
- Open or enclosed _____

Landscaping:

- Trees   _____
- Shrubbery, flowers   _____
- Lawns   _____
- Automatic sprinklers   _____

Condition and upkeep of exterior   _____

C. Interior Factors

Intercom system   _____

Medical alert system   _____

Fire safety system (fire alarms, smoke detectors, sprinklers)   _____

Burglar alarm system   _____

General safety:

- TV surveillance   _____
- Controlled access   _____

Pre-wired for television and telephone cable   _____

Lobby:

- Cleanliness   _____
- Decor   _____
- Security guard   _____

Public corridors:

- Material used   _____
- Condition   _____
- Plaster (free of cracks, stains)   _____
- Decor   _____

Stairs:

- General accessibility   _____
- Number of stairwells   _____

Elevators   _____

Wheelchair accessibility   _____

Storage facilities:

- Location   _____
- Size   _____

Insulation: (The R factor is the measure of heating and cooling efficiency; the higher the R factor, the more efficient)

- R rating in walls (minimum of R-19; depends on geographic location)   _____
- R rating in ceiling (minimum of R-30; depends on geographic location)   _____

- Heat pumps   _____
- Windows (insulated, storm, screen) _____

Temperature controls:
- Individually controlled _____
- Convenient location _____

Plumbing:
- Functions well _____
- Convenient fixtures _____
- Quietness of plumbing _____

Suitable water pressure _____

Heating and air conditioning (gas, electric, hot water, oil) _____

Utility costs:
- Gas _____
- Electric _____
- Other _____

Laundry facilities _____

Soundproofing features _____

D. Management

Apartment management company _____

Condominium management company _____

Owner-managed _____

Resident manager _____

Management personnel:
- Front desk _____
- Maintenance _____
- Gardener _____
- Trash removal _____
- Snow removal _____
- Security (number of guards, hours, location, patrol) _____

E. Condominium Corporation

Experience of directors of corporation _____

Average age of other owners _____

F. Recreation Facilities (if condominium or apartment building)

Clubhouse _____

Club membership fees (included, not included) _____

Sports:
- Courts (tennis, squash, racquetball, handball, basketball) _____
- Games room (ping-pong, billiards) _____
- Exercise room _____
- Bicycle path/jogging track _____
- Organized sports and activities _____

Children's playground:
- Location (accessibility) _____
- Noise factor _____
- Organized sports and activities (supervised) _____

Swimming pool:
- Location (outdoor, indoor) _____
- Children's pool _____
- Noise factor _____

Visitors' accommodation _____

G. Individual Unit (if condominium or apartment building)

Location in complex _____

Size of unit _____

Is the floor plan and layout suitable? _____

Will your furnishings fit in? _____

Is the unit exposed to the sunlight? _____

Does the unit have a scenic view? _____

Is the unit in a quiet location (away from
garbage unit, elevator noise, playgrounds, etc.)? _____

Accessibility (stairs, elevators, fire exits) _____

Closets:
- Number _____
- Location _____

Carpet:
- Colour _____
- Quality/texture _____

Hardwood floors _____

Living room:
- Size/shape _____
- Windows/view _____
- Sunlight (morning, afternoon) _____
- Fireplace _____
- Privacy (from outside, from rest of condo) _____

Dining room:
- Size   _____
- Accessibility to kitchen   _____
- Windows/view   _____

Den or family room:
- Size/shape   _____
- Windows/view (morning or afternoon sunlight)   _____
- Fireplace   _____
- Privacy (from outside, from rest of condo)   _____

Laundry room:
- Work space available   _____
- Washer and dryer   _____
- Size/capacity   _____
- Warranty coverage   _____

Kitchen:
- Size   _____
- Eating facility (table, nook, no seating)   _____
- Floors (linoleum, tile, wood)   _____
- Exhaust system   _____
- Countertop built in   _____
- Countertop material   _____
- Work space   _____
- Kitchen cabinets (number, accessibility)   _____
- Cabinet material   _____
- Sink (size, single, double)   _____
- Sink material   _____
- Built-in cutting boards   _____
- Oven (single, double, self-cleaning)   _____
- Gas or electric oven   _____
- Age of oven   _____
- Microwave (size)   _____
- Age of microwave   _____
- Refrigerator/freezer (size/capacity)   _____
- Refrigerator (frost-free, ice maker, single/double door)   _____
- Age of refrigerator   _____
- Dishwasher (age)   _____
- Trash compactor/garbage disposal   _____
- Pantry or storage area   _____
- Is there warranty coverage on all appliances?   _____

Number of bedrooms   _____

Master bedroom:

- Size/shape   _____
- Privacy (from outside, from rest of condo)   _____
- Closets/storage space   _____
- Fireplace   _____
- Floor and wall covering   _____

Master bathroom (en suite):

- Size   _____
- Bathtub   _____
- Whirlpool tub/jacuzzi   _____
- Shower   _____
- Steam room   _____
- Vanity   _____
- Sink (single, double, integrated sink bowls)   _____
- Medicine cabinet   _____

Number of bathrooms   _____

Complete, or sink and toilet only?   _____

Overall condition of condo, apartment, or house   _____

Overall appearance and decor of condo, apartment, or house _____

H. Legal and Financial Matters

Project documents (e.g., disclosure/declaration)
received and read (if new condominium)   _____

Bylaws received and read (if condominium)   _____

Rules and regulations received and read
(if condominium or apartment)   _____

Financial statements received and read
(if condominium or revenue-generating property)   _____

Condo council minutes, and annual general meeting and
special general meeting minutes over past two years received
and read (if condominium or revenue-generating property)   _____

No litigation or pending litigation   _____

No outstanding or pending special assessments   _____

No pending repairs, or leaky condo problems   _____

Other documents (list):

- _____   _____
- _____   _____
- _____   _____
- _____   _____

All above documentation (as applicable) reviewed by your
lawyer and legal advice on investment obtained   _____

Financial statements reviewed by your accountant
and tax advice on investment obtained   _____

All assessments, maintenance fees, and taxes detailed   _____

Condominium corporation insurance coverage adequate   _____

Restrictions acceptable (e.g., pets, renting of unit, number of
people living in suite, children, etc.) for rental property   _____

All verbal promises or representations of sales representative
or vendor's agent that you are relying on written into the
offer to purchase   _____

Other

- _____   _____
- _____   _____
- _____   _____
- _____   _____

CHECKLIST 2: Mortgage Checklist
(See Chapter 5)

A. Ask Yourself These Questions

1. Is your income secure?   _____

2. Will your income increase or decrease in the future?   _____

3. Are you planning on increasing the size of your family
   (e.g., children, relatives) and therefore your living expenses?   _____

4. Will you be able to put aside a financial buffer
   for unexpected expenses or emergencies?   _____

5. Are you planning to purchase the property with someone else?   _____

6. If the answer is yes to the above question, will you be able
   to depend on your partner's financial contribution
   without interruption?   _____

7. If you are relying on an income from renting out all
   or part of your purchase, have you determined:

   • If city zoning and use bylaws permit it?   _____

   • If the condominium corporation bylaws permit it?   _____

   • If the mortgage company policies permit it?   _____

8. Have you thoroughly compared mortgage rates and
   features so that you know what type of mortgage and
   mortgage company you want?   _____

9. Have you determined the amount of mortgage
   that you would be eligible for?   _____

10. Have you considered the benefits of a pre-approved
    mortgage?   _____

11. Have you considered talking to a mortgage broker?   _____

12. Have you considered assuming an existing mortgage?   _____

13. Have you considered the benefits of a portable mortgage?   _____

14. Have you considered having the vendor give you a mortgage?   _____

15. Have you determined all the expenses you will incur
    relating to the purchase transaction? (See Checklist 3.)   _____

16. Have you completed your present and projected financial
    needs analysis (income and expenses)? (See Form 1.)   _____

17. Have you completed the mortgage application form, including
    net worth statement (assets and liabilities)? (See Form 2.)   _____

B. Ask the Lender These Questions

Interest Rates

18. What is the current interest rate? _____

19. How frequently is the interest calculated?
(semi-annually, monthly, etc.) _____

20. What is the effective interest rate on an annual basis? _____

21. How long will the lender guarantee a quoted interest rate? _____

22. Will the lender put the above guarantee in writing? _____

23. Will you receive a lower rate of interest if the rates fall
before you finalize your mortgage? _____

24. Will the lender put the above reduction assurance in writing? _____

25. Will the lender show you the total amount of interest you
will have to pay over the lifetime of the mortgage? _____

Amortization

26. What options do you have for amortization periods?
(10, 15 years, etc.) _____

27. Will the lender provide you with an amortization schedule
for your loan showing your monthly payments apportioned
into principal and interest? _____

28. Have you calculated what your monthly payments
will be based on each amortization rate? _____

29. Are you required to maintain the amortized monthly
payment schedule if annual pre-payments are made,
or will they be adjusted accordingly? _____

Term of the Mortgage

30. What different terms are available?
(six months, one, two, three, five years, etc.) _____

31. What is the best term for your personal circumstances? _____

32. What are the different interest rates available
relating to the different terms? _____

Payments

33. What is the amount of your monthly payments
(based on amortization period)? _____

34. Are you permitted to increase the amount of
your monthly payments if you want to without penalty? _____

35. Does the lender have a range of payment periods
available, such as weekly, biweekly, monthly, etc.? _____

36. What is the best payment period in your personal
circumstances? _____

Prepayment

37. What are your prepayment privileges?

- Completely open? _____
- Open with a fixed penalty or notice requirement? _____
- Limited open with no penalty or notice requirement? _____
- Limited open with fixed penalty or notice requirement? _____
- Completely closed? _____
- Some combination of the above? _____

38. What amount can be prepaid and what is the penalty or notice required, if applicable? _____

39. How long does the privilege apply in each of the above categories, if applicable? _____

40. When does the prepayment privilege commence? (six months, one year, anytime, etc.) _____

41. Is there a minimum amount that has to be prepaid? _____

42. What form does your prepayment privilege take—increase in payments or lump sum? _____

43. Is your prepayment privilege cumulative (e.g., make last year's lump sum prepayment next year)? _____

Taxes

44. How much are the property taxes? _____

45. Does the lender require a property tax payment monthly (based on projected annual tax), or is it optional? _____

46. Does the lender pay interest on the property tax account? If yes, what is the interest rate? _____

Mortgage Transaction Fees and Expenses

47. What is the appraisal fee? Is an appraisal necessary? _____

48. What is the survey fee? Is a survey necessary? _____

49. Will you be able to select a lawyer of your choice to do the mortgage work? _____

50. Does the lender charge a processing or administrative fee? _____

51. Does the lender arrange for a lawyer to do the mortgage documentation work at a flat fee, regardless of the amount of the mortgage? _____

52. Does the lender know what the out-of-pocket disbursements for the mortgage transaction will be? _____

53. Does the mortgage have a renewal administration fee? How much is it? _____

Mortgage Assumption Privileges

54. Can the mortgage be assumed if the property is sold?   _____

55. Is the mortgage assumable with or without the
lender's approval?   _____

56. What are the assumption administrative fees, if any?   _____

57. Will the lender release the vendor of all personal
obligations under the terms of the mortgage if it is assumed?   _____

Portability

58. Is the mortgage portable, e.g., can you transfer it to
another property that you may buy?   _____

CHECKLIST 3: Real Estate Purchase Expenses Checklist
(See Chapter 4)

In addition to the actual purchase price of your investment, there are a number of other expenses to be paid on or prior to closing. Not all of these expenses will be applicable. Some provinces may have additional expenses.

Type of expense	When paid	Estimated amount
Deposits	At time of offer	_____
Mortgage application fee	At time of application	_____
Property appraisal	At time of mortgage application	_____
Property inspection	At inspection	_____
Balance of purchase price	On closing	_____
Legal fees re property transfer	On closing	_____
Legal fees re mortgage preparation	On closing	_____
Legal disbursements re property transfer	On closing	_____
Legal disbursements re mortgage preparation	On closing	_____
Mortgage broker commission	On closing	_____
Property survey	On closing	_____
Property tax holdback (by mortgage company)	On closing	_____
Land transfer or deed tax (provincial)	On closing	_____
Property purchase tax (provincial)	On closing	_____
Property tax (local/municipal) adjustment	On closing	_____
Goods and services tax (GST) (federal)	On closing	_____
New Home Warranty Program fee	On closing	_____
Mortgage interest adjustment (by mortgage company)	On closing	_____
Sales tax on chattels purchased from vendor (provincial)	On closing	_____
Adjustments for fuel, taxes, etc.	On closing	_____
Mortgage lender insurance premium (CMHC or GEM)	On closing	_____
Condominium maintenance fee adjustment	On closing	_____
Building insurance	On closing	_____

Life insurance premium on amount of outstanding mortgage   On closing   _____

Moving expenses   At time of move   _____

Utility connection charges   At time of move   _____

Redecorating and refurbishing costs   Shortly after purchase   _____

Immediate repair and maintenance costs   Shortly after purchase   _____

House and garden improvements   Shortly after purchase   _____

Other expenses (list):

_____   _____   _____

_____   _____   _____

_____   _____   _____

TOTAL CASH REQUIRED $_____

CHECKLIST 4: Business Deductions Checklist
(See Chapter 7)

Note: The tax laws are constantly changing, so be sure to verify annually the following deductible items with a professionally qualified accountant or other tax authority. Some exceptions to the following deductions may apply.

_____ Accounting or bookkeeping services

_____ Advertising expenses

_____ Automobile expenses

_____ Bad debts/bounced cheques

_____ Books related to business

_____ Business development expenses

_____ Business gifts

_____ Cable charges (T.V., Internet)

_____ Cleaning services (supplies, equipment, service)

_____ Commissions (sales representatives, agents, others)

_____ Computer hardware and software (depreciated)

_____ Consulting fees

_____ Delivery charges

_____ Donations (charitable or business-related)

_____ Dues to professional organizations

_____ Educational expenses (business seminars, workshops, classes, handbooks, manuals)

_____ Entertainment (e.g., meals), business-related (50% deductible; must be carefully documented)

_____ Equipment purchases (may be depreciated or expensed)

_____ Freight and shipping charges

_____ House-related expenses (mortgage interest, depreciation, utilities, services, repairs)

_____ Internet charges

_____ Insurance premiums (special riders on homeowner's policy, i.e., computer insurance, etc.)

_____ Interest on business loans or charge cards, bank charges

_____ Labour costs (independent contractors or employees)

_____ Lease payments (equipment, etc.)

_____ Legal and professional fees

_____ Licences and permits

_____ Maintenance contracts on office equipment and other repairs

_____ Membership fees in business-related organizations

_____ Office furnishings (depreciated)

_____ Office supplies

_____ Postage

_____ Rent (apartment or house)

_____ Safety deposit box (if it holds documents related to business)

_____ Salaries (including those paid to spouse or children)

_____ Salary expense (employer's contributions to CPP, EI, WCB, etc.)

_____ Stationery and printing

_____ Subscriptions to business magazines and periodicals

_____ Supplies and materials

_____ Tax preparer's fee

_____ Telephone (equipment, monthly service charges, long-distance calls, etc.)

_____ Telephone-answering service/machine

_____ Travel expenses connected with business (meals and lodging for overnight stays, airfare, train, bus, taxi, auto expenses, tips, tolls)

_____ Other (itemize)

CHECKLIST 5: Landlord/Tenant Suite Inspection Checklist

(See Chapter 10)

Apartment number:________ Apartment address: ______________________________

Modify this checklist as necessary.

ITEM	CONDITION Poor =1	2	3	4	5 = Excellent	INITIALS Landlord	Tenant
Kitchen							
Drawers	1	2	3	4	5	____	____
Countertop	1	2	3	4	5	____	____
Table (built-in or nook)	1	2	3	4	5	____	____
Sink	1	2	3	4	5	____	____
Windows	1	2	3	4	5	____	____
Screens	1	2	3	4	5	____	____
Cupboards	1	2	3	4	5	____	____
Doors	1	2	3	4	5	____	____
Floor	1	2	3	4	5	____	____
Ceiling	1	2	3	4	5	____	____
Walls	1	2	3	4	5	____	____
Dining Room							
Floors	1	2	3	4	5	____	____
Ceiling	1	2	3	4	5	____	____
Walls	1	2	3	4	5	____	____
Carpet	1	2	3	4	5	____	____
Doors	1	2	3	4	5	____	____
Hanging light	1	2	3	4	5	____	____
Living Room							
Bookcase	1	2	3	4	5	____	____
Fireplace	1	2	3	4	5	____	____
Windows	1	2	3	4	5	____	____
Screens	1	2	3	4	5	____	____
Doors	1	2	3	4	5	____	____
Ceilings	1	2	3	4	5	____	____
Walls	1	2	3	4	5	____	____
Carpet	1	2	3	4	5	____	____

ITEM	Poor =1	2	3	4	5 = Excellent	INITIALS Landlord/Tenant
			CONDITION			

Bedroom #1

ITEM	Poor =1	2	3	4	5 = Excellent	Landlord	Tenant
Closet	1	2	3	4	5	_____	_____
Drapes	1	2	3	4	5	_____	_____
Lights	1	2	3	4	5	_____	_____
Floor	1	2	3	4	5	_____	_____
Ceiling	1	2	3	4	5	_____	_____
Walls	1	2	3	4	5	_____	_____
Windows	1	2	3	4	5	_____	_____
Screens	1	2	3	4	5	_____	_____
Doors	1	2	3	4	5	_____	_____
Carpet	1	2	3	4	5	_____	_____
Thermostat	1	2	3	4	5	_____	_____

Bedroom #2

ITEM	Poor =1	2	3	4	5 = Excellent	Landlord	Tenant
Closet	1	2	3	4	5	_____	_____
Drapes	1	2	3	4	5	_____	_____
Lights	1	2	3	4	5	_____	_____
Floor	1	2	3	4	5	_____	_____
Ceiling	1	2	3	4	5	_____	_____
Walls	1	2	3	4	5	_____	_____
Windows	1	2	3	4	5	_____	_____
Screens	1	2	3	4	5	_____	_____
Doors	1	2	3	4	5	_____	_____
Carpet	1	2	3	4	5	_____	_____
Thermostat	1	2	3	4	5	_____	_____

Bedroom #3

ITEM	Poor =1	2	3	4	5 = Excellent	Landlord	Tenant
Closet	1	2	3	4	5	_____	_____
Drapes	1	2	3	4	5	_____	_____
Lights	1	2	3	4	5	_____	_____
Floor	1	2	3	4	5	_____	_____
Ceiling	1	2	3	4	5	_____	_____
Walls	1	2	3	4	5	_____	_____
Windows	1	2	3	4	5	_____	_____
Screens	1	2	3	4	5	_____	_____
Doors	1	2	3	4	5	_____	_____

ITEM	Poor =1	CONDITION 2	3	4	5 = Excellent	INITIALS Landlord/Tenant	
Carpet	1	2	3	4	5	_____	_____
Thermostat	1	2	3	4	5	_____	_____
Bathroom							
Sink	1	2	3	4	5	_____	_____
Toilet tank	1	2	3	4	5	_____	_____
Toilet seat	1	2	3	4	5	_____	_____
Shower (door, curtain)	1	2	3	4	5	_____	_____
Bathtub	1	2	3	4	5	_____	_____
Shower head	1	2	3	4	5	_____	_____
Door	1	2	3	4	5	_____	_____
Walls	1	2	3	4	5	_____	_____
Ceiling	1	2	3	4	5	_____	_____
Floor	1	2	3	4	5	_____	_____
Windows	1	2	3	4	5	_____	_____
Screens	1	2	3	4	5	_____	_____
Towel racks	1	2	3	4	5	_____	_____
Cabinet	1	2	3	4	5	_____	_____
Tissue holder	1	2	3	4	5	_____	_____
Countertop	1	2	3	4	5	_____	_____
Mirror	1	2	3	4	5	_____	_____
Common Areas							
Front hallway	1	2	3	4	5	_____	_____
Floor	1	2	3	4	5	_____	_____
Ceiling	1	2	3	4	5	_____	_____
Walls	1	2	3	4	5	_____	_____
Lights	1	2	3	4	5	_____	_____
Carpet	1	2	3	4	5	_____	_____
Stairwells	1	2	3	4	5	_____	_____
Upper							
• floor	1	2	3	4	5	_____	_____
• ceiling	1	2	3	4	5	_____	_____
• walls	1	2	3	4	5	_____	_____

ITEM	Poor =1	CONDITION 2	3	4	5 = Excellent	INITIALS Landlord/Tenant
Lower						
• floor	1	2	3	4	5	_____ _____
• ceiling	1	2	3	4	5	_____ _____
• walls	1	2	3	4	5	_____ _____
Thermostat	1	2	3	4	5	_____ _____
Front door	1	2	3	4	5	_____ _____
Rear door	1	2	3	4	5	_____ _____
Basement						
Washer	1	2	3	4	5	_____ _____
Dryer	1	2	3	4	5	_____ _____
Freezer	1	2	3	4	5	_____ _____
Furnace	1	2	3	4	5	_____ _____
Sink	1	2	3	4	5	_____ _____
Floors	1	2	3	4	5	_____ _____
Ceiling	1	2	3	4	5	_____ _____
Walls	1	2	3	4	5	_____ _____
Windows	1	2	3	4	5	_____ _____
Screens	1	2	3	4	5	_____ _____
Doors	1	2	3	4	5	_____ _____
Other items	1	2	3	4	5	_____ _____

The apartment conditions are confirmed as of the date noted by our signatures below.

Date: _____ Tenant _____

Date: _____ Landlord _____

CHECKLIST 6: Master Checklist for Successful
Real Estate Investing
(See Chapter 1)

1. Understand why real estate could be a good investment for you.

_____ Learn the advantages and potential disadvantages of real estate investing.

_____ Make a list of the benefits of investing in real estate.

_____ Make a list of any potential disadvantages of investing in real estate.

2. Know how the real estate market works.

_____ Understand the cycles involved in the real estate market and how they work.

_____ Understand what factors affect the real estate market and prices.

_____ Understand when the best time is to buy and sell.

3. Educate yourself about real estate.

_____ Take courses or seminars offered locally through school boards, colleges, institutes, universities, or private seminar companies.

_____ Read books on real estate and real estate investment.

_____ Familiarize yourself with mortgage tables, mortgage calculations, accounting, management and real estate investment computer software and spreadsheets.

_____ Familiarize yourself with on-line mortgage calculators.

_____ Research the Internet for property search opportunities, e.g., **www.mls.ca**

_____ Use **www.google.ca** for research information.

_____ Subscribe to publications, including newspapers, magazines, or newsletters that cover real estate issues.

_____ Subscribe to free publications such as the Royal LePage *Survey of Canadian House Prices* and the various Canada Mortgage and Housing Corporation (CMHC) surveys and forecasts.

_____ Receive free weekly real estate publications possibly available in your community.

4. Analyze your present financial situation.

_____ Determine your personal cost-of-living budget (income and expenses). Calculate your personal net worth statement (assets and liabilities).

_____ Calculate your gross debt-service ratio (GDS).

_____ Calculate your total debt-service ratio (TDS).

_____ Determine the maximum amount of mortgage that you could be eligible for.

_____ Determine the maximum amount of mortgage that you would feel comfortable with.

_____ Utilize on-line mortgage calculators.

5. Establish your investment goals.

_____ Determine your real estate investment needs and goals in the short, medium, and long term.

_____ Determine your personal and family needs and goals in the short, medium, and long term.

_____ Do a detailed and candid self-assessment. Prepare an objective analysis of your personal strengths, weaknesses, skills, talents, and goals, and compare them to the attributes required to invest in and manage real estate. If you assess that certain skills, etc., are needed, determine how you will acquire them.

_____ Determine what time and talent involvement that you expect or require from your family.

_____ Do a SWOT (strengths, weaknesses, opportunities, and threats) analysis of your investment plans on a periodic basis.

_____ Develop a written investment strategic plan.

_____ Prepare a projected personal cash flow statement over the next five years (monthly).

_____ Prepare a projected personal income and expense statement over the next five years (annually).

_____ Prepare a projected personal balance sheet (assets and liabilities) over next the five years (annually).

_____ Determine how much money you believe you will need to maintain your desired standard of living after retirement.

_____ Make sure you take into account the value of your money in real terms, in terms of buying power, after inflation is taken into account. Allow a factor of 3% inflation each year. Of course, inflation might be less or more than 3% at any given time.

_____ Determine the degree of financial risk you are prepared to take, if any.

6. Understand the basic real estate guidelines.

_____ Learn the common rules of thumb used to quickly analyze a potential real estate investment. Recognize which methods are more or less reliable in determining the value of a property.

_____ Always perform a thorough property analysis before deciding to seriously consider a property purchase.

_____ Know how appraisers determine the value of property. Learn the various formulas that experts use to determine value.

7. Determine your desired degree of involvement in property management.

_____ Determine if you want to do all the management yourself.

_____ Determine if you want to employ a resident manager who lives in the building and deals with common problems that can occur or tasks that have to be performed. This may include collecting rents, renting apartments, cleaning apartments, and general building cleaning and maintenance.

_____ Determine if you want to employ a professional property-management company to handle the investment. This may include renting, collecting rent and paying bills, bookkeeping, maintenance, and overall management.

8. Select the type of investment ideal for your needs.

_____ Review the various types of real estate investments that fit within your investment goals and needs.

_____ Look for the availability of the type of real estate investment that you are considering.

_____ Thoroughly do your research and compare and contrast alternative properties.

_____ Determine if you will purchase the property yourself or with others.

9. Select your professional and business advisers carefully.

_____ Select your lawyer.

_____ Select your accountant.

_____ Select your financial planner.

_____ Select your building inspector.

_____ Select your realtor.

_____ Select your insurance broker.

_____ Select a lender/mortgage broker.

10. Determine the form of legal ownership of property.

_____ Proprietorship

_____ Partnership

_____ Limited partnership

_____ Limited company (corporation)

_____ Joint tenancy

_____ Tenants in common

_____ Freehold

_____ Leasehold

11. Locate your investment property.

_____ Review the amount of money you have available for purchase purposes.

_____ Review the maximum amount you are willing to pay for the property.

_____ Review your real estate investment criteria.

_____ Select the geographic area or areas in which you want to have your investment.

_____ Obtain copies of all municipal zoning maps in the selected investment area, as well as any municipal zoning regulations that may affect your purchase. Find out future policy plans for the specific street area that you intend to purchase in, e.g., rezoning from existing single-family to multi-family.

_____ Obtain a municipal street map showing the geographic area in detail.

_____ Contact your realtors and provide them with the guidelines of what you are looking for. Have them utilize the MLS, if they are on it, to search for properties within your guidelines.

_____ Review all real estate newspapers in your area to become aware of what is available in your areas of interest, as not all listings are on MLS.

_____ Use the Internet as an effective research tool.

_____ Read the real estate section of local newspapers under the types of property you are looking for, such as houses, condominiums, apartment buildings, etc.

_____ Research the market thoroughly in every way, using the guidelines and check-lists in this book.

_____ Shortlist three potential purchases that fall within your investment criteria and then negotiate for the best overall price and package. Make sure that you put in conditions or "subject clauses" to give yourself room to get out of the deal if need be, and to satisfy all your needs.

_____ Consult with your lawyer and tax accountant to make sure that you have covered everything necessary in the offer, either before making the offer or after making the offer, but with the condition that the offer is subject to your lawyer's and accountant's approval.

12. Analyze your prospective investment property.

_____ Thoroughly and carefully analyze your prospective investment. Have all details, essential information, and representations verified in writing. Make sure that the financial information is accurate, especially the income and expense statement.

_____ Make sure you have compared your prospective investment with other alternative choices.

_____ Complete an initial property analysis using a system that you understand and that works for you. Develop a prepared form that will have all the critical factors for comparative and evaluative purposes that you need to know. This would include such factors as lot size, age of property, price, rent breakdown per unit, vacancy history, financing, expenses, income, tax benefits, rezoning potential, etc.

_____ Make sure that the property makes financial sense or don't buy it.

_____ Make sure that you obtain your accountant's and lawyer's opinion before finally committing yourself to a purchase.

13. Utilize the most effective financing techniques.

_____ Familiarize yourself with the many conventional and creative financing techniques.

_____ Determine how much financing you feel comfortable with. Some people, especially with principal residences, want to put in as much down payment as possible because the interest on the mortgage is not deductible (unless you are writing off a portion as a home office). Others want to have high-ratio financing of 90% and put in just a 10% down payment, so that they have cash available for other purposes. Some people worry about mortgage debt and feel uncomfortable having more than their threshold level.

_____ Determine which financing technique meets your investment objectives, e.g., 30-year amortization period because of lower monthly payments, vendor-take-back financing to save on bank financing, or assuming an existing mortgage because of lower interest rates.

_____ Prepare your reasons for requesting the financing package to sell the vendor and/or lender.

_____ Be aware of the benefits and pitfalls of leveraging your real estate investment, e.g., borrowing on increasing equity.

14. Consider the tax implications.

_____ Obtain all the documentation and information you can about the financial aspects of the investment for review and analysis.

_____ Analyze your investment from a tax perspective. The important thing is not the amount of money you make but the amount you can keep after taxes.

_____ Analyze your investment from the perspective of how you should structure the initial purchase. For example, if you are buying a small apartment building, you would want to structure the allocation of value given for leasehold improvements, building, land, chattels, and goodwill (if any) to be to your benefit. This is part of your initial negotiating.

_____ Analyze your investment from the tax perspective of the legal ownership and nature of ownership. For example, principal residence with or without rental suite, revenue property, single or joint ownership, capital gains exemption implications, etc.

_____ Make sure that you obtain the advice of a professional accountant (CA or CGA) who is knowledgeable on the tax aspects of real estate investment before you commit yourself to a purchase.

15. Consider the legal implications.

_____ Analyze your purchase in terms of issues such as ownership, control, and management.

_____ Decide if you want to purchase through a limited liability company or in your personal name.

_____ Determine if you want to purchase the property with partners and, if so, make sure the arrangement is clearly documented in writing in advance.

_____ Make sure that you insert appropriate conditions or "subject clauses" in the agreement of purchase and sale to protect your interests.

_____ Make sure that you obtain the advice of a lawyer who specializes in real estate before you submit an offer of purchase and sale. An alternative is to put a condition in the offer that the agreement has to meet the approval of the purchaser's lawyer. The advantage of the first approach is that it is easier to make the terms of the first offer the best terms, rather than attempt to change the terms later after speaking with a lawyer.

16. Negotiate the purchase.

_____ Determine your best terms for an agreement and your bottom-line fallback position in advance, after advance consultation with your lawyer and, if you are intending to generate revenue from your investment, after speaking with your accountant.

_____ Determine your persuasive reasons for your negotiating position, so that you can convince the vendor through the realtor.

_____ Make sure that you feel comfortable with the terms of the offer with regard to the overall package.

_____ Insert all the necessary conditions in the agreement for your protection, e.g., receipt and verification by your accountant of income and expense statements.

_____ Make sure you understand the real estate market and the value to you of the property, and make sure you have alternative property options so that you can make realistic decisions comparatively.

_____ Make sure that you have assessed the property objectively, using the checklists in this book.

_____ Offer less than the listing price. How much less depends on each individual situation. Look for reasons why the property is worth less to you than the asking price.

_____ Determine the factors that are motivating the vendor to sell.

_____ Make sure that you have listed all items that are part of the purchase price and all documents that you want from the vendor.

_____ Never buy a property without viewing it thoroughly inside and out, and on several occasions beforehand. Be very cautious about buying a property that is more than a three-hour drive from where you live.

_____ Make sure that you are satisfied with the overall deal before removing the conditions in the agreement and thereby having a firm legal commitment.

17. Take necessary steps before and after closing the purchase.

_____ Make sure you have selected a lawyer who is experienced in the type of real estate purchase you are making; e.g., new or resale house, condominium, duplex, apartment building, raw land, renovation, property development, etc. Never attempt to close your own real estate transaction.

_____ Ask your lawyer in advance what the anticipated fees and disbursement costs will be for the property transfer and mortgage.

_____ Calculate realistically all your closing costs. Refer to Checklist 3.

_____ Make an itemized list of all the documents or items you want to receive from the vendor at the time of closing. All these matters should have been referred to in the agreement of purchase and sale, so there is no misunderstanding.

_____ Visit your property on the day of closing. Make sure that it is in the same condition as when you last inspected it.

_____ Make a point of meeting your tenants, if it is a revenue property, as soon as convenient after you have purchased the property.

18. Set up a record-keeping system.

_____ Keep your personal bank accounts separate from your revenue property accounts in order to simplify your bookkeeping.

_____ Before closing the purchase, open up two separate bank accounts so you can order cheques and have the accounts ready for operation. One account is a chequing account for operational and management expenses relating to your revenue property, in other words for income and expenses. The second account is a savings account to hold the tenants' security deposits. In most provinces you have to pay interest on the security deposits of residential tenants.

_____ Set up a bookkeeping and accounting system that is simple to understand and operate. You can use a manual or computerized system, depending on the number of tenants. Speak to your accountant. The key point is to set up a system that works for you. This will provide a convenient record for the purpose of completing your tax returns. There are excellent accounting and management software programs available.

19. Monitor your investment.

_____ Monitor your investment on a regular basis, at least semi-annually.

_____ Make sure that your real estate investment continues to meet the investment goals that you have set for yourself. If you are not getting the return on your investment you anticipated, or if you can anticipate that there will be unacceptable future expenses, or if you no longer enjoy dealing with the property, then consider selling it.

_____ Have your professional accountant advise you on the performance of your revenue investment, ideally every six months, to make sure that you are keeping your expenses as low as possible, keeping your income as high as possible, and minimizing personal and investment tax payable. For example, you may want to renew your mortgage if the interest rate is low for a longer period of time, e.g., three or five years or longer, rather than one year, depending on your long-term plans.

20. Structure the sale to meet your needs.

_____ Determine the basis on which you would like to sell before you buy. This is part of your advance planning.

_____ Make a decision to sell your property and set a price based on objective assessment of market reality rather than emotion.

_____ Don't be influenced to sell your property unless you believe, based on the facts, that the timing is right for you to sell.

_____ Consider the benefits of listing your property with a realtor on the MLS to maximize sale price and market exposure.

_____ Consider the advantages and disadvantages of vendor-back financing.

_____ Insert appropriate conditions to protect your interests, such as "72-hour clause" for the purchaser to remove conditions if another offer comes in.

_____ Attempt to negotiate as large a deposit as possible and attempt to negotiate that the deposit is non-refundable and goes directly to the vendor after all the purchaser's conditions are removed.

_____ Obtain your lawyer's and tax accountant's advice before accepting an offer.

21. Continue implementing your real estate investment goal plans.

_____ Remember to reassess your investment plans on a regular basis, based on your tax accountant's advice and your own evolving and changing needs, goals, and comfort zone.

_____ Refer back to the sequence of steps in this checklist for your next purchase.

_____ Be prudent about leveraging and pyramiding your real estate investments.

_____ Make sure that your property produces net positive income; that it is a viable investment as a revenue business.

_____ Make sure that you yourself verify the income and expenses and that you have control over your investment.

_____ Avoid high-risk, get-rich-quick schemes. Concentrate on sound real estate investment techniques.

Glossary

To know how the real estate market operates and to function within that market successfully, you have to use and understand the language of real estate investment. People who buy and sell property, who borrow or make loans, all communicate with a common set of terms and concepts. Review this glossary and become familiar with the terms. In many cases, these terms are discussed in more depth in various chapters of this book.

ACB: See Adjusted cost base below.

Acceleration clause: Usually written into a mortgage to allow the lender to accelerate or call the entire principal balance of the mortgage, plus accrued interest, when the payments become delinquent.

Adjusted cost base (ACB): The value of the real property established for tax purposes. It is the original cost plus any allowable capital improvements, plus certain acquisition costs, plus any mortgage interest costs, and less any depreciation taken.

Agreement of purchase and sale: A written agreement between the owner and a purchaser for the purchase of real estate on a predetermined price and terms.

Amenities: Generally, those parts of the condominium or apartment building that are intended to beautify the premises and that are for the enjoyment of occupants rather than for utility.

Amortization: The reduction of a loan through periodic payments in which interest is charged only on the unpaid balance.

Amortization period: The actual number of years it will take to repay a mortgage loan in full. This can be well in excess of the loan's term. For example, mortgages often have 5-year terms, but 25-year amortization periods.

Analysis of property: The systematic method of determining the performance of investment real estate using a property analysis form.

Appraised value: An estimate of the fair market value of the property, usually performed by an appraiser.

Assessment fee: Also referred to as maintenance fee. A monthly fee that condominium owners must pay, usually including management fees, costs of common property upkeep, heating costs, garbage-removal costs, the owner's contribution to the contingency reserve fund, and so on. In the case of time-shares, the fee is normally levied annually.

Assumption agreement: A legal document signed by a homebuyer to assume responsibility for the obligations of a mortgage made by a former owner.

Balance sheet: A financial statement that indicates the financial status of a condominium corporation or apartment building, or other revenue property, at a specific point in time by listing its assets and liabilities.

Base rent: The fixed rent paid by a tenant. This is separate from any rent paid as a result of extra charges or percentage rents.

Blended payments: Equal payments consisting of both a principal and an interest component, paid each month during the term of the mortgage. The principal portion increases each month, while the interest portion decreases, but the total monthly payment does not change.

Budget: An annual estimate of a condominium corporation or apartment building's expenses and the revenues needed to balance those expenses. There are operating budgets and capital budgets. (See also Capital budget.)

Buildings: The buildings included in a property. In the case of a condominium purchase, usually refers to the parts that are divided into the units and the common area.

Canada Mortgage and Housing Corporation (CMHC): The federal Crown corporation that is governed by the *National Housing Act*. CMHC services include providing housing information and assistance, financing, and insuring home purchase loans for lenders.

Canada Revenue Agency (CRA): This is the current name of the former Revenue Canada. However, as the name Revenue Canada is so familiar, that term is used frequently throughout the book.

Canadian Real Estate Association (CREA): An association of members of the real estate industry, principally real estate agents and brokers.

Capital budget: An estimate of costs to cover replacements and improvements, and the corresponding revenues needed to balance them, usually for a 12-month period. Different from an operating budget.

Capital gain: Profit on the sale of an asset that is subject to taxation. Capital improvements. Major improvements made to a property that are written off over several years rather than expensed off in the year in which they are made.

Capitalization rate (CAP): The percentage of return on an investment when purchased on a free-and-clear or all-cash basis.

Charge: A document registered against a property, stating that someone has or believes he or she has a claim on the property.

Closing: The actual completion of the transaction acknowledging satisfaction of all legal and financial obligations between buyer and seller, and acknowledging the deed or transfer of title and disbursement of funds to appropriate parties.

Closing costs: The expenses over and above the purchase price of buying and selling real estate.

Closing date: The date on which the sale of a property becomes final and the new owner takes possession.

Collateral mortgage: A loan backed up by a promissory note and the security of a mortgage on a property. The money borrowed may be used for the purchase of a property or for another purpose, such as home renovations or a vacation.

Common area: The area in a condominium project that is shared by all of the condominium owners, such as elevators, hallways, and parking lots.

Common area maintenance (CAM): The charge to owners to maintain the common areas, normally due on a monthly basis.

Condominium: A housing unit to which the owner has title and of which the owner also owns a share in the common area (elevators, hallways, swimming pool, land, etc.).

Condominium corporation: The condominium association of unit owners incorporated under some provincial condominium legislation, automatically at the time of registration of the project. It is called a strata corporation in British Columbia. Under each of the provincial statutes, it will differ from an ordinary corporation in many respects. The condominium corporation, unlike a private business corporation, usually does not enjoy limited liability, and any judgment against the corporation for the payment of money is usually a judgment against each owner. The objects of the corporation are to manage the property and any assets of the corporation, and its duties include effecting compliance by the owners with the requirements of the *Act*, the declaration, the bylaws, and the rules.

Condominium council: The governing body of the condominium corporation, elected at the annual general meeting of the corporation.

Conventional mortgage: A mortgage loan that does not exceed 75% of the appraised value or of the purchase price of the property, whichever is less. Mortgages that exceed this limit generally must be insured by mortgage insurance, such as that provided by CMHC and GEM.

Conversion: The changing of a structure from some other use, such as changing a rental apartment to a condominium apartment.

Conveyancing: The transfer of property, or title to property, from one party to another.

CRA: Stands for Canada Revenue Agency, i.e., the current name for Canada Revenue Agency.

Debt service: Cost of paying interest for use of mortgage money.

Deductions: The expenses that Revenue Canada (CRA) allows you to deduct from your gross income.

Deed: This document conveys the title of the property to the purchaser. Different terminology may be used in different provincial jurisdictions.

Depreciation: The amount by which you write off the value of your real estate investment over the useful life of the investment. Does not include the value of your land.

Down payment: An initial amount of money (in the form of cash) put forward by the purchaser. Usually it represents the difference between the purchase price and the amount of the mortgage loan.

Encumbrance: See Charge.

Equity: The difference between the price for which a property could be sold and the total debts registered against it.

Equity return: The percentage ratio between your equity in the property and the total of cash flow plus mortgage principal reduction.

Escrow: The holding of a deed or contract by a third party until fulfillment of certain stipulated conditions between the contracting parties.

Estate: The title or interest one has in property such as real estate and personal property that can, if desired, be passed on to survivors at the time of one's death.

Fair market value: The value established on real property that is determined to be one that a buyer is willing to pay and a seller is willing to sell.

Fee simple: A manner of owning land, in one's own name and free of any conditions, limitations, or restrictions.

Financial statements: Documents that show the financial status of the condominium corporation, apartment building, or other revenue property at a given point in time. Generally includes income and expense statement and balance sheet.

Fiscal year: The 12-month period in which financial affairs are calculated.

Floating-rate mortgage: Another term for variable-rate mortgage.

Foreclosure: A legal procedure whereby the lender obtains ownership of, or right to sell, the property following default by the borrower.

GE Mortgage Insurance Canada (GEM): This is a private company providing mortgage insurance in Canada.

GEM: The initials for GE Mortgage Insurance Canada. See above.

High-ratio mortgage: A conventional mortgage loan that exceeds 75% of the appraised value or purchase price of the property. Such a mortgage must be insured.

Income, gross: Income or cash flow before expenses.

Income, net: Income or cash flow after expenses (but generally before income tax).

Interest averaging: The method of determining the overall average interest rate being paid when more than one mortgage is involved.

Interim financing: The temporary financing by a lender during the construction of real property for resale, or while other funds are due in.

Leases, sub: The lessee leases part of his or her premises to another user.

Legal description: Identification of a property that is recognized by law, that identifies that property from all others.

Lessee: The tenant in rental space.

Lessor: The owner of the rental space.

Letter of intent: Used in place of a formal written contract with a deposit. The prospective purchaser informs the seller, in writing, that he or she is willing to enter into a formal purchase contract upon certain terms and conditions if they are acceptable to the seller.

Leverage: The use of financing or other people's money to control large pieces of real property with a small amount of invested capital.

Limited partnership: An investment group in which one partner serves as the general partner and the others as limited partners. The general partner bears all of the financial responsibility and management of the investment. The limited partners are obligated only to the extent of their original investment plus possible personal guarantees.

Listings, exclusive agency: A signed agreement by a seller in which he or she agrees to co-operate with one broker. All other brokers must go through the listing broker.

Listings, multiple: (See also Multiple listing service.) A system of agency/subagency relationships. If Broker A lists the property for sale, "A" is the vendor's agent. If Broker B sees the MLS listing and offers it for sale, "B" is the vendor's subagent.

Listings, open: A listing given to one or more brokers, none of whom have any exclusive rights or control over the sale by other brokers or the owner of the property.

Marginal tax rate: That point in income at which any additional income will be taxed at a higher tax rate.

MLS: See Multiple listing service.

Mortgage: The document that pledges real property as collateral for an indebtedness.

Mortgage, balloon: A mortgage amortized over a number of years, but which requires the entire principal balance to be paid at a certain time, short of the full amortization period.

Mortgage, constant: The interest rate charged on a mortgage consisting of both the rate being charged by the lender and the rate that represents the amount of principal reduction each period.

Mortgage, deferred payment: A mortgage allowing for payments to be made on a deferred or delayed basis. Usually used where present income is not sufficient to make the payments.

Mortgage, discounted: The selling of a mortgage to another party at a discount or an amount less than the face value of the mortgage.

Mortgage, first: A mortgage placed on a property in first position.

Mortgage, fixed: This is a conventional mortgage, with payments of interest and principal. Fixed terms with a fixed rate can vary from 6 months to 10 years or more.

Mortgage insurance: This is insurance provided by the lender as an option for the borrower. It would pay out the balance outstanding on your mortgage, in the event of your death.

Mortgage, interest only: Payments to interest only are made. There is no principal reduction in the payment.

Mortgage, points: The interest rate charged by the lender.

Mortgage, second: A mortgage placed on a property in second position to an already existing first mortgage.

Mortgage, variable: This is a mortgage with an interest rate that fluctuates with the Bank of Canada interest rate. You just pay the interest, with optional pay-down on the principal. Different than a fixed-rate mortgage. See above.

Mortgage wraparound: Sometimes called an all-inclusive mortgage. A mortgage that includes any existing mortgages on the property. The buyer makes one large payment on the wraparound and the seller continues making the existing mortgage payments out of that payment.

Mortgagee: The lender.

Mortgagor: The borrower.

Multiple listing service (MLS): A service licensed to member real estate boards by CREA. Used to compile and disseminate information by publication and computer concerning a given property to a large number of agents and brokers.

NAA: The Federal National Housing Act

NHWP: New Home Warranty Program, which is provincial in nature and provides warranty protection for new homes.

New Home Warranty Program: See NHWP.

National Housing Act (NHA) Loan: A mortgage loan that is insured by CMHC to certain maximums.

Offer to purchase: The document that sets forth all the terms and conditions under which a purchaser offers to purchase property. This offer, when accepted by the seller, becomes a binding agreement of purchase and sale once all conditions have been removed.

Operating budget: An estimate of costs to operate a building or condominium complex and corresponding revenues needed to balance them, usually for a 12 month period. Different from a capital budget.

Operating costs: Those expenses required to operate an investment property, generally excluding mortgage payments.

Option agreement: A contract, with consideration, given to a potential purchaser of a property, giving him or her the right to purchase at a future date. If he or she chooses not to purchase, the deposit to the seller is forfeited.

Personal property: Property in an investment property, such as carpeting, draperies, refrigerators, etc., that can be depreciated over a shorter useful life than the structure itself.

PI: Principal and interest due on a mortgage.

PIT: Principal, interest, and taxes due on a mortgage.

Prepayment penalty: A penalty charge written into many mortgages that must be paid if the mortgage is paid off ahead of schedule.

Principal: The amount you actually borrowed, or the portion of it still owing on the original loan.

Property manager: A manager or management company hired to run an investment property for the owner.

Purchase-and-sale agreement: See Agreement of purchase and sale.

Pyramiding: The process of building real estate wealth by allowing appreciation and mortgage principal reduction to increase the investors' equity in a series of ever larger properties.

Resident manager: An individual, usually living in the building, who handles all of the day-to-day problems in the building.

Revenue Canada: You know what this agency does. Its current name is Canada Revenue Agency (CRA). However, for the purpose of this book, the name Revenue Canada will be used primarily, as that name is the most familiar to most people, as well as for nostalgic reasons.

Sale/leaseback: The tenant in a building sells it to an investor and leases it back for a period of years.

Tax shelter: The tax write-off possible through the depreciation benefits available on investment real estate ownership.

Time value of money: The value of a future sum of money if it is paid today. Usually there is a discount factor as you would be getting the benefit of the money today even though it is not due until sometime in the future.

Title: Generally, the evidence of right that a person has to the possession of property.

Title insurance: This insurance covers the purchaser or vendor, in case of any defects in the property or title that existed at the time of sale, but were not known about until after the sale.

Trust account: The separate account in which a lawyer or real estate broker holds funds until the real estate closing takes place or other legal disbursement is made.

Trust funds: Funds held in trust, either held as a deposit for the purchase of real property or to pay taxes and insurance.

Unit: Normally refers to the rental suite or that part of a condominium owned and occupied or rented by the owner.

Useful life: The term during which an asset is expected to have useful value.

Vacancy allowance: A projected deduction from the scheduled gross income of a building to allow for loss of income due to vacant apartments or other rental units.

Value, assessed: The property value as determined by local, regional, or provincial assessment authority.

Vendor: A person selling a piece of property.

Vendor take-back: A procedure wherein the seller (vendor) of a property provides some or all of the mortgage financing in order to sell the property. Also referred to as vendor financing.

Zoning: Rules for land use established by local governments.

Further Education and Information

If you would like further information about real estate investment in Canada, including seminars, books, software programs, and consulting, please write to the address below:

Canadian Real Estate Education Group

3665 Kingsway , Suite 300

Vancouver, B.C.   V5R 5W2

Or visit the Web site at www.homebuyer.ca

Index